THE

COLUMBIAD,

A POEM.

BY JOEL BARLOW.

Tu spiegherai, Colombo, a un novo polo
Lontane sì le fortunate antenne,
Ch'a pena seguirà con gli occhi il volo
La Fama, ch' hà mille occhi e mille penne.
Canti ella Alcide, e Bacco; e di te solo
Basti a i posteri tuoi, ch' alquanto accenne:
Chè quel poco darà lunga memoria
Di poema degnissima, e d'istoria.
GIERUS. LIB. Can. XV.

LONDON:
PRINTED FOR RICHARD PHILLIPS, BRIDGE STREET,
BLACKFRIARS.
1809.

Richard Taylor and Co., Printers, Shoe Lane.

PREFACE.

In preparing this work for publication it seems proper to offer some observations explanatory of its design. The classical reader will perceive the obstacles which necessarily presented themselves in reconciling the nature of the subject with such a manner of treating it as should appear the most poetical, and at the same time the most likely to arrive at that degree of dignity and usefulness to which it ought to aspire.

The Columbiad is a patriotic poem; the subject is national and historical. Thus far it must be interesting to my countrymen. But most of the events were so recent, so important and so well known, as to render them inflexible to the hand of fiction. The poem therefore could not with propriety be modelled after that regular epic form which the more splendid works of this kind have taken, and on which their success is supposed in a great measure to depend. The attempt would have been highly injudicious; it must have diminished and debased a series of actions which were really great in themselves, and could not be disfigured without losing their interest.

I shall enter into no discussion on the nature of the epopea, nor attempt to prove by any latitude of reasoning that I have written an Epic Poem. The subject indeed is vast; far superior to any one of those on which the celebrated poems of this description have been constructed; and I have no doubt but the form I have given to the work is the best that the subject would admit. It may be added that in no poem are the unities of time, place and action more rigidly observed: the action, in the technical sense of the word, consisting only of what takes place between Columbus and Hesper; which must be supposed to occupy but few hours, and is confined to the prison and the mount of vision.

But these circumstances of classical regularity are of little consideration in estimating the real merit of any work of this nature. Its merit must depend on the importance of the action, the disposition of the parts, the invention and application of incidents, the propriety of the illustrations, the liveliness and chastity of the images, the suitable intervention of machinery, the moral tendency of the manners, the strength and sublimity of the sentiments; the whole being clothed in language whose energy, harmony and elegance shall constitute a style every where suited to the matter they have to treat.

It is impossible for me to determine how far I may have succeeded in any of these particulars. This must be decided by others, the result of whose decision I shall never know. But there is one point of view in which I wish the reader to place the character of my work, before he pronounces on its merit: I mean its political tendency. There are two distinct objects to be kept in view in the conduct of a narrative poem; the *poetical* object and the *moral* object. The poetical is the fictitious design of the action; the moral is the real design of the poem.

In the Iliad of Homer the poetical object is to kindle, nourish, sustain and allay the anger of Achilles. This end is constantly kept in view; and the action proper to attain it is conducted with wonderful judgment thro a long series of incidents, which elevate the mind of the reader, and excite not only a veneration for the creative powers of the poet, but an ardent emulation of his heroes, a desire to imitate and rival some of the great actors in the splendid scene; perhaps to endeavor to carry into real life the fictions with which we are so much enchanted.

Such a high degree of interest excited by the first object above mentioned, the fictitious design of the action, would make it extremely important that the second object, the real design of the poem, should be beneficial to society. But the real design in the

Iliad was directly the reverse. Its obvious tendency was to inflame the minds of young readers with an enthusiastic ardor for military fame; to inculcate the pernicious doctrine of the divine right of kings; to teach both prince and people that military plunder was the most honorable mode of acquiring property; and that conquest, violence and war were the best employment of nations, the most glorious prerogative of bodily strength and of cultivated mind.

How much of the fatal policy of states, and of the miseries and degradations of social man, have been occasioned by the false notions of honor inspired by the works of Homer, it is not easy to ascertain. The probability is, that however astonishing they are as monuments of human intellect, and how long soever they have been the subject of universal praise, they have unhappily done more harm than good. My veneration for his genius is equal to that of his most idolatrous readers; but my reflections on the history of human errors have forced upon me the opinion that his existence has really proved one of the signal misfortunes of mankind.

The moral tendency of the Eneid of Virgil is nearly as pernicious as that of the works of Homer. Its poetical or fictitious design, the settlement of his hero in Italy, is well delineated and steadily pursued. This object must have been far more interesting to the Romans than the anger of Achilles could have been to the Greeks. Had Virgil written his poem one or two centuries earlier than he did, while his countrymen felt that they had a country and were not themselves the property of a master, they must have glowed with enthusiasm in reciting the fabulous labors of their ancestors, and adored the songster who could have thus elevated so endearing a subject; who could have adorned it with such an interesting variety of incidents, such weight of pathos, such majesty of sentiment and harmony of verse. But Virgil wrote and felt like a subject, not like a citizen. The real design of his poem was to increase the veneration of the people for a master, whoever he might be, and to encourage like Homer the great system of military depredation.

Lucan is the only republican among the ancient epic poets. But the action of his rambling tho majestic poem is so badly arranged as to destroy, in a poetical sense, the life and interest of the great national subject on which it is founded; at the same time that it abounds in the most exalted sentiments and original views of manners, highly favorable to the love of justice and the detestation of war. If a mind, formed like that of Lucan, as to its moral and political cast, and endowed with the creative energy of Homer, had sung to the early Greeks the fall of Troy or the labors of Hercules, his work (taking the place which those of Homer have unfortunately occupied) as a splendid model for all succeeding ages, would have given a very different turn to the pursuits of heroes and the policy of nations. Ambition might then have become a useful passion, instead of a destructive disease.

In the poem here presented to the public the objects, as in other works of the kind, are two, the fictitious object of the action and the real object of the poem. The first of these is to sooth and satisfy the desponding mind of Columbus; to show him that his labors, tho ill rewarded by his cotemporaries, had not been performed in vain; that he had opened the way to the most extensive career of civilization and public happiness; and that he would one day be recognised as the author of the greatest benefits to the human race. This object is steadily kept in view; and the actions, images and sentiments are so disposed as probably to attain the end. But the real object of the poem embraces a larger scope; it is to inculcate the love of rational liberty, and to discountenance the deleterious passion for violence and war; to show that on the basis of the republican principle all good morals, as well as good government and hopes of permanent peace, must be founded; and to convince the student in political science, that the theoretical question of the future advancement of human society, till states as well as individuals arrive at universal civilization, is held in dispute and still unsettled only because we have had too little experience of organized liberty in the government of nations to have well considered its effects.

I cannot expect that every reader, nor even every republican reader, will join me in opinion with respect to the future progress of society and the civilization of states; but there are two sentiments in which I think all men will agree: that the event is desirable, and that to believe it practicable is one step towards rendering it so. This being the case, they ought to pardon a writer, if not applaud him, for endeavoring to inculcate this belief.

I have taken the liberty, notwithstanding the recency of the events, to make some changes in the order of several of the principal battles described in this poem. I have associated the actions of Starke, Herkimer, Brown and Francis in the battle of Saratoga, tho they happened at some distance from that battle, both as to time and place. A like circumstance will be noticed with respect to Sumter, Jackson of Georgia and some others in the battle of Eutaw. I have supposed a citadel mined and blown up in the siege of York, and two ships of war grappled and blown up in the naval battle of Degrasse and Graves. It is presumed that these circumstances require no apology; as in the two latter cases the events are incidental to such situations, and they here serve the principal purpose, being meant to increase our natural horror for the havoc and miseries of war in general. And with regard to the two former cases we ought to consider that, in the epic field, the interest to be excited by the action cannot be sustained by following the gazette, as Lucan has done. The desultory parts of the historical action must be brought together and be made to elevate and strengthen each other, so as to press upon the mind with the full force of their symmetry and unity. Where the events are recent and the actors known, the only duty imposed by that circumstance on the poet is to do them historical justice, and not ascribe to one hero the actions of another. But the scales of justice in this case are not necessarily accompanied by the calendar and the map.

It will occur to most of my readers that the modern modes of fighting, as likewise the instruments and terms now used in war, are not yet rendered familiar in poetical language. It is doubtless from an unwarrantable timidity, or want of confidence in their own powers of description, that modern poets have made so little use of this kind of riches that lay before them. I confess that I imbibed the common prejudice, and remained a long time in the error of supposing that the ancients had a poetical advantage over us in respect to the dignity of the names of the weapons used in war, if not in their number and variety. And when I published a sketch of the present poem, under the title of The

Vision of Columbus, I labored under the embarrassment of that idea. I am now convinced that the advantage, at least as to the weapons, is on the side of the moderns. There are better sounding names and more variety in the instruments, works, stratagems and other artifices employed in our war system than in theirs. In short, the modern military dictionary is more copious than the ancient, and the words at least as poetical.

As to the mode of fighting, we have, poetically speaking, lost something in one respect, but we have gained much in another. Our battles indeed admit but few single combats, or trials of individual prowess. They do admit them however; and it is not impossible to describe them with as much detail and interest as the nature of the action requires; as Voltaire has proved in the single combat of Aumale and Turenne in the Henriad. Had he managed his general descriptions and the other parts of the conduct of his poem as well, he would have made it a far more interesting work than he has. However, since our single combats must be insignificant in their consequences, not deciding any thing as to the result of the battle, it would be inconvenient and misplaced to make much use of them in our descriptions. And here lies our disadvantage, compared with the ancients.

But in a general engagement, the shock of modern armies is, beyond comparison, more magnificent, more sonorous and more discoloring to the face of nature, than the ancient could have been; and is consequently susceptible of more pomp and variety of description. Our heaven and earth are not only shaken and tormented with greater noise, but filled and suffocated with fire and smoke. If Homer, with his Grecian tongue and all its dialects, had had the battle of Blenheim to describe, the world would have possessed a picture and a piece of music which now it will never possess. The description would have astonished all ages, and enriched every language into which it might have been translated.

With regard to naval battles the moderns have altogether the advantage. But there has been no naval battle described in modern poetry; neither is there any remaining to us from the ancients, except that in the bay of Marseilles by Lucan, and that near Syracuse by Silius. It would seem strange indeed that Homer, whose wonderful powers of fiction were not embarrassed by historical realities, and who in other respects is so insatiable of variety, did not introduce a sea fight either in the defence of Troy, or in the disastrous voyages of Ulysses. But the want of this in Homer's two poems amounts almost to a proof that in his time the nations had not yet adopted any method of fighting at sea; so that the poet could have no such image in his mind.

The business of war, with all its varieties, makes but a small part of the subject of my poem; it ought therefore to occupy but a small portion of its scenery. This is the reason why I have not been more solicitous to vary and heighten the descriptions of battles and other military operations. I make this observation to satisfy those readers who being accustomed to see a long poem chiefly occupied with this sort of bustle conceive that the life and interest of such compositions depend upon it. How far the majesty or interest of epic song really depends upon the tumultuous conflicts of war I will not decide; but I can assure the reader, so far as my experience goes, that these parts of the work are not the most difficult to write. They are scenes that exhibit those vigorous traits of human character which strike the beholder most forcibly and leave the deepest impression. They delight in violent attitudes; and, painting themselves in the strongest colors on the poet's fancy, they are easy at any time to recal. He varies them at pleasure, he adorns them readily with incidents, and imparts them with spirit to the reader.

My object is altogether of a moral and political nature I wish to encourage and strengthen in the rising generation, a sense of the importance of republican institutions; as being the great foundation of public and private happiness, the necessary aliment of future and permanent ameliorations in the condition of human nature.

This is the moment in America to give such a direction to poetry, painting and the other fine arts, that true and useful ideas of glory may be implanted in the minds of men here, to take place of the false and destructive ones that have degraded the species in other countries; impressions which have become so wrought into their most sacred institutions, that it is there thought impious to detect them and dangerous to root them out, tho acknowledged to be false. Wo be to the republican principle and to all the institutions it supports, when once the pernicious doctrine of the holiness of error shall creep into the creed of our schools and distort the intellect of our citizens!

The Columbiad, in its present form, is such as I shall probably leave it to its fate. Whether it be destined to survive its author, is a question that gives me no other concern than what arises from the most pure and ardent desire of doing good to my country. To my country therefore, with every sentiment of veneration and affection I dedicate my labors.

INTRODUCTION.

Every circumstance relating to the discovery and settlement of America is an interesting object of inquiry, especially to the great and growing nations of this hemisphere, who owe their existence to those arduous labors. Yet it is presumed that many persons, who might be entertained with a poem on this subject, are but slightly acquainted with the life and character of the hero whose extraordinary genius led him to discover the continent, and whose singular sufferings, arising from that service, ought to excite the indignation of the world.

Christopher Columbus was born in Genoa about the year 1447, when the navigation of Europe was scarcely extended beyond the limits of the Mediterranean and the other narrow seas that border the great ocean. The mariner's compass had been invented and in common use for more than a century; yet with the help of this sure guide, and prompted by a laudable spirit of discovery, the mariners of those days rarely ventured from the sight of land.

They acquired wonderful applause by sailing along the coast of Africa, and discovering some of the neighboring islands; and after pushing their researches with great industry for half a century, the Portuguese, who were the most fortunate and enterprising, extended their voyages southward no farther than the equator.

The rich commodities of the East had, for several ages, been brought into Europe by the Red Sea and the Mediterranean; and it had now become the object of the Portuguese to find a passage to India by sailing round the southern extremity of Africa, and then taking an eastern course. This great object engaged the general attention, and drew into the Portuguese service adventurers from the other maritime nations of Europe. Every year added to their experience in navigation, and seemed to promise some distant reward to their industry. The prospect however of arriving at India by that route was still by no means encouraging. Fifty years perseverance in the same track having brought them only to the equator, it was probable that as many more would elapse before they could accomplish their purpose.

But Columbus, by an uncommon exertion of genius, formed a design no less astonishing to the age in which he lived than beneficial to posterity. This design was to sail to India by taking a western direction. By the accounts of travellers who had visited that part of Asia, it seemed almost without limits on the east; and by attending to the spherical figure of the earth Columbus drew the natural conclusion, that the Atlantic ocean must be bounded on the west either by India itself, or by some continent not far distant from it.

This illustrious navigator, who was then about twenty-seven years of age, appears to have possessed every talent requisite to form and execute the greatest enterprises. He was early educated in such of the useful sciences as were taught in that day. He had made great proficiency in geography, astronomy and drawing, as they were necessary to his favorite pursuit of navigation. He had been a number of years in the service of the Portuguese, and had acquired all the experience that their voyages and discoveries could afford. His courage had been put to the severest test; and the exercise of every amiable as well as heroic virtue, the kindred qualities of a great mind, had secured him an extensive reputation. He had married a Portuguese lady, by whom he had two sons, Diego and Ferdinand; the younger of these is the historian of his life.

Such was the situation of Columbus, when he formed and digested a plan, which, in its operation and consequences, has unfolded to the view of mankind one half of the globe, diffused wealth and industry over the other, and is extending commerce and civilization thro the whole. To corroborate the theory he had formed of the existence of a western continent, his discerning mind, which knew the application of every circumstance that fell in his way, had observed several facts which by others would have passed unnoticed. In his voyages to the African islands he had found, floating ashore after a long western storm, pieces of wood carved in a curious manner, canes of a size unknown in that quarter of the world, and human bodies with very singular features.

The opinion being well established in his mind that a considerable portion of the earth still remained to be discovered, his temper was too vigorous and persevering to suffer an idea of this importance to rest merely in speculation, as it had done with Plato and Seneca, who seem to have entertained conjectures of a similar nature. He determined therefore to bring his theory to the test of experiment. But an object of that magnitude required the patronage of a prince; and a design so extraordinary met with all the obstructions that an age of superstition could invent, and personal jealousy enhance.

It is happy for mankind that, in this instance, a genius capable of devising the greatest undertakings associated in itself a degree of patience and enterprise, modesty and confidence, which rendered him superior to these misfortunes, and enabled him to meet with fortitude all the future calamities of his life. Excited by an ardent enthusiasm to become a discoverer of new countries, and fully sensible of the advantages that would result to mankind from such discoveries, he had the cruel mortification to wear away eighteen years of his life, after his system was well established in his own mind, before he could obtain the means of executing his projected voyage. The greatest part of this period was spent in successive solicitations in Genoa, Portugal and Spain.

As a duty to his native country he made his first proposal to the senate of Genoa, where it was soon rejected. Conscious of the truth of his theory, and of his own abilities to execute his plan, he retired without dejection from a body of men who were incapable of forming any just ideas upon the subject, and applied with fresh confidence to John Second, king of Portugal; who had distinguished himself as the great patron of navigation, and in whose service Columbus had acquired a reputation which entitled him and his project to general confidence. But here he experienced a treatment much more insulting than a direct refusal. After referring the examination of his scheme to the council who had the direction of naval affairs, and drawing from him his general ideas of the length of the voyage and the course he meant to take, that splendid monarch had the meanness to conspire with this council to rob Columbus of the glory and advantage he expected to derive from his undertaking. While Columbus was amused with the negotiation, in hopes of having his scheme adopted, a vessel was secretly dispatched by order of the king to make the intended discovery. Want of skill or courage in the pilot rendered the plot unsuccessful; and Columbus, on discovering the treachery, retired with an ingenuous indignation from a court which could be capable of such duplicity.

Having now performed what was due to the country that gave him birth, and to the one that had adopted him as a subject, he was at liberty to court the patronage of any other which should have the wisdom to accept his proposals. He had communicated his ideas to his brother Bartholomew, whom he sent to England to negotiate with Henry Seventh; at the same time he went himself into Spain to apply in person to Ferdinand and Isabella, who governed the united kingdoms of Arragon and Castile.

The circumstances of his brother's application in England, which appears to have been unsuccessful, are not to my purpose to relate; and the limits prescribed to this biographical sketch will prevent the detail of particulars respecting his own negotiation in Spain. This occupied him eight years; in which the various agitations of suspense, expectation and disappointment must have borne hard upon his patience. At length his scheme was adopted by Isabella; who undertook, as queen of Castile, to defray the expenses of the expedition, and declared herself ever after the friend and patron of the hero who projected it.

Columbus, who during his ill success in the negotiation never abated any thing of the honors and emoluments which he expected to acquire in the expedition, obtained from Ferdinand and Isabella a stipulation of every article contained in his first proposals. He was constituted high admiral and viceroy of all the seas, islands and continents which he should discover; with power to receive one tenth of the profits arising from their productions and commerce. Which offices and emoluments were to be made hereditary in his family.

These articles being adjusted, the preparations for the voyage were brought forward with rapidity; but they were by no means adequate to the importance of the expedition. Three small vessels, scarcely sufficient in size to be employed in the coasting business, were appointed to traverse the vast Atlantic, and to encounter the storms and currents always to be expected in tropical climates, uncertain seasons and unknown seas. These vessels, as we must suppose them in the infancy of navigation, were ill constructed, in a poor condition, and manned by seamen unaccustomed to distant voyages. But the tedious length of time which Columbus had passed in solicitation and suspense, and the prospect of being able soon to obtain the object of his wishes, induced him to overlook what he could not easily remedy; and led him to disregard those circumstances which would have intimidated any other mind. He accordingly equipped his small squadron with as much expedition as possible, manned with ninety men and victualled for one year. With these, on the third of August 1492, amidst a vast crowd of spectators, he set sail on an enterprise which, if we consider the ill condition of his ships, the inexperience of his sailors, the length and precarious nature of his voyage, and the consequences that flowed from it, was the most daring and important that ever was undertaken. He touched at some of the Portuguese settlements in the Canary Isles; where, altho he had been but a few days at sea, he found his vessels needed refitting. He soon made the necessary repairs, and took his departure from the westermost islands that had hitherto been discovered. Here he left the former track of navigation, and steered his course due west.

Not many days after he laid this course he perceived the symptoms of a new scene of difficulty. The sailors now began to contemplate the dangers and uncertain issue of a voyage, the nature and length of which were left entirely open to conjecture. Besides the fickleness and timidity natural to men unaccustomed to the discipline of a seafaring life, several circumstances contributed to inspire an obstinate and mutinous disposition;

which required the most consummate art as well as fortitude in the admiral to control. Having been three weeks at sea, and experienced the uniform course of the trade winds, they contended that, should they continue the same course for a longer time, the same winds would never permit them to return to Spain. The magnetic needle began to vary its direction. This being the first time that this phenomenon was ever noticed, it was viewed by the sailors with astonishment; they thought it an indication that nature itself had changed its laws, and that Providence was about to punish their audacity in venturing so far beyond the bounds of man. They declared that the commands of the government had been fully obeyed in their proceeding so many days in the same course, and so far surpassing all former navigators in quest of discoveries.

Every talent requisite for governing, soothing and tempering the passions of men is conspicuous in the conduct of Columbus on this occasion. The dignity and affability of his manners, his surprising knowledge and experience in naval affairs, his unwearied and minute attention to the duties of his command, gave him a great ascendency over the minds of his men, and inspired that degree of confidence which would have maintained his authority in almost any circumstances. But here, from the nature of the undertaking, every man had leisure to feed his imagination with the gloominess and uncertainty of the prospect. They found from day to day the same steady gales wafting them with rapidity from their native country, and indeed from all countries of which they had any knowledge.

He addressed himself to their passions with all the variety of management that the situation would admit, sometimes by soothing them with the prognostics of approaching land, sometimes by flattering their ambition and feasting their avarice with the glory and wealth they would acquire from discovering the rich countries beyond the Atlantic, and sometimes by threatening them with the displeasure of their king, should their disobedience defeat so great an object. But every argument soon lost its effect; and their uneasiness still increased. From secret whisperings it arose to open mutiny and dangerous conspiracy. At length they determined to rid themselves of the remonstrances of Columbus by throwing him into the sea. The infection spread from ship to ship, and involved officers as well as sailors. They finally lost all sense of subordination and addressed their commander in an insolent manner, demanding to be conducted immediately back to Spain; or, they assured him, they would seek their own safety by taking away his life.

Columbus, whose sagacity had discerned every symptom of the disorder, was prepared for this last stage of it; and was sufficiently apprized of the danger that awaited him. He found it vain to contend with passions he could no longer control. He therefore proposed that they should obey his orders for three days longer; and should they not discover land in that time, he would then direct his course for Spain. They complied with his proposal; and, happily for mankind, in three days they discovered land. This was a small island, to which he gave the name of San Salvador. His first interview with the natives was a scene of compassion on the one part and astonishment on the other, but highly interesting to both. The natives were entirely naked, simple and timorous; and they viewed the Spaniards as a superior order of beings descended from the sun; which, in that island and in most parts of America, was worshipped as a Deity. By this it was easy for Columbus to perceive the line of conduct proper to be observed toward that simple and inoffensive people. Had his companions and successors of the Spanish nation possessed the wisdom and humanity of this great discoverer, the benevolent mind would have had to experience no sensations of regret in contemplating the extensive advantages arising to mankind from the discovery of America.

In this voyage Columbus discovered the islands of Cuba and Hispaniola, on the latter of which he erected a small fort; and having left a garrison of thirty-eight men he set sail for Spain. Returning across the Atlantic, he was overtaken by a violent storm, which lasted several days, and increased to such a degree as baffled his naval skill and threatened immediate destruction. In this situation, when all were in a state of despair, and it was expected that every sea would swallow up the crazy vessel, he manifested a serenity and presence of mind seldom equalled in cases of like extremity. He wrote a short account of his voyage and of the discoveries he had made; this he hastily wrapt in an oiled cloth, then enclosed it in a cake of wax and put it into an empty cask, which he threw overboard, in hopes that some fortunate accident might preserve a deposit of so much importance to the world.

The storm however abated, and he at length arrived in Spain, after having been driven by stress of weather into the port of Lisbon; where he had opportunity, in an interview with the king of Portugal, to prove the truth of his system by arguments more convincing than those he had before advanced in the character of a bold projector but humble suitor. He was received every where in Spain with royal honors; his family was ennobled, and his former stipulation respecting his offices and emoluments was ratified in the most solemn manner by Ferdinand and Isabella; while all Europe resounded his praises, and reciprocated their joy and congratulations on the discovery of what they called a new world.

The immediate consequence was a second voyage, in which Columbus took charge of a squadron of seventeen ships of considerable burden. Volunteers of all ranks solicited to be employed in this expedition. He carried over fifteen hundred persons, with the necessaries for establishing a colony and extending his discoveries. In this voyage he explored most of the West India islands; but on his arrival at Hispaniola he found that the garrison he had left there had been all destroyed by the natives, and the fort demolished. He proceeded however in the planting of his colony; and by his prudent and humane conduct towards the natives he effectually established the Spanish authority in that island. But while he was thus laying the foundation of European dominion in America, some discontented persons, who had returned to Spain, uniting with his former opponents and powerful enemies at court, conspired to accomplish his ruin.

They represented his conduct in such a light as to create uneasiness in the jealous mind of Ferdinand, and make it necessary for Columbus again to return to Spain, to counteract their machinations aud obtain such farther supplies as were necessary to his great political and beneficent purposes. On his arriving at court, and stating with his usual dignity and confidence the whole history of his transactions abroad, every thing wore a favorable appearance. He was received with the same honors as before, and solicited to take charge of another squadron, to carry out farther supplies, to pursue his discoveries, and in every respect to use his discretion in extending the Spanish empire in the new world.

In this third voyage he discovered the continent of America at the mouth of the river Orinoco. He rectified many disorders in his government of Hispaniola, which had happened in his absence; and every thing was going on in a prosperous train, when an event was announced to him, which completed his own ruin and gave a fatal turn to the Spanish policy and conduct in America. This was the arrival of Francis de Bovadilla, with a commission to supersede Columbus in his government, to arraign him as a criminal, and pronounce judgment on all his former administration.

It seems that by this time the enemies of Columbus, despairing to complete his overthrow by groundless insinuations of malconduct, had taken the more effectual method of exciting the jealousy of their sovereigns. From the promising samples of gold and other valuable commodities brought from America, they took occasion to represent to the king and queen that the prodigious wealth and extent of the countries he had discovered would soon throw such power into the hands of the viceroy, that he would trample on the royal authority and bid defiance to the Spanish power. These arguments were well calculated for the cold and suspicious temper of Ferdinand; and they must have had some effect upon the mind of Isabella. The consequence was the appointment of Bovadilla, the inveterate enemy of Columbus, to take the government from his hands. This first tyrant of the Spanish nation in America began his administration by ordering Columbus to be put in chains on board of a ship, and sending him prisoner to Spain. By relaxing all discipline he introduced disorder and licentiousness thro the colony. He subjected the unhappy natives to a most miserable servitude, and apportioned them out in large numbers among his adherents. Under this severe treatment perished in a short time many thousands of those innocent people.

Columbus was carried in his fetters to the Spanish court, where the king and queen either feigned or felt a sufficient regret at the conduct of Bovadilla towards their illustrious prisoner. He was not only released from confinement; he was treated with all imaginable respect. But, altho the king endeavored to expiate the offence by censuring and recalling Bovadilla, yet we may judge of his sincerity from his appointing Nicholas de Ovando, another well known enemy of Columbus, to succeed in the government; and from his ever after refusing to reinstate Columbus, or to fulfil any of the conditions on which the discoveries had been undertaken.

After two years of solicitation for this or some other employment, he at length obtained a squadron of four small vessels to attempt new discoveries. He then set out, with the enthusiasm of a young adventurer, in quest of what was always his favorite object, a passage into the South Sea, by which he might sail to India. He touched at Hispaniola, where Ovando the governor refused him admittance on shore, even to take shelter during a hurricane, the prognostics of which his experience had taught him to discern. By putting into a creek he rode out the storm, and then bore away for the continent. He spent several months, the most boisterous of the year, in exploring the coast round the gulph of Mexico, in hopes of finding the intended navigation to India. At length he was shipwrecked, and driven ashore on the island of Jamaica.

His cup of calamities seemed now to be full. He was cast upon an island of savages, without provisions, without a vessel, and thirty leagues from any Spanish settlement. But the greatest physical misfortunes are capable of being imbittered by the insults of our fellow creatures. A few of his companions generously offered, in two Indian canoes, to attempt a voyage to Hispaniola, in hopes of obtaining a vessel for the relief of the unhappy crew. After suffering every extremity of danger and fatigue, they arrived at the Spanish colony in ten days. Ovando, excited by personal malice against Columbus, detained these messengers for eight months, and then despatched a vessel to Jamaica to spy out the condition of Columbus and his crew, with positive instructions to the captain not to afford them any relief. This order was punctually executed. The captain approached the shore, delivered a letter of empty compliment from Ovando to the admiral, received his answer and returned. About four months afterwards a vessel came to their relief; and Columbus, worn out with fatigues and broken by misfortunes, returned for the last time to Spain. Here a new distress awaited him, which he considered as one of the greatest of his whole life: this was the death of queen Isabella, his last and most powerful friend.

He did not suddenly abandon himself to despair. He called upon the gratitude and justice of the king; and in terms of dignity demanded the fulfilment of his former contract. Notwithstanding his age and infirmities, he even solicited to be farther employed in extending the career of discovery, without a prospect of any other reward than the pleasure of doing good to mankind. But Ferdinand, cold ungrateful and timid, dared not comply with any proposal of this kind, lest he should increase his own obligations to a man, whose services he thought it dangerous to reward. He therefore delayed and avoided any decision on these subjects, in hopes that the declining health of Columbus would soon rid the court of the remonstrances of a suitor, whose unexampled merit was, in their opinion, a sufficient reason for destroying him. In this they were not disappointed. Columbus languished a short time, and gladly resigned a life which had been worn out in the most signal services perhaps that have been rendered by any one man to an ungrateful world.

Posterity is sometimes more just to the memory of great men than cotemporaries were to their persons. But even this consolation, if it be one, has been wanting to the discoverer of our hemisphere. The continent, instead of bearing his name, has been called after one of his followers, a man of no particular merit. And in the modern city of Mexico there is instituted and perpetuated, by order of government, an annual festival in honour of Hernando Cortez, the perfidious butcher of its ancient race; while no public honors have been decreed to Christopher Columbus, one of the wisest and best among the benefactors of mankind.

After his last return from America he seems to have past the short remainder of his life at Valladolid, the capital of Old Castile, and then the seat of the Spanish government. He died in that city on the twentieth of August 1506, and was buried in one of its churches. Over his body is a plain stone inscribed simply with his name, as it is written in Spanish, CHRISTOVAL COLON.

His son, who wrote his life, has left us a particular description of his person, manners and private character; all of which were agreeable and interesting. His portrait is in possession of the author of this poem. It is painted in oil, half length and the size of life, copied from an original picture in the gallery of Florence.

THE

COLUMBIAD.

BOOK I.

ARGUMENT.

Subject of the Poem, and invocation to Freedom. Condition of Columbus in a Spanish prison. His monologue on the great actions of his life, and the manner in which they had been rewarded. Appearance and speech of Hesper, the guardian Genius of the western continent. They quit the dungeon, and ascend the mount of vision, which rises over the western coast of Spain; Europe settling from their sight, and the Atlantic ocean spreading far beneath their feet. Continent of America draws into view, and is described by its mountains, rivers, lakes, soil and some of the natural productions.

THE

COLUMBIAD.

BOOK I.

I SING the Mariner who first unfurl'd
An eastern banner o'er the western world,
And taught mankind where future empires lay
In these fair confines of descending day;
Who sway'd a moment, with vicarious power,
Iberia's sceptre on the new found shore,
Then saw the paths his virtuous steps had trod
Pursued by avarice and defiled with blood,
The tribes he foster'd with paternal toil
Snatch'd from his hand, and slaughter'd for their spoil.
Slaves, kings, adventurers, envious of his name,
Enjoy'd his labours and purloin'd his fame,
And gave the Viceroy, from his high seat hurl'd,
Chains for a crown, a prison for a world

Long overwhelm'd in woes, and sickening there,
He met the slow still march of black despair,
Sought the last refuge from his hopeless doom,
And wish'd from thankless men a peaceful tomb:
Till vision'd ages, opening on his eyes,
Cheer'd his sad soul, and bade new nations rise;
He saw the Atlantic heaven with light o'ercast,
And Freedom crown his glorious work at last.

Almighty Freedom! give my venturous song
The force, the charm that to thy voice belong;
'Tis thine to shape my course, to light my way,
To nerve my country with the patriot lay,
To teach all men where all their interest lies,
How rulers may be just and nations wise:
Strong in thy strength I bend no suppliant knee,
Invoke no miracle, no Muse but thee.

Night held on old Castile her silent reign,
Her half orb'd moon declining to the main;
O'er Valladolid's regal turrets hazed
The drizzly fogs from dull Pisuerga raised;
Whose hovering sheets, along the welkin driven,
Thinn'd the pale stars, and shut the eye from heaven.
Cold-hearted Ferdinand his pillow prest,
Nor dream'd of those his mandates robb'd of rest,

Of him who gemm'd his crown, who stretch'd his
reign
To realms that weigh'd the tenfold poise of Spain;
Who now beneath his tower indungeon'd lies,
Sweats the chill sod and breathes inclement skies.
His feverish pulse, slow laboring thro his frame,
Feeds with scant force its fast expiring flame;
A far dim watch-lamp's thrice reflected beam
Throws thro his grates a mist-encumber'd gleam,
Paints the dun vapors that the cell invade,
And fills with spectred forms the midnight shade;
When from a visionary short repose,
That nursed new cares and temper'd keener woes,
Columbus woke, and to the walls addrest
The deep felt sorrows bursting from his breast:
Here lies the purchase, here the wretched spoil
Of painful years and persevering toil.
For these damp caves, this hideous haunt of
pain,
I traced new regions o'er the chartless main,
Tamed all the dangers of untraversed waves,
Hung o'er their clefts, and topt their surging graves,
Saw traitorous seas o'er coral mountains sweep,
Red thunders rock the pole and scorch the deep,

Death rear his front in every varying form,
Gape from the shoals and ride the roaring storm,
My struggling bark her seamy planks disjoin,
Rake the rude rock and drink the copious brine.
Till the tired elements are lull'd at last,
And milder suns allay the billowing blast,
Lead on the trade winds with unvarying force,
And long and landless curve our constant course.
Our homeward heaven recoils; each night forlorn
Calls up new stars, and backward rolls the morn;
The boreal vault descends with Europe's shore,
And bright Calisto shuns the wave no more,
The Dragon dips his fiery-foaming jole,
The affrighted magnet flies the faithless pole;
Nature portends a general change of laws,
My daring deeds are deemed the guilty cause;
The desperate crew, to insurrection driven,
Devote their captain to the wrath of heaven,
Resolve at once to end the audacious strife,
And buy their safety with his forfeit life.
In that sad hour, this feeble frame to save,
(Unblest reprieve) and rob the gaping wave,
The morn broke forth, these tearful orbs descried
The golden banks that bound the western tide.

With full success I calm'd the clamorous race,
Bade heaven's blue arch a second earth embrace;
And gave the astonish'd age that bounteous shore,
Their wealth to nations, and to kings their power.
  Land of delights! ah, dear delusive coast,
To these fond aged eyes forever lost!
No more thy flowery vales I travel o'er,
For me thy mountains rear the head no more,
For me thy rocks no sparkling gems unfold,
Nor streams luxuriant wear their paths in gold;
From realms of promised peace forever borne,
I hail mute anguish, and in secret mourn.
  But dangers past, a world explored in vain,
And foes triumphant show but half my pain.
Dissembling friends, each early joy who gave,
And fired my youth the storms of fate to brave,
Swarm'd in the sunshine of my happier days,
Pursued the fortune and partook the praise,
Now pass my cell with smiles of sour disdain,
Insult my woes and triumph in my pain.
  One gentle guardian once could shield the brave;
But now that guardian slumbers in the grave.
Hear from above, thou dear departed shade;
As once my hopes, my present sorrows aid,

Burst my full heart, afford that last relief,
Breathe back my sighs and reinspire my grief;
Still in my sight thy royal form appears,
Reproves my silence and demands my tears.
Even on that hour no more I joy to dwell,
When thy protection bade the canvass swell;
When kings and churchmen found their factions vain,
Blind superstition shrunk beneath her chain,
The sun's glad beam led on the circling way,
And isles rose beauteous in Atlantic day.
For on those silvery shores, that new domain,
What crowds of tyrants fix their murderous reign!
Her infant realm indignant Freedom flies,
Truth leaves the world, and Isabella dies.
  Ah, lend thy friendly shroud to veil my sight,
That these pain'd eyes may dread no more the light;
These welcome shades shall close my instant doom,
And this drear mansion moulder to a tomb.
  Thus mourn'd the hapless man: a thundering sound
Roll'd thro the shuddering walls and shook the ground;
O'er all the dungeon, where black arches bend,
The roofs unfold, and streams of light descend;

The growing splendor fills the astonish'd room,
And gales etherial breathe a glad perfume.
Robed in the radiance, moves a form serene,
Of human structure, but of heavenly mien;
Near to the prisoner's couch he takes his stand,
And waves, in sign of peace, his holy hand.
Tall rose his stature, youth's endearing grace
Adorn'd his limbs and brighten'd in his face;
Loose o'er his locks the star of evening hung, 139
And sounds melodious moved his cheerful tongue:

Rise, trembling chief, to scenes of rapture rise;
This voice awaits thee from the western skies;
Indulge no longer that desponding strain,
Nor count thy toils, nor deem thy virtues vain.
Thou seest in me the guardian Power who keeps
The new found world that skirts Atlantic deeps,
Hesper my name, my seat the brightest throne
In night's whole heaven, my sire the living sun.
My brother Atlas with his name divine
Stampt the wild wave; the solid coast is mine.

Atlas and Hesper were of the race of Titans. They were sons of Uranus, or of Japetus, according as the fable is traced to different countries, whose supreme God (originally the sun) was called by different names. Atlas, from being king of Mauritania, became a mountain to support the heavens, and gave his name to

This hand, which form'd, and in the tides of time
Laves and improves the meliorating clime,
Which taught thy prow to cleave the trackless way,
And hail'd thee first in occidental day,
To all thy worth shall vindicate thy claim,
And raise up nations to revere thy name.

---

the western ocean. Hesper frequented that mountain in the study of astronomy; till one evening he disappeared, and returned no more. He was then placed in the western heaven; and, having been a beautiful young man, he became a beautiful planet, called the evening star. This circumstance gave his name to the western regions of the earth indefinitely. Italy was called Hesperia by the Greeks, because it lay west from them, and seemed under the influence of the star of evening; Spain was called Hesperia by the Romans, for the same reason.

If the nations which adopted this fable had known of a country west of the Atlantic, that country must have been Hesperia to them all; and pursuing this analogy I have so named it, in several instances, in the course of this poem. Considering Hesper as the guardian Genius, and Columbus as the Discoverer, of the western continent, it may derive its name, in poetical language, from either of theirs indifferently, and be called Hesperia or Columbia.

Atlas is considered in this poem as the guardian Genius of Africa. See his speech, in the eighth book, on the slavery of his people.

This explanation seemed of such immediate importance for understanding the machinery of the poem, as to require its being placed here. The other notes, being numerous and some of them long, have been forced to yield to typographical elegance; and are placed at the end of the volume, with suitable reference to the passages to which they belong.

In this dark age tho blinded faction sways,
And wealth and conquest gain the palm of praise;
Awed into slaves while groveling millions groan,
And blood-stain'd steps lead upward to a throne;
Far other wreaths thy virtuous temples twine,
Far nobler triumphs crown a life like thine;
Thine be the joys that minds immortal grace,
As thine the deeds that bless a kindred race.
Now raise thy sorrow'd soul to views more bright,
The vision'd ages rushing on thy sight;
Worlds beyond worlds shall bring to light their stores,
Time, nature, science blend their utmost powers,
To show, concentred in one blaze of fame,
The ungather'd glories that await thy name.

As that great seer, whose animating rod
Taught Jacob's sons their wonder-working God,
Who led thro dreary wastes the murmuring band,
And reach'd the confines of their promised land,
Opprest with years, from Pisgah's towering height,
On fruitful Canaan feasted long his sight;
The bliss of unborn nations warm'd his breast,
Repaid his toils and sooth'd his soul to rest;
Thus o'er thy subject wave shalt thou behold
Far happier realms their future charms unfold,

In nobler pomp another Pisgah rise,
Beneath whose foot thy new found Canaan lies;
There, rapt in vision, hail my favorite clime,
And taste the blessings of remotest time.
 So Hesper spoke; Columbus raised his head;
His chains dropt off; the cave, the castle fled.
Forth walk'd the Pair; when steep before them stood,
Slope from the town, a heaven-illumined road;
That thro disparting shades arose on high,
Reach'd o'er the hills, and lengthen'd up the sky,
Show'd a clear summit, rich with rising flowers,
That breathe their odors thro celestial bowers.
O'er the proud Pyrenees it looks sublime,
Subjects the Alps, and levels Europe's clime;
Spain, lessening to a chart, beneath it swims,
And shrouds her dungeons in the void she dims.
 Led by the Power, the Hero gain'd the height,
New strength and brilliance flush'd his mortal sight;
When calm before them flow'd the western main,
Far stretch'd, immense, a sky-encircled plain.
No sail, no isle, no cloud invests the bound,
Nor billowy surge disturbs the vast profound;
Till, deep in distant heavens, the sun's blue ray
Topt unknown cliffs and call'd them up to day;

Slow glimmering into sight wide regions drew,
And rose and brighten'd on the expanding view;
Fair sweep the waves, the lessening ocean smiles,
In misty radiance loom a thousand isles;
Near and more near the long drawn coasts arise,
Bays stretch their arms and mountains lift the skies,
The lakes, high mounded, point the streams their way,
Slopes, ridges, plains their spreading skirts display,
The vales branch forth, high walk approaching groves,
And all the majesty of nature moves.

O'er the wild hemisphere his glances fly,
Its form unfolding as it still draws nigh,
As all its salient sides force far their sway,
Crowd back the ocean and indent the day.
He saw, thro central zones, the winding shore
Spread the deep Gulph his sail had traced before,
The Darien isthmus check the raging tide,
Join distant lands, and neighboring seas divide;
On either hand the shores unbounded bend,
Push wide their waves, to each dim pole ascend;
The two twin continents united rise,
Broad as the main, and lengthen'd with the skies.

Long gazed the Mariner; when thus the Guide:
Here spreads the world thy daring sail descried,

Hesperia call'd, from my anterior claim;
But now Columbia, from thy patriarch name.
So from Phenicia's peopled strand of yore
Europa sail'd, and sought an unknown shore;
There stampt her sacred name; and thence her race,
Hale, venturous, bold, from Jove's divine embrace,
Ranged o'er the world, predestined to bestride
Earth's elder continents and each far tide.

Ages unborn shall bless the happier day,
That saw thy streamer shape the guideless way,
Their bravest heroes trace the path you led,
And sires of nations thro the regions spread.
Behold yon isles, where first thy flag unfurl'd
In bloodless triumph o'er the younger world;
As, awed to silence, savage bands gave place,
And hail'd with joy the sun-descended race.

Retrace the banks yon rushing waters lave;
There Orinoco checks great ocean's wave;
Thine is the stream; it cleaves the well known coast,
Where Paria's walks thy former footsteps boast.
But these no more thy wide discoveries bound;
Superior prospects lead their swelling round;
Nature's remotest scenes before thee roll,
And years and empires open on thy soul.

To yon dim rounds first elevate thy view;
See Quito's plains o'erlook their proud Peru;
On whose huge base, like isles amid sky driven,
A vast protuberance props the cope of heaven;
Earth's loftiest turrets there contend for height,
And all our Andes fill the bounded sight.
From south to north what long blue swells arise,
Built thro the clouds, and lost in ambient skies!
Approaching slow they heave expanding bounds,
The yielding concave bends sublimer rounds;
Whose wearied stars, high curving to the west,
Pause on the summits for a moment's rest;
Recumbent there they renovate their force,
And roll rejoicing on their downward course.
Round each bluff base the sloping ravine bends;
Hills forms on hills, and croupe o'er croupe extends;
Ascending, whitening, how the crags are lost,
O'erhung with headcliffs of eternal frost!
Broad fields of ice give back the morning ray,
Like walls of suns, or heaven's perennial day.
There folding storms on eastern pinions ride,
Veil the black void, and wrap the mountains side,
Rude thunders rake the crags, the rains descend,
And the long lightnings o'er the vallies bend;

While blasts unburden'd sweep the cliffs of snow,
The whirlwinds wheel above, the floods convolve below.
There molten rocks explosive rend their tomb;
Volcanos, laboring many a nation's doom,
Wild o'er the regions pour their floods of fire;
The shores heave backward, and the seas retire.
There lava waits my late reluctant call,
To roar aloft and shake some guilty wall;
Thy pride, O Lima, swells the sulphurous wave,
And fanes and priests and idols crowd thy grave.
But cease, my son, these dread events to trace,
Nor learn the woes that here await thy race.
Anorth from that broad gulph, where verdant rise
Those gentler mounds that skirt the temperate skies,
A happier hemisphere invites thy view;
Tis there the old world shall embrace the new:
There Europe's better sons their seat shall trace,
And change of government improve the race.
Thro all the midsky zones, to yon blue pole,
Their green hills lengthen, their bright rivers roll;
And swelling westward, how their champaigns run!
How slope their uplands to the morning sun!
So spoke the blest Immortal; when more near
His northern wilds in all their breadth appear;

Lands yet unknown, and streams without a name
Rise into vision and demand their fame.
As when some saint first gains his bright abode,
Vaults o'er the spheres and views the works of God,
Sees earth, his kindred orb, beneath him roll,
Here glow the centre, and there point the pole;
O'er land and sea his eyes delighted rove,
And human thoughts his heavenly joys improve;
With equal scope the raptured Hero's sight
Ranged the low vale, or climb'd the cloudy height,
As, fixt in ardent look, his opening mind,
Explored the realms that here invite mankind.
   From sultry Mobile's gulph-indented shore
To where Ontario hears his Laurence roar,
Stretch'd o'er the broadback'd hills, in long array,
The tenfold Alleganies meet the day.
And show, far sloping from the plains and streams,
The forest azure streak'd with orient beams.
High moved the scene, Columbus gazed sublime,
And thus in prospect hail'd the happy clime:
Blest be the race my guardian guide shall lead
Where these wide vales their various bounties spread!
What treasured stores the hills must here combine!
Sleep still ye diamonds, and ye ores refine;

Exalt your heads ye oaks, ye pines ascend,
Till future navies bid your branches bend;
Then spread the canvass o'er the watery way,
Explore new worlds and teach the old your sway.
He said, and northward cast his curious eyes
On other cliffs of more exalted size.
Where Maine's bleak breakers line the dangerous coast,
And isles and shoals their latent horrors boast,
High lantern'd in his heaven the cloudless White
Heaves the glad sailor an eternal light;
Who far thro troubled ocean greets the guide,
And stems with steadier helm the stormful tide.
Nor could those heights unnoticed raise their head,
That swell sublime o'er Hudson's shadowy bed;
Tho fiction ne'er has hung them in the skies,
Tho White and Andes far superior rise,
Yet hoary Kaatskill, where the storms divide,
Would lift the heavens from Atlas' laboring pride.
Land after land his passing notice claim,
And hills by hundreds rise without a name;
Hills yet unsung, their mystic powers untold;
Celestials there no sacred senates hold;
No chain'd Prometheus feasts the vulture there,
No Cyclop forges thro their summits glare,

To Phrygian Jove no victim smoke is curl'd,
Nor ark high landing quits a deluged world.
But were these masses piled on Asia's shore,
Taurus would shrink, Hemodia strut no more,
Indus and Ganges scorn their humble sires,
And rising suns salute superior fires;
Whose watchful priest would meet, with matin blaze,
His earlier God, and sooner chaunt his praise.
For here great nature, with a bolder hand,
Roll'd the broad stream, and heaved the lifted land;
And here from finish'd earth, triumphant trod
The last ascending steps of her creating God.

He saw these mountains ope their watery stores,
Floods quit their caves and seek the distant shores;
Wild thro disparting plains their waves expand,
And lave the banks where future towns must stand.
Whirl'd from the monstrous Andes' bursting sides,
Maragnon leads his congregating tides;
A thousand Alps for him dissolve their snow,
A thousand Rhones obedient bend below,
From different zones their ways converging wind,
Sweep beds of ore, and leave their gold behind,
In headlong cataracts indignant rave,
Rush to his banks and swell the swallowing wave.

Ucayla, first of all his mighty sons,
From Cusco's walls a wearied journey runs;
Pastaza mines proud Pambamarca's base,
And holds thro sundering hills his lawless race;
Aloft, where Cotopaxa flames on high,
The roaring Napo quits his misty sky,
Down the long steeps in whitening torrents driven,
Like Nile descending from his fabled heaven;
Mound after mound impetuous Tigris rends,
Curved Ista folds whole countries in his bends;
Vast Orinoco, summon'd forth to bring
His far fetch'd honors to the sateless king,
Drives on his own strong course to gain the shore,
But sends Catuba here with half his store;
Like a broad Bosphorus here Negro guides
The gather'd mass of fifty furious tides;
From his waste world, by nameless fountains fed,
Wild Purus wears his long and lonely bed;
O'er twelve degrees of earth Madera flows,
And robs the south of half its treasured snows;
Zingus, of equal length and heavier force,
Rolls on, for months, the same continuous course
To reach his master's bank; that here constrains
Topayo, charged with all Brazilla's rains;

While inland seas, and lakes unknown to fame,
Send their full tributes to the monarch stream;
Who, swell'd with growing conquest, wheels abroad,
Drains every land, and gathers all his flood;
Then far from clime to clime majestic goes,
Enlarging, widening, deepening as he flows;
Like heaven's broad milkyway he shines alone,
Spreads o'er the globe its equatorial zone,
Weighs the cleft continent, and pushes wide
Its balanced mountains from each crumbling side.
Sire Ocean hears his proud Maragnon roar,
Moves up his bed, and seeks in vain the shore,
Then surging strong, with high and hoary tide,
Whelms back the Stream and checks his rolling pride.
The stream ungovernable foams with ire,
Climbs, combs tempestuous, and attacks the Sire;
Earth feels the conflict o'er her bosom spread,
Her isles and uplands hide their wood-crown'd head;
League after league from land to water change,
From realm to realm the seaborn monsters range;
Vast midland heights but pierce the liquid plain,
Old Andes tremble for their proud domain;
Till the fresh Flood regains his forceful sway,
Drives back his father Ocean, lash'd with spray;

Whose ebbing waters lead the downward sweep,
And waves and trees and banks roll whirling to the deep.
Where suns less ardent cast their golden beams,
And minor Andes pour a waste of streams,
The marsh of Moxoe scoops the world, and fills
(From Bahia's coast to Cochabamba's hills)
A thousand leagues of bog ; he strives in vain
Their floods to centre and their lakes retain ;
His gulphs o'ercharged their opening sides display,
And southern vales prolong the seaward way.
Columbus traced, with swift exploring eye,
The immense of waves that here exalted lie,
The realms that mound the unmeasured magazine,
The far blue main, the climes that stretch between.
He saw Xaraya's diamond banks unfold,
And Paraguay's deep channel paved with gold,
Saw proud Potosi lift his glittering head,
And pour down Plata thro his tinctured bed.
Rich with the spoils of many a distant mine,
In his broad silver sea their floods combine ;
Wide over earth his annual freshet strays,
And highland drains with lowland drench repays ;
Her thirsty regions wait his glad return,
And drink their future harvest from his urn.

Where the cold circles gird the southern sky,
Brave Magellan's wild channel caught his eye;
The long cleft ridges wall'd the spreading way,
That gleams far westward to an unknown sea.
Soon as the distant swell was seen to roll,
His ancient wishes reabsorb'd his soul;
Warm from his heaving heart a sudden sigh
Burst thro his lips; he turn'd his moisten'd eye,
And thus besought his Angel: speak, my guide,
Where leads the pass? and what yon purple tide?
How the dim waves in blending ether stray!
No lands behind them rise, no pinions on them play.
There spreads, belike, that other unsail'd main
I sought so long, and sought, alas, in vain;
To gird this watery globe, and bring to light
Old India's coast; and regions wrapt in night.
Restore, celestial friend, my youthful morn,
Call back my years, and let my fame return;
Grant me to trace, beyond that pathless sea,
Some happier shore from lust of empire free;
To find in that far world a peaceful bower,
From envy safe and curst Ovando's power.
Earth's happiest realms let not their distance hide,
Nor seas forever roll their useless tide.

For nations yet unborn, that wait thy time,
Demand their seats in that secluded clime;
Ah, grant me still, their passage to prepare,
One venturous bark, and be my life thy care.
So pray'd the Hero; Hesper mild replies,
Divine compassion softening in his eyes,
Tho still to virtuous deeds thy mind aspires,
And these glad visions kindle new desires,
Yet hear with reverence what attends thy state,
Nor wish to pass the eternal bounds of fate.
Led by this sacred light thou soon shalt see
That half mankind shall owe their seats to thee,
Freedom's first empire claim its promised birth
In these rich rounds of sea-encircled earth;
Let other years, by thine example prest,
Call forth their heroes to explore the rest.
Thro different seas a twofold passage lies
To where sweet India scents a waste of skies.
The circling course, by Madagascar's shores,
Round Afric's cape, bold Gama now explores;
Thy well plann'd path these gleamy straits provide,
Nor long shall rest the daring search untried.
This idle frith must open soon to fame,
Here a lost Lusitanian fix his name,

From that new main in furious waves be tost,
And fall neglected on the barbarous coast.
  But lo the Chief! bright Albion bids him rise,
Speed in his pinions, ardor in his eyes!
Hither, O Drake, display thy hastening sails,
Widen ye passes, and awake ye gales,
March thou before him, heaven-revolving sun,
Wind his long course, and teach him where to run;
Earth's distant shores, in circling bands unite,
Lands, learn your fame, and oceans, roll in light,
Round all the watery globe his flag be hurl'd,
A new Columbus to the astonish'd world.
  He spoke; and silent tow'rd the northern sky
Wide o'er the hills the Hero cast his eye,
Saw the long floods thro devious channels pour,
And wind their currents to the opening shore;
Interior seas and lonely lakes display
Their glittering glories to the beams of day.
Thy capes, Virginia, towering from the tide,
Raise their blue banks, and slope thy barriers wide,
To future sails unfold an inland way,
And guard secure thy multifluvian Bay;
That drains uncounted realms, and here unites
The liquid mass from Alleganian heights.

York leads his wave, imbank'd in flowery pride,
And nobler James falls winding by his side;
Back to the hills, thro many a silent vale,
While Rappahanok seems to lure the sail,
Patapsco's bosom courts the hand of toil,
Dull Susquehanna laves a length of soil;
But mightier far, in sealike azure spread,
Potowmak sweeps his earth disparting bed.
Long dwelt his eye where these commingling pour'd,
Their waves unkeel'd, their havens unexplored;
Where frowning forests stretch the dusky wing,
And deadly damps forbid the flowers to spring;
No seasons clothe the field with cultured grain,
No buoyant ship attempts the chartless main;
Then with impatient voice: My Seer, he cried,
When shall my children cross the lonely tide?
Here, here my sons, the hand of culture bring,
Here teach the lawn to smile, the grove to sing:
Ye laboring floods, no longer vainly glide,
Ye harvests load them, and ye forests ride;
Bear the deep burden from the joyous swain,
And tell the world where peace and plenty reign.
Hesper to this return'd him no reply,
But raised new visions to his roving eye.

He saw broad Delaware the shores divide,
He saw majestic Hudson pour his tide;
Thy stream, my Hartford, thro its misty robe,
Play'd in the sunbeams, belting far the globe;
No watery glades thro richer vallies shine,
Nor drinks the sea a lovelier wave than thine.

Mystick and Charles refresh their seaward isles,
And gay Piscateway pays his passing smiles;
Swift Kenebec, high bursting from his lakes,
Shoots down the hillsides thro the clouds he makes;
And hoarse resounding, gulphing wide the shore,
Dread Laurence labors with tremendous roar;
Laurence, great son of Ocean! lorn he lies,
And braves the blasts of hyperborean skies.
Where hoary winter holds his howling reign,
And April flings her timid showers in vain,
Groans the choked Flood, in frozen fetters bound,
And isles of ice his angry front surround.

As old Enceladus, in durance vile,
Spreads his huge length beneath Sicilia's isle,
Feels mountains, crush'd by mountains, on him prest,
Close not his veins, nor still his laboring breast;
His limbs convulse, his heart rebellious rolls,
Earth shakes responsive to her utmost poles,

While rumbling, bursting, boils his ceaseless ire,
Flames to mid heaven, and sets the skies on fire.
So the contristed Laurence lays him low,
And hills of sleet and continents of snow
Rise on his crystal breast; his heaving sides
Crash with the weight, and pour their gushing tides.
Asouth, whence all his hundred branches bend,
Relenting airs with boreal blasts contend;
Far in his vast extremes he swells and thaws,
And seas foam wide between his ice-bound jaws.
Indignant Frost, to hold his captive, plies
His hosted fiends that vex the polar skies,
Unlocks his magazines of nitric stores,
Azotic charms and muriatic powers;
Hail, with its glassy globes, and brume congeal'd,
Rime's fleecy flakes, and storm that heaps the field
Strike thro the sullen Stream with numbing force,
Obstruct his sluices and impede his course.
In vain he strives; his might interior fails;
Nor spring's approach, nor earth's whole heat avails;
He calls his hoary Sire; old Ocean roars
Responsive echoes thro the Shetland shores.
He comes, the Father! from his bleak domains,
To break with liquid arms the sounding chains;

Clothed in white majesty, he leads from far
His tides high foaming to the wintry war.
Billows on billows lift the maddening brine,
And seas and clouds in battling conflict join,
O'erturn the vast gulph glade with rending sweep,
And crash the crust that bridged the boiling deep;
Till forced aloft, bright bounding thro the air,
Moves the blear ice, and sheds a dazzling glare;
The torn foundations on the surface ride,
And wrecks of winter load the downward tide.
  The loosen'd ice-isles o'er the main advance,
Toss on the surge, and thro the concave dance;
Whirl'd high, conjoin'd, in crystal mountains driven,
Alp over Alp, they build a midway heaven;
Whose million mirrors mock the solar ray,
And give condensed the tenfold glare of day.
As tow'rd the south the mass enormous glides,
And brineless rivers furrow down its sides;
The thirsty sailor steals a glad supply,
And sultry trade winds quaff the boreal sky.
  But oft insidious death, with mist o'erstrown,
Rides the dark ocean on this icy throne;
When ships thro vernal seas with light airs steer
Their midnight march, and deem no danger near.

The steerman gaily helms his course along,
And laughs and listens to the watchman's song,
Who walks the deck, enjoys the murky fog,
Sure of his chart, his magnet and his log;
Their shipmates dreaming, while their slumbers last,
Of joys to come, of toils and dangers past.
Sudden a chilling blast comes roaring thro
The trembling shrouds, and startles all the crew;
They spring to quarters, and perceive too late
The mount of death, the giant strides of fate.
The fullsail'd ship, with instantaneous shock,
Dash'd into fragments by the floating rock,
Plunges beneath its basement thro the wave,
And crew and cargo glut the watery grave.
  Say, Palfrey, brave good man, was this thy doom?
Dwells here the secret of thy midsea tomb?
But, Susan, why that tear? my lovely friend,
Regret may last, but grief should have an end.
An infant then, thy memory scarce can trace
The lines, tho sacred, of thy father's face;
A generous spouse has well replaced the sire;
New duties hence new sentiments require.
  Now where the lakes, those midland oceans, lie,
Columbus turn'd his heaven-illumined eye.

Ontario's banks, unable to retain
The five great Caspians from the distant main,
Burst with the ponderous mass, and forceful whirl'd
His Laurence forth, to balance thus the world.
Above, bold Erie's wave sublimely stood,
Look'd o'er the cliff, and heaved his headlong flood;
Where dread Niagara bluffs high his brow,
And frowns defiance to the world below.
White clouds of mist expanding o'er him play,
That tinge their skirts in all the beams of day;
Pleased Iris wantons in perpetual pride,
And bends her rainbows o'er the dashing tide.
Far glimmering in the north, bleak Huron runs,
Clear Michigan reflects a thousand suns,
And bason'd high, on earth's broad bosom gay,
The bright Superior silvers down the day.
Blue mounds beyond them far in ether fade,
Deep groves between them cast a solemn shade,
Slow moves their settling mist in lurid streams,
And dusky radiance streaks the solar beams.
Fixt on the view the great discoverer stood,
And thus addrest the messenger of good:
But why these seats, that seem reserved to grace
The social toils of some illustrious race,

Why spread so wide and form'd so fair in vain?
And why so distant rolls the bounteous main?
These happy regions must forever rest,
Of man unseen, by native beasts possest;
And the best heritage my sons could boast
Illude their search in far dim deserts lost.
For see, no ship can point her pendants here,
No stream conducts nor ocean wanders near;
Frost, crags and cataracts their north invest,
And the tired sun scarce finds their bounds awest.
  To whom the Seraph: Here indeed retires
The happiest land that feels my fostering fires;
Here too shall numerous nations found their seat,
And peace and freedom bless the kind retreat.
Led by this arm thy sons shall hither come,
And streams obedient yield the heroes room,
Spread a broad passage to their well known main,
Nor sluice their lakes, nor form their soils in vain.
  Here my bold Missisippi bends his way,
Scorns the dim bounds of yon bleak boreal day,
And calls from western heavens, to feed his stream,
The rains and floods that Asian seas might claim.
Strong in his march, and charged with all the fates
Of regions pregnant with a hundred states,

He holds in balance, ranged on either hand,
Two distant oceans and their sundering land;
Commands and drains the interior tracts that lie
Outmeasuring Europe's total breadth of sky.
  High in the north his parent fountains wed,
And oozing urns adorn his infant head;
In vain proud Frost his nursing lakes would close,
And choke his channel with perennial snows;
From all their slopes he curves his countless rills,
Sweeps their long marshes, saps their settling hills;
Then stretching, straightening south, he gaily gleams,
Swells thro the climes, and swallows all their streams;
From zone to zone, o'er earth's broad surface curl'd,
He cleaves his course, he furrows half the world,
Now roaring wild thro bursting mountains driven,
Now calm reflecting all the host of heaven;
Where Cynthia pausing, her own face admires,
And suns and stars repeat their dancing fires.
Wide o'er his meadowy lawns he spreads and feeds
His realms of canes, his waving world of reeds;
Where mammoth grazed the renovating groves,
Slaked his huge thirst, and chill'd his fruitless loves;
Where elks, rejoicing o'er the extinguish'd race,
By myriads rise to fill the vacant space.

Earth's widest gulph expands to meet his wave,
Vast isles of ocean in his current lave;
Glad Thetis greets him from his finish'd course,
And bathes her Nereids in his freshening source.
To his broad bed their tributary stores
Wisconsin here, there lonely Peter pours;
Croix, from the northeast wilds his channel fills,
Ohio, gather'd from his myriad hills,
Yazoo and Black, surcharged by Georgian springs,
Rich Illinois his copious treasure brings;
Arkansa, measuring back the sun's long course,
Moine, Francis, Rouge augment the father's force.
But chief of all his family of floods
Missouri marches thro his world of woods;
He scorns to mingle with the filial train,
Takes every course to reach alone the main;
Orient awhile his bending sweep he tries,
Now drains the southern, now the northern skies,
Searches and sunders far the globe's vast frame,
Reluctant joins the sire, and takes at last his name.
There lies the path thy future sons shall trace,
Plant here their arts, and rear their vigorous race:
A race predestined, in these choice abodes,
To teach mankind to tame their fluvial floods,

Retain from ocean, as their work requires,
These great auxiliars, raised by solar fires,
Force them to form ten thousand roads, and girth
With liquid belts each verdant mound of earth,
To aid the colon's as the carrier's toil,
To drive the coulter, and to fat the soil,
Learn all mechanic arts, and oft regain
Their native hills in vapor and in rain.

So taught the Saint. The regions nearer drew,
And raised resplendent to their Hero's view
Rich nature's triple reign; for here elate
She stored the noblest treasures of her state,
Adorn'd exuberant this her last domain,
As yet unalter'd by her mimic man,
Sow'd liveliest gems, and plants of proudest grace,
And strung with strongest nerves her animated race.

Retiring far round Hudson's frozen bay,
Earth's lessening circles shrink beyond the day;
Snows ever rising with the toils of time
Choke the chill shrubs that brave the dismal clime;
The beasts all whitening roam the lifeless plain,
And caves unfrequent scoop the couch for man.

Where Spring's coy steps in cold Canadia stray,
And joyless seasons hold unequal sway,

He saw the pine its daring mantle rear,
Break the rude blast, and mock the brumal year,
Shag the green zone that bounds the boreal skies,
And bid all southern vegetation rise.
Wild o'er the vast impenetrable round
The untrod bowers of shadowy nature frown'd;
Millennial cedars wave their honors wide,
The fir's tall boughs, the oak's umbrageous pride,
The branching beech, the aspen's trembling shade
Veil the dim heaven, and brown the dusky glade.
For in dense crowds these sturdy sons of earth,
In frosty regions, claim a stronger birth;
Where heavy beams the sheltering dome requires,
And copious trunks to feed its wintry fires.

But warmer suns, that southern zones emblaze,
A cool thin umbrage o'er their woodland raise;
Floridia's shores their blooms around him spread,
And Georgian hills erect their shady head;
Whose flowery shrubs regale the passing air
With all the untasted fragrance of the year.
Beneath tall trees, dispersed in loose array,
The rice-grown lawns their humble garb display;
The infant maize, unconscious of its worth,
Points the green spire and bends the foliage forth;

In various forms unbidden harvests rise,
And blooming life repays the genial skies.
  Where Mexic hills the breezy gulph defend,
Spontaneous groves with richer burdens bend.
Anana's stalk its shaggy honors yields,
Acassia's flowers perfume a thousand fields,
Their cluster'd dates the mast-like palms unfold,
The spreading orange waves a load of gold,
Connubial vines o'ertop the larch they climb,
The long-lived olive mocks the moth of time,
Pomona's pride, that old Grenada claims,
Here smiles and reddens in diviner flames;
Pimento, citron scent the sky serene,
White woolly clusters fringe the cotton's green,
The sturdy fig, the frail deciduous cane
And foodful cocoa fan the sultry plain.
  Here, in one view, the same glad branches bring
The fruits of autumn and the flowers of spring;
No wintry blasts the unchanging year deform,
Nor beasts unshelter'd fear the pinching storm;
But vernal breezes o'er the blossoms rove,
And breathe the ripen'd juices thro the grove.
  Beneath the crystal wave's inconstant light
Pearls burst their shells to greet the Hero's sight;

From opening earth in living lustre shine
The various treasures of the blazing mine;
Hills cleft before him all their stores unfold,
The pale platina and the burning gold;
Silver whole mounds, and gems of dazzling ray
Illume the rocks and shed the beams of day.

THE

COLUMBIAD.

BOOK II.

ARGUMENT.

Natives of America appear in vision. Their manners and characters. Columbus demands the cause of the dissimilarity of men in different countries. Hesper replies, That the human body is composed of a due proportion of the elements suited to the place of its first formation; that these elements, differently proportioned, produce all the changes of health, sickness, growth and decay; and may likewise produce any other changes which occasion the diversity of men; that these elemental proportions are varied, not more by climate than temperature and other local circumstances; that the mind is likewise in a state of change, and will take its physical character from the body and from external objects: examples. Inquiry concerning the first peopling of America. View of Mexico. Its destruction by Cortez. View of Cusco and Quito, cities of Peru. Tradition of Capac and Oella, founders of the Peruvian empire. Columbus inquires into their real history. Hesper gives an account of their origin, and relates the stratagems they used in establishing that empire.

THE

COLUMBIAD.

BOOK II.

High o'er his world as thus Columbus gazed,
And Hesper still the changing scene emblazed,
Round all the realms increasing lustre flew,
And raised new wonders to the Patriarch's view.
He saw at once, as far as eye could rove,
Like scattering herds, the swarthy people move
In tribes innumerable; all the waste,
Wide as their walks, a varying shadow cast.
As airy shapes, beneath the moon's pale eye,
People the clouds that sail the midnight sky,
Dance thro the grove and flit along the glade,
And cast their grisly phantoms on the shade;
So move the hordes, in thickets half conceal'd,
Or vagrant stalking thro the fenceless field.

Here tribes untamed, who scorn to fix their home,
O'er shadowy streams and trackless deserts roam;
While others there in settled hamlets rest,
And corn-clad vales a happier state attest.
The painted chiefs, in guise terrific drest,
Rise fierce to war, and beat their savage breast;
Dark round their steps collecting warriors pour,
Some fell revenge begins the hideous roar;
From hill to hill the startling war-song flies,
And tribes on tribes in dread disorder rise,
Track the mute foe and scour the howling wood,
Loud as a storm, ungovern'd as a flood;
Or deep in groves the silent ambush lay,
Lead the false flight, decoy and seize their prey,
Their captives torture, butcher and devour,
Drink the warm blood and paint their cheeks with gore.
Awhile he paused, with dubious thoughts opprest,
And thus to Hesper's ear his doubts addrest:
Say, to what class of nature's sons belong
The countless tribes of this untutor'd throng?
Where human frames and brutal souls combine,
No force can tame them, and no arts refine.
Can these be fashion'd on the social plan,
Or boast a lineage with the race of man?

When first we found them in yon hapless isle,
They seem'd to know and seem'd to fear no guile;
A timorous herd, like harmless roes, they ran,
And call'd us Gods, from whom their tribes began.
But when, their fears allay'd, in us they trace
The well-known image of a mortal race,
When Spanish blood their wondering eyes beheld,
A frantic rage their changing bosoms swell'd;
They roused their bands from numerous hills afar,
To feast their souls on ruin, waste and war.
Nor plighted vows nor sure defeat control
The same indignant savageness of soul.

Tell then, my Seer, from what dire sons of earth
The brutal people drew their ancient birth;
If these forgotten shores and useless tides
Have form'd them different from the world besides,
Born to subjection, when in happier time
A nobler race should reach their fruitful clime;
Or, if a common source all nations claim,
Their lineage, form and faculties the same,
What sovereign secret cause, yet undisplay'd,
This wondrous change in nature's work has made;
Why various powers of soul and tints of face
In different lands diversify the race;

To whom the Guide: Unnumber'd causes lie,
In earth and sea, in climate, soil and sky,
That fire the soul, or damp the genial flame,
And work their wonders on the human frame.
See beauty, form and color change with place;
Here charms of health the lively visage grace;
There pale diseases float in every wind,
Deform the figure, and degrade the mind.

From earth's own elements thy race at first
Rose into life, the children of the dust;
These kindred elements, by various use,
Nourish the growth and every change produce;
In each ascending stage the man sustain,
His breath, his food, his physic and his bane.
In due proportions where these atoms lie,
A certain form their equal aids supply;
And while unchanged the efficient causes reign,
Age following age the certain form maintain.
But where crude atoms disproportion'd rise,
And cast their sickening vapors round the skies,
Unlike that harmony of human frame,
That moulded first and reproduce the same,
The tribes ill form'd, attempering to the clime,
Still vary downward with the years of time;

More perfect some, and some less perfect yield
Their reproductions in this wondrous field;
Till fixt at last their characters abide,
And local likeness feeds their local pride.
The soul too, varying with the change of clime,
Feeble or fierce, or groveling or sublime,
Forms with the body to a kindred plan,
And lives the same, a nation or a man.
  Yet think not clime alone the tint controls,
On every shore, by altitude of poles;
A different cast the glowing zone demands,
In Paria's groves, from Tombut's burning sands.
Unheeded agents, for the sense too fine,
With every pulse, with every thought combine,
Thro air and ocean, with their changes run,
Breathe from the ground, or circle with the sun.
Where these long continents their shores outspread,
See the same form all different tribes pervade;
Thro all alike the fertile forests bloom,
And all, uncultured, shed a solemn gloom;
Thro all great nature's boldest features rise,
Sink into vales or tower amid the skies;
Streams darkly winding stretch a broader sway,
The groves and mountains bolder walks display;

A dread sublimity informs the whole,
And rears a dread sublimity of soul.
  Yet time and art shall other changes find,
And open still and vary still the mind.
The countless clans that tread these dank abodes,
Who glean spontaneous fruits and range the woods,
Fixt here for ages, in their swarthy face
Display the wild complexion of the place.
Yet when the hordes to happy nations rise,
And earth by culture warms the genial skies,
A fairer tint and more majestic grace
Shall flush their features and exalt the race;
While milder arts, with social joys refined,
Inspire new beauties in the growing mind.
  Thy followers too, old Europe's noblest pride,
When future gales shall wing them o'er the tide,
A ruddier hue and deeper shade shall gain,
And stalk, in statelier figures, on the plain.
While nature's grandeur lifts the eye abroad
O'er these last labors of the forming God,
Wing'd on a wider glance the venturous soul
Bids greater powers and bolder thoughts unrol;
The sage, the chief, the patriot unconfined,
Shield the weak world and meliorate mankind.

But think not thou, in all the range of man,
That different pairs each different cast began;
Or tribes distinct, by signal marks confest,
Were born to serve or subjugate the rest.
The Hero heard, and thus resumed the strain:
Who led these wanderers o'er the dreary main?
Could their weak sires, unskill'd in human lore,
Build the bold bark, to seek an unknown shore?
A shore so distant from the world beside,
So dark the tempests, and so wild the tide,
That Greece and Tyre, and all who tempt the sea,
Have shunn'd the task, and left the fame to me.
When first thy roving race, the Power replied,
Learn'd by the stars the devious sail to guide,
From stormy Hellespont explored the way,
And sought the limits of the Midland sea;
Before Alcides form'd his impious plan
To check the sail, and bound the steps of man,
This hand had led them to this rich abode,
And braved the wrath of that strong demigod.
Driven from the Calpian strait, a hapless train
Roll'd on the waves that sweep the western main;
Storms from the orient blacken'd heaven with shade,
Nor sun nor stars could yield their wonted aid.

For many a darksome day o'erwhelm'd and tost,
Their sails, their oars in swallowing surges lost,
At length, the clouds withdrawn, they sad descry
Their course directing from their native sky.
No hope remains; far onward o'er the zone
The trade wind bears them with the circling sun;
Till wreck'd and stranded here, the sylvan coast
Receives to lonely seats the suffering host.
The fruitful vales invite their steps to roam,
Renounce their sorrows and forget their home;
Revolving years their ceaseless wanderings led,
And from their sons descending nations spread.
  These in the torrid tracts began their sway,
Whose cultured fields their growing arts display;
The northern tribes a later stock may boast,
A race descended from the Asian coast.
High in the Arctic, where Anadir glides,
A narrow strait the impinging worlds divides;
There Tartar fugitives from famine sail,
And migrant tribes these fruitful shorelands hail.
  He spoke; when Behren's pass before them lay,
And moving nations on the margin stray,
Thick swarming, venturous; sail and oar they ply,
Climb on the surge and o'er the billows fly.

As when autumnal storms awake their force,
The storks foreboding tempt their southern course;
From all the fields collecting throngs arise,
Mount on the wing and crowd along the skies:
Thus, to his eye, from bleak Tartaria's shore,
Thro isles and seas, the gathering people pour,
Change their cold regions for a happier strand,
Leap from the wave and tread the welcome land;
In growing tribes extend their southern sway,
And wander wide beneath a warmer day.

But why, the Chief replied, if ages past
Led the bold vagrants to so mild a waste;
If human souls, for social compact given,
Inform their nature with the stamp of heaven,
Why the wild woods for ever must they rove,
Nor arts nor social joys their passions move?
Long is the lapse of ages, since thy hand
Conducted here thy first adventurous band.
On other shores, in every eastern clime,
Since that unletter'd, distant tract of time,
What arts have sprung, imperial powers to grace!
What sceptres sway'd the many-master'd race!
Guilt, grandeur, glory from their seats been hurl'd,
And dire divulsions shook the changing world!

Ere Rome's first Eagle clave the frighted air,
Ere Sparta form'd her deathlike sons of war,
Ere Tyre and Ilion saw their towers arise,
Or Memphian pyramids usurp'd the skies,
These tribes have forester'd the fruitful zone,
Their seats unsettled, and their name unknown.

Hesper to this replied: A scanty train,
In that far age, approach'd the wide domain;
The wide domain, with game and fruitage crown'd,
Supplied their food uncultured from the ground.
By nature form'd to rove, the humankind,
Of freedom fond, will ramble unconfined,
Till all the region fills, and rival right
Restrains their steps, and bids their force unite;
When common safety builds a common cause,
Conforms their interest and inspires their laws;
By mutual checks their different manners blend,
Their fields bloom joyous, and their walls ascend.
Here to the vagrant tribes no bounds arose,
They form'd no union, as they fear'd no foes;
Wandering and wild, from sire to son they stray,
A thousand ages, scorning every sway.
And what a world their seatless nations led!
A total hemisphere around them spread;

See the lands lengthen, see the rivers roll,
To each far main, to each extended pole!
  But lo, at last the destined course is run,
The realms are peopled and their arts begun.
Where yon mid region elevated lies,
A few famed cities glitter to the skies;
There move, in eastern pomp, the toils of state,
And temples heave, magnificently great.
  The Hero turn'd to greet the novel sight;
When three far splendors, yet confusedly bright,
Rose like a constellation; till more near,
Distinctly mark'd their different sites appear;
Diverging still, beneath their roofs of gold,
Three cities gay their mural towers unfold.
So, led by visions of his guiding God,
The seer of Patmos o'er the welkin trod,
Saw the new heaven its flamy cope unbend,
And walls and gates and spiry domes descend;
His well known sacred city grows, and gains
Her new built towers, her renovated fanes;
With golden skies and suns and rainbows crown'd,
Jerusalem looks forth and lights the world around.
  Bright on the north imperial Mexic rose;
A mimic morn her sparkling vanes disclose,

Her opening streets concentred hues display,
Give back the sun, and shed internal day;
The circling wall with guardian turrets frown'd,
And look'd defiance to the realms around;
A glimmering lake without the wall retires,
Inverts the towers, and seems a grove of spires.
Proud o'er the midst, on columns lifted high,
A giant structure claims a loftier sky;
O'er the tall gates sublimer arches bend,
Courts larger lengthen, bolder walks ascend,
Starr'd with superior gems the porches shine,
And speak the royal residence within.
There, deck'd in state robes, on his golden throne,
Mid suppliant kings, dread Montezuma shone;
Mild in his eye a temper'd grandeur sate,
High seem'd his soul, with conscious power elate;
In aspect open, social and serene,
Enclosed by favorites, and of friends unseen.
Round the rich throne, in various lustre dight,
Gems undistinguish'd cast a changing light;
Sapphire and emerald soften down the scene,
Cold azure mingling with the vernal green,
Pearl, amber, ruby warmer flames unfold,
And diamonds brighten from the burning gold;

Thro all the dome the living blazes blend,
And shoot their rainbows where the arches bend.
On every ceiling, painted light and gay,
Symbolic forms their graphic art display;
Recording, confident of endless fame,
Each feat of arms, each patriarchal name;
Like Memphian hieroglyphs, to stretch the span
Of memory frail in momentary man.
  Pour'd thro the gates a hundred nations greet,
Throng the rich mart and line each ample street,
Ply different labors, walls and structures rear,
Or till the fields, or train the ranks of war.
Thro spreading states the skirts of empire bend,
New temples rise and other plains extend;
Thrice ten wide provinces, in culture gay,
Bless the same king, and daily firm the sway.
  A smile benignant kindling in his eyes,
O happy realm! the glad Columbus cries,
Far in the midland, safe from every foe,
Thy arts shall flourish as thy virtues grow,
To endless years thy rising fame extend,
And sires of nations from thy sons descend.
May no gold-thirsty race thy temples tread,
Insult thy rites, nor heap thy plains with dead;

No Bovadilla seize the tempting spoil,
No dark Ovando, no religious Boyle,
In mimic priesthood grave, or robed in state,
O'erwhelm thy glories in oblivious fate!
Vain are thy hopes, the sainted Power replied,
These rich abodes from Spanish hordes to hide,
Or teach hard guilt and cruelty to spare
The guardless prize of sacrilegious war.
Think not the vulture, mid the field of slain,
Where base and brave promiscuous strow the plain,
Where the young hero in the pride of charms
Pours brighter crimson o'er his spotless arms,
Will pass the tempting prey, and glut his rage
On harder flesh, and carnage black with age;
O'er all alike he darts his eager eye,
Whets the blunt beak and hovers down the sky,
From countless corses picks the dainty food,
And screams and fattens in the purest blood.
So the vile hosts, that hither trace thy way,
On happiest tribes with fiercest fury prey.
Thine the dread task, O Cortez, here to show
What unknown crimes can heighten human woe,
On these fair fields the blood of realms to pour,
Tread sceptres down, and print thy steps in gore,

With gold and carnage swell thy sateless mind,
And live and die the blackest of mankind.
He gains the shore. Behold his fortress rise,
His fleet high flaming suffocates the skies.
The march begins; the nations in affright
Quake as he moves, and wage the fruitless fight;
Thro the rich provinces he bends his way,
Kings in his chain, and kingdoms for his prey;
Full on the imperial town infuriate falls,
And pours destruction o'er its batter'd walls.
In quest of peace great Montezuma stands,
A sovereign supplicant with lifted hands,
Brings all his treasure, yields the regal sway,
Bids vassal millions their new lord obey;
And plies the victor with incessant prayer,
Thro ravaged realms the harmless race to spare.
But treasures, tears and sceptres plead in vain,
Nor threats can move him, nor a world restrain;
While blind religion's prostituted name
And monkish fury guide the sacred flame.
O'er crowded fanes their fires unhallow'd bend,
Climb the wide roofs, the lofty towers ascend,
Pour thro the lowering skies the smoky flood,
And stain the fields, and quench the blaze in blood.

Columbus heard; and, with a heaving sigh,
Dropt the full tear that started in his eye:
O hapless day! his trembling voice replied,
That saw my wandering pennon mount the tide.
Had but the lamp of heaven to that bold sail
Ne'er mark'd the passage nor awoke the gale,
Taught foreign prows these peopled shores to find,
Nor led those tigers forth to fang mankind;
Then had the tribes beneath these bounteous skies
Seen their walls widen and their harvests rise;
Down the long tracts of time their glory shone,
Broad as the day and lasting as the sun.
The growing realms, behind thy shield that rest,
Paternal monarch, still thy power had blest,
Enjoy'd the pleasures that surround thy throne,
Survey'd thy virtues and improved their own.

Forgive me, prince; this luckless arm hath led
The storm unseen that hovers o'er thy head;
Taught the dark sons of slaughter where to roam,
To seize thy crown and seal the nation's doom.
Arm, sleeping empire, meet the murderous band,
Drive back the invaders, save the sinking land.—
But vain the call! behold the streaming blood!
Forgive me, Nature! and forgive me, God!

While sorrows thus his patriarch pride control,
Hesper reproving soothes his tender soul:
Father of this new world, thy tears give o'er,
Let virtue grieve and heaven be blamed no more.
Enough for man, with persevering mind,
To act his part and strive to bless his kind;
Enough for thee, o'er thy dark age to soar,
And raise to light that long-secluded shore.
For this my guardian care thy youth inspired,
To virtue rear'd thee, and with glory fired,
Bade in thy plan each distant world unite,
And wing'd thy vessel for the venturous flight.
Nor think the labors vain; to good they tend;
Tyrants like these shall ne'er defeat their end;
Their end that opens far beyond the scope
Of man's past efforts and his present hope.
Long has thy race, to narrow shores confined,
Trod the same round that fetter'd fast the mind;
Now, borne on bolder plumes, with happier flight,
The world's broad bounds unfolding to the sight,
The mind shall soar; the coming age expand
Their arts and lore to every barbarous land;
And buried gold, drawn copious from the mine,
Give wings to commerce and the world refine.

Now to yon southern cities turn thy view,
And mark the rival seats of rich Peru.
See Quito's airy plains, exalted high,
With loftier temples rise along the sky;
And elder Cusco's shining roofs unfold,
Flame on the day, and shed their suns of gold.
Another range, in these pacific climes,
Spreads a broad theatre for unborn crimes;
Another Cortez shall their treasures view,
His rage rekindle and his guilt renew;
His treason, fraud, and every fell design,
O curst Pizarro, shall revive in thine.

Here reigns a prince, whose heritage proclaims
A long bright lineage of imperial names;
Where the brave roll of Incas love to trace
The distant father of their realm and race,
Immortal Capac. He, in youthful pride,
With young Oella his illustrious bride,
Announced their birth divine; a race begun
From heaven, the children of their God the Sun;
By him sent forth a polish'd state to frame,
Crush the fiend Gods that human victims claim,
With cheerful rites their pure devotions pay
To the bright orb that gives the changing day.

On this great plan, as children of the skies,
They plied their arts and saw their hamlets rise.
First of their works, and sacred to their fame,
Yon proud metropolis received its name,
Cusco the seat of states, in peace design'd
To reach o'er earth, and civilize mankind.
Succeeding sovereigns spread their limits far,
Tamed every tribe, and sooth'd the rage of war;
Till Quito bow'd; and all the heliac zone
Felt the same sceptre, and confirm'd the throne.

Near Cusco's walls, where still their hallow'd isle
Bathes in its lake and wears its verdant smile,
Where these prime parents of the sceptred line
Their advent made, and spoke their birth divine,
Behold their temple stand; its glittering spires
Light the glad waves and aid their father's fires.
Arch'd in the walls of gold, its portal gleams
With various gems of intermingling beams;
And flaming from the front, with borrow'd ray,
A diamond circlet gives the rival day;
In whose bright face forever looks abroad
The labor'd image of the radiant God.
There dwells the royal priest, whose inner shrine
Conceals his lore; tis there his voice divine

Proclaims the laws; and there a cloister'd quire
Of holy virgins keep the sacred fire.
  Columbus heard; and curious to be taught
What pious fraud such wondrous changes wrought,
Ask'd by what mystic charm, in that dark age,
They quell'd in savage souls the barbarous rage,
By leagues of peace combined a wide domain,
And taught the virtues in their laws to reign.
  Long is the tale; but tho their labors rest
By years obscured, in flowery fiction drest,
My voice, said Hesper, shall revive their name,
And give their merits to immortal fame.
Led by his father's wars, in early prime
Young Capac left his native northern clime;
The clime where Quito since hath rear'd her fanes,
And now no more her barbarous rites maintains.
He saw these vales in richer blooms array'd,
And tribes more numerous haunt the woodland shade,
Saw rival clans their local Gods adore,
Their altars staining with their children's gore,
Yet mark'd their reverence for the Sun, whose beam
Proclaims his bounties and his power supreme;
Who sails in happier skies, diffusing good,
Demands no victim and receives no blood.

In peace return'd with his victorious sire,
New charms of glory all his soul inspire;
To conquer nations on a different plan,
And build his greatness on the good of man.
By nature form'd for hardiest deeds of fame,
Tall, bold and full-proportion'd rose his frame;
Strong moved his limbs, a mild majestic grace
Beam'd from his eyes and open'd in his face;
O'er the dark world his mind superior shone,
And seem'd the semblance of his parent Sun.
But tho fame's airy visions lift his eyes,
And future empires from his labors rise;
Yet softer fires his daring views control,
And mixt emotions fill his changing soul.
Shall genius rare, that might the world improve,
Bend to the milder voice of careless love,
That bounds his glories, and forbids to part
From bowers that woo'd his fluctuating heart?
Or shall the toils imperial heroes claim
Fire his brave bosom with a patriot flame,
Bid sceptres wait him on Peruvia's shore,
And loved Oella meet his eyes no more?
Still unresolved he sought the lonely maid,
Who plied her labors in the silvan shade;

Her locks loose rolling mantle deep her breast,
And wave luxuriant round her slender waist,
Gay wreaths of flowers her pensive brows adorn,
And her white raiment mocks the light of morn.
Her busy hand sustains a bending bough,
Where cotton clusters spread their robes of snow,
From opening pods unbinds the fleecy store,
And culls her labors for the evening bower.
For she, the first in all Hesperia, fed
The turning spindle with the twisting thread;
The woof, the shuttle follow'd her command,
Till various garments grew beneath her hand.
And now, while all her thoughts with Capac rove
Thro former scenes of innocence and love,
In distant fight his fancied dangers share,
Or wait him glorious from the finish'd war;
Blest with the ardent hope, her sprightly mind
A vesture white had for the prince design'd;
And here she seeks the wool to web the fleece,
The sacred emblem of returning peace.
Sudden his near approach the maid alarms;
He flew enraptured to her yielding arms,
And lost, dissolving in a softer flame,
His distant empire and the fire of fame.

At length, retiring thro the homeward field,
Their glowing souls to cooler converse yield;
O'er various scenes of blissful life they ran,
When thus the warrior to the maid began:
  Long have we mark'd the inauspicious reign
That waits our sceptre in this rough domain;
A soil ungrateful and a wayward race,
Their game but scanty, and confined their space.
Where late my steps the southern war pursued,
The fertile plains grew boundless as I view'd;
More numerous nations trod the grassy wild,
And joyous nature more delightful smiled.
No changing seasons there the flowers deform,
No dread volcano and no mountain storm;
Rains ne'er invade, nor livid lightnings play,
Nor clouds obscure the radiant King of day.
But while his orb, in ceaseless glory bright,
Rolls the rich day and fires his stars by night,
Unbounded fulness flows beneath his reign,
Seas yield their treasures, fruits adorn the plain;
His melting mountains spread their annual flood,
Night sheds her dews, the day-breeze fans the God.
Tis he inspires me with the vast design
To form those nations to a sway divine;

Destroy the rites of every demon Power,
Whose altars smoke with sacrilegious gore;
To laws and labor teach the tribes to yield,
And richer fruits to grace the cultured field.
  But great, my charmer, is the task of fame,
Their faith to fashion and their lives to tame;
Full many a spacious wild these eyes must see
Spread dreary bounds between my love and me;
And yon bright Godhead circle thrice the year,
Each lonely evening number'd with a tear.
Long robes of white my shoulders must embrace,
To speak my lineage of ethereal race;
That simple men may reverence and obey
The radiant offspring of the Power of day.
  When these my deeds the faith of nations gain,
And happy millions bless thy Capac's reign,
Then shall he feign a journey to the Sun,
To bring the partner of his well-earn'd throne;
So shall descending kings the line sustain,
Till earth's whole regions join the vast domain.
  Will then my fair, at my returning hour,
Forsake these wilds and hail a happier bower?
Will she consenting now resume her smiles,
Send forth her warrior to his glorious toils;

And, sweetly patient, wait the flight of days,
That crown our labors with immortal praise?
  Silent the damsel heard; her moistening eye
Spoke the full soul, nor could her voice reply;
Till softer accents sooth'd her wounded ear,
Composed her tumult and allay'd her fear:
Think not, heroic maid, my steps would part
While silent sorrows heave that tender heart.
Oella's peace more dear shall prove to me
Than all the realms that bound the raging sea;
Nor thou, bright Sun, shalt bribe my soul to rest,
And leave one struggle in her lovely breast.
  Yet think in tribes so vast, my gentle fair,
What millions merit our instructive care;
How age to age leads on their joyless gloom,
Habitual slaughter their poor piteous doom;
No social ties their wayward passions prove,
Nor peace nor pleasure treads the howling grove;
Mid thousand heroes and a thousand fair
No fond Oella meets her Capac there.
Yet, taught by thee domestic joys to prize,
With softer charms the virgin race shall rise,
Awake new virtues, every grace improve,
And form their minds for happiness and love.

Ah think, as future years thro time descend,
What wide creations on thy voice depend;
And, like the Sun, whose all-delighting ray
To those mild regions gives his purest day,
Diffuse thy bounties, let me instant fly;
In three short moons the generous task I'll try;
Then swift returning, I'll conduct my fair
Where realms submissive wait her fostering care.

And will my prince, my Capac, borne away,
Thro those dark wilds in quest of empire stray,
Where tigers fierce command the shuddering wood,
And men like tigers thirst for human blood?
Think'st thou no dangerous deed the course attends,
Alone, unaided by thy sire and friends?
Even chains and death may meet my hero there,
Nor his last groan could reach Oella's ear.

But no! nor death nor chains shall Capac prove
Unknown to her, while she has power to rove.
Close by thy side, where'er thy wanderings stray,
My equal steps shall measure all the way;
With borrow'd soul each chance of fate I'll dare,
Thy toils to lessen and thy dangers share.
Quick shall my ready hand two garments weave,
Whose sunny whiteness shall the tribes deceive;

Thus clad, their homage shall secure our sway,
And hail us children of the God of day.
The lovely counsel pleased. The smiling chief
Approved her courage and dispell'd her grief;
Then to their homely bower in haste they move,
Begin their labors and prepare to rove.
Soon grow the robes beneath her forming care,
And the fond parents wed the wondrous pair;
But whelm'd in grief beheld the following dawn,
Their joys all vanish'd and their children gone.
Nine days they march'd; the tenth effulgent morn
Saw their white forms that sacred isle adorn.
The work begins; they preach to every band
The well-form'd fiction, and their faith demand;
With various miracles their powers display,
To prove their lineage and confirm their sway.
They form to different arts the hand of toil,
To whirl the spindle and to spade the soil,
The Sun's bright march with pious finger trace,
And his pale sister with her changing face;
Show how their bounties clothe the labor'd plain,
The green maize shooting from its golden grain,
How the white cotton tree's expanding lobes
File into threads, and swell to fleecy robes;

While the tamed Llama aids the wondrous plan,
And lends his garment to the loins of man.
The astonish'd tribes believe, with glad surprise,
The Gods descended from the favoring skies,
Adore their persons robed in shining white,
Receive their laws and leave each horrid rite,
Build with assisting hands the golden throne,
And hail and bless the sceptre of the Sun.

THE

COLUMBIAD.

BOOK III.

ARGUMENT.

Actions of the Inca Capac. A general invasion of his dominions threatened by the mountain savages. Rocha, the Inca's son, sent with a few companions to offer terms of peace. His embassy. His adventure with the worshippers of the volcano. With those of the storm, on the Andes. Falls in with the savage armies. Character and speech of Zamor, their chief. Capture of Rocha and his companions. Sacrifice of the latter. Death song of Azonto. War dance. March of the savage armies down the mountains to Peru. Incan army meets them. Battle joins. Peruvians terrified by an eclipse of the sun, and routed. They fly to Cusco. Grief of Oella, supposing the darkness to be occasioned by the death of Rocha. Sun appears. Peruvians from the city wall discover Rocha on an altar in the savage camp. They march in haste out of the city and engage the savages. Exploits of Capac. Death of Zamor. Recovery of Rocha, and submission of the enemy.

THE

COLUMBIAD.

BOOK III.

Now twenty years these children of the skies
Beheld their gradual growing empire rise.
They ruled with rigid but with generous care,
Diffused their arts and sooth'd the rage of war,
Bade yon tall temple grace their favorite isle,
The mines unfold, the cultured valleys smile,
Those broad foundations bend their arches high,
And rear imperial Cusco to the sky;
Wealth, wisdom, force consolidate the reign
From the rude Andes to the western main.
But frequent inroads from the savage bands
Lead fire and slaughter o'er the labor'd lands;
They sack the temples, the gay fields deface,
And vow destruction to the Incan race.

The king, undaunted in defensive war,
Repels their hordes, and speeds their flight afar;
Stung with defeat, they range a wider wood,
And rouse fresh tribes for future fields of blood.
   Where yon blue ridges hang their cliffs on high,
And suns infulminate the stormful sky,
The nations, temper'd to the turbid air,
Breathe deadly strife, and sigh for battle's blare;
Tis here they meditate, with one vast blow,
To crush the race that rules the plains below.
Capac with caution views the dark design,
Learns from all points what hostile myriads join,
And seeks in time by proffer'd leagues to gain
A bloodless victory, and enlarge his reign.
   His eldest hope, young Rocha, at his call,
Resigns his charge within the temple wall;
In whom began, with reverend forms of awe,
The functions grave of priesthood and of law.
   In early youth, ere yet the ripening sun
Had three short lustres o'er his childhood run,
The prince had learnt, beneath his father's hand,
The well-framed code that sway'd the sacred land;
With rites mysterious served the Power divine,
Prepared the altar and adorn'd the shrine,

Responsive hail'd, with still returning praise,
Each circling season that the God displays,
Sooth'd with funereal hymns the parting dead,
At nuptial feasts the joyful chorus led;
While evening incense and the morning song
Rose from his hand or trembled on his tongue.
Thus form'd for empire ere he gain'd the sway,
To rule with reverence and with power obey,
Reflect the glories of the parent Sun,
And shine the Capac of his future throne,
Employ'd his docile years; till now from far
The rumor'd leagues proclaim approaching war;
Matured for active scenes he quits the shrine,
To aid in council or in arms to shine.
Amid the chieftains that the court compose,
In modest mien the stripling pontiff rose,
With reverence bow'd, conspicuous o'er the rest,
Approach'd the throne, and thus the sire addrest:
Great king of nations, heaven-descended sage,
Thy second heir has reach'd the destined age
To take these priestly robes; to his pure hand
I yield them pure, and wait thy kind command.
Should foes invade, permit this arm to share
The toils, the triumphs, every chance of war;

For this dread conflict all our force demands,
In one wide field to whelm the brutal bands,
Pour to the mountain gods their wonted food,
And save thy realms from future leagues of blood.
Yet oh, may sovereign mercy first ordain
Propounded compact to the savage train!
I'll go with terms of peace to spread thy sway,
And teach the blessings of the God of day.

The sire return'd: My great desire you know,
To shield from slaughter and preserve the foe,
In bands of concord all their tribes to bind,
And live the friend and guardian of mankind.
Should strife begin, thy youthful arm shall share
The toils of glory thro the walks of war;
But o'er their hills to seek alone the foes,
To gain their confidence or brave their blows,
Bend their proud souls to reason's voice divine,
Claims hardier limbs and riper years than thine.
Yet one of heavenly race the task requires,
Whose mystic rites control the solar fires;
So the sooth'd Godhead proves to faithless eyes
His love to man, his empire of the skies.

Some veteran chief, in those rough labors tried,
Shall aid thee on, and go thy faithful guide;

O'er dreary heights thy sinking limbs sustain,
Teach the dark wiles of each insidious train,
Thro all extremes of life thy voice attend,
In counsel lead thee, or in arms defend.
And three firm youths, thy chosen friends, shall go
To learn the climes and meditate the foe;
That wars of future years their skill may find,
To serve the realm and save the savage kind.
  Rise then, my son, first partner of my fame,
With early toils to build thy sacred name;
In high behest, for his own legate known,
Proclaim the bounties of our sire the Sun.
Tell how his fruits beneath our culture rise,
His stars, how glorious, gem our cloudless skies;
And how to us his hand hath kindly given
His peaceful laws, the purest grace of heaven,
With power to widen his terrestrial sway,
And give our blessings where he gives the day.
Yet, should the stubborn nations still prepare
The shaft of slaughter for the barbarous war,
Tell them we know to tread the crimson plain,
And God's own children never yield to man.
  But ah, my child, with steps of caution go,
The ways are hideous, and enraged the foe;

Blood stains their altars, all their feasts are blood,
Death their delight, and darkness reigns their God;
Tigers and vultures, storms and earthquakes share
Their rites of worship and their spoils of war.
Shouldst thou, my Rocha, tempt too far their ire,
Should those dear relics feed a murderous fire,
Deep sighs would rend thy wretched mother's breast,
The pale Sun sink in clouds of darkness drest,
Thy sire and mournful nations rue the day
That drew thy steps from these sad walls away.

Yet go; tis virtue calls; and realms unknown,
Won by these works, may bless thy future throne;
Millions of unborn souls in time may see
Their doom reversed, and owe their peace to thee,
Deluded sires, with murdering hands, no more
Feed fancied demons with their children's gore,
But, sway'd by happier sceptres, here behold
The rites of freedom and the shrines of gold.
Be wise, be mindful of thy realm and throne;
God speed thy labors and preserve my son!

Soon the glad prince, in robes of white array'd,
Call'd his attendants and the sire obey'd.
A diamond broad, in burning gold imprest,
Display'd the sun's bright image on his breast;

A pearl-dropt girdle bound his waist below,
And the white lautu graced his lofty brow.
They journey'd forth, o'ermarching far the mound
That flank'd the kingdom on its Andean bound;
Ridge after ridge thro vagrant hordes they past,
Where each new tribe seem'd wilder than the last;
To all they preach and prove the solar sway,
And climb fresh mountains on their tedious way.

At length, as thro disparting clouds they rise,
And hills above them still obstruct the skies,
While a dead calm o'er all the region stood,
And not a leaf could fan its parent wood,
Sudden a strange portentous noise began;
The birds fled wild, the beasts for shelter ran;
Slow, sullen, loud, with deep astounding blare,
Swell the strong tones of subterranean war;
Behind, before, beneath them groans the ground,
Earth heaves and labors with the shuddering sound;
Columns of smoke, that cap the rumbling height,
Roll reddening far thro heaven, and choke the light;
From tottering steeps descend their cliffs of snow,
The mountains reel, the valleys rend below;
The headlong streams forget their usual round,
And shrink and vanish in the gaping ground.

The sun descends; but night recals in vain
Her silent shades, to recommence her reign;
The bursting mount gapes high, a sudden glare
Coruscates wide, till all the purpling air
Breaks into flame, and wheels and roars and raves
And wraps the welkin in its folding waves;
Light sailing cinders, thro its vortex driven,
Stream high and brighten to the midst of heaven;
And, following slow, full floods of boiling ore
Swell, swoop aloft and thro the concave roar.
Torrents of molten rocks, on every side,
Lead o'er the shelves of ice their fiery tide;
Hills slide before them, skies around them burn,
Towns sink beneath and heaving plains upturn;
O'er many a league the flaming deluge hurl'd,
Sweeps total nations from the staggering world.
  Meanwhile, at distance thro the livid light,
A busy concourse met their wondering sight;
The prince drew near; where lo! an altar stood,
Rude in its form, and fill'd with burning wood;
Wrapt in the flames a youth expiring lay,
And the fond father thus was heard to pray:
Receive, O dreadful Power, from feeble age,
This last pure offering to thy sateless rage;

Thrice has thy vengeance on this hated land
Claim'd a dear infant from my yielding hand;
Thrice have those lovely lips the victim prest,
And all the mother torn that tender breast;
When the dread duty stifled every sigh,
And not a tear escaped her beauteous eye.
Our fourth and last now meets the fatal doom;
Groan not, my child, thy God remands thee home;
Attend once more, thou dark infernal Name,
From yon far streaming pyramid of flame;
Snatch from his heaving flesh the blasted breath,
Sacred to thee and all the fiends of death;
Then in thy hall, with spoils of nations crown'd,
Confine thy walks beneath the rending ground;
No more on earth the embowel'd flames to pour,
And scourge my people and my race no more.

Thus Rocha heard; and to the trembling crowd
Turn'd the bright image of his beaming God.
The afflicted chief, with fear and grief opprest,
Beheld the sign, and thus the prince addrest:
From what far land, O royal stranger, say,
Ascend thy wandering steps this nightly way?
From plains like ours, by holy demons fired?
Have thy brave people in the flames expired?

And hast thou now, to stay the whelming flood,
No son to offer to the furious God?
From happier lands I came, the prince returns,
Where no red flaming flood the concave burns,
No furious God bestorms our soil and skies,
Nor yield our hands the bloody sacrifice;
But life and joy the Power delights to give,
And bids his children but rejoice and live.
Thou seest thro heaven the day-dispensing Sun
In living radiance wheel his golden throne,
O'er earth's gay surface send his genial beams,
Force from yon cliffs of ice the vernal streams;
While fruits and flowers adorn the cultured field,
And seas and lakes their copious treasures yield;
He reigns our only God. In him we trace
The friend, the father of our happy race.
Late the lone tribes, on those unlabor'd shores,
Ran wild and served imaginary Powers;
Till he, in pity, taught their feuds to cease,
Devised their laws, and fashion'd all for peace.
My sacred parents first the reign began,
Sent from his courts to guide the paths of man,
To plant his fruits, to manifest his sway,
And give their blessings where he gives the day.

The sachem proud replied: Thy garb and face
Proclaim thy lineage of superior race;
And our progenitors, no less than thine,
Sprang from a God, and own a birth divine.
From that sky-scorching mount, on floods of flame,
In elder times my great forefathers came;
There dwells the Sire, and from his dark abode
Oft claims, as now, the tribute of a God.
This victim due when willing mortals pay,
His terrors lessen and his fires decay;
While purer sleet regales the mountain air,
And our glad hosts are fired for fiercer war.
Yet know, dread chief, the pious youth rejoin'd,
Some one prime Power produced all human kind;
Some Sire supreme, whose ever-ruling soul
Creates, preserves, and regulates the whole.
That Sire supreme must roll his radiant eye
Round the wide earth and thro the boundless sky;
That all their habitants, their gods and men,
May rise unveil'd beneath his careful ken.
Could thy dark fiend, that hides his blind abode,
And cauldrons in his cave that fiery flood,
Yield the rich fruits that distant nations find?
Or praise or punish or behold mankind?

But when my God, resurging from the night,
Shall gild his chambers with the morning light,
By mystic rites he'll vindicate his throne,
And own thy servant for his duteous son.
  Meantime, the chief replied, thy cares releast,
Rest here the night and share our scanty feast;
Which, driven in hasty rout, our train supplied,
When trembling earth foretold the boiling tide.
They fared, they rested; till with lucid horn
All-cheering Phosphor led the lively morn;
The prince arose, an altar rear'd in haste,
And watch'd the splendors of the reddening east.
  As o'er the mountain flamed the sun's broad eye,
He call'd the host, his holy rites to try;
Then took the loaves of maize, the bounties brake,
Gave to the chief, and bade them all partake;
The hallow'd relics on the pile he placed,
With tufts of flowers the simple offering graced,
Held to the sun the image from his breast,
Whose glowing concave all the God exprest;
O'er the dried leaves the rays concentred fly,
And thus his voice ascends the listening sky:
O thou, whose splendors kindle heaven with fire,
Great Soul of nature, man's immortal Sire,

If e'er my father found thy sovereign grace,
Or thy blest will ordain'd the Incan race,
Give these lorn tribes to learn thy awful name,
Receive this offering, and the pile inflame;
So shall thy laws o'er wider bounds be known,
And earth's whole race be happy as thy own.
Thus pray'd the prince; the focal flames aspire,
The mute beholders tremble and retire,
Gaze on the miracle, full credence own,
And vow obedience to the sacred Sun.
The legates now their farther course descried,
A young cazique attending as a guide,
O'er craggy cliffs pursued their eastern way,
Trod loftier champaigns, meeting high the day,
Saw timorous tribes, in these sublime abodes,
Adore the blasts and turn the storms to gods;
While every cloud that thunders thro the skies
Claims from their hands a human sacrifice.
Awhile the youth, their better faith to gain,
Strives with his usual art, but strives in vain;
In vain he pleads the mildness of the sun;
A gale refutes him ere his speech be done;
Continual tempests from their orient blow,
And load the mountains with eternal snow.

The sun's own beam, the timid clans declare,
Drives all their evils on the tortured air;
He draws the vapors up their eastern sky,
That sail and centre round his dazzling eye;
Leads the loud storms along his midday course,
And bids the Andes meet their sweeping force;
Builds their bleak summits with an icy throne,
To shine thro heaven, a semblance of his own;
Hence the sharp sleet, these lifted lawns that wait,
And all the scourges that attend their state.
Two toilsome days the virtuous Inca strove
To social life their savage minds to move;
When the third morning glow'd serenely bright,
He led their elders to an eastern height;
The world unlimited beneath them lay,
And not a cloud obscured the rising day.
Vast Amazonia, starr'd with twinkling streams,
In azure drest, a heaven inverted seems;
Dim Paraguay extends the aching sight,
Xaraya glimmers like the moon of night,
Land, water, sky in blending borders play,
And smile and brighten to the lamp of day.
When thus the prince: What majesty divine!
What robes of gold! what flames about him shine!

There walks the God! his starry sons on high
Draw their dim veil and shrink behind the sky;
Earth with surrounding nature's born anew,
And men by millions greet the glorious view!
Who can behold his all-delighting soul
Give life and joy, and heaven and earth control,
Bid death and darkness from his presence move,
Who can behold, and not adore and love?
Those plains, immensely circling, feel his beams,
He greens the groves, he silvers gay the streams,
Swells the wild fruitage, gives the beast his food,
And mute creation hails the genial God.
But richer boons his righteous laws impart,
To aid the life and mould the social heart,
His arts of peace thro happy realms to spread,
And altars grace with sacrificial bread;
Such our distinguish'd lot, who own his sway,
Mild as his morning stars and liberal as the day.
His unknown laws, the mountain chief replied,
May serve perchance your boasted race to guide;
And yon low plains, that drink his partial ray,
At his glad shrine their just devotions pay.
But we nor fear his frown nor trust his smile;
Vain as our prayers is every anxious toil;

Our beasts are buried in his whirls of snow,
Our cabins drifted to his slaves below.
Even now his placid looks thy hopes beguile,
He lures thy raptures with a morning smile;
But soon (for so those saffron robes proclaim)
His own black tempest shall obstruct his flame,
Storm, thunder, fire, against the mountains driven,
Rake deep their sulphur'd sides, disgorging here his heaven.

He spoke; they waited, till the fervid ray
High from the noontide shot the faithless day;
When lo, far gathering under eastern skies,
Solemn and slow, the dark red vapors rise;
Full clouds, convolving on the turbid air,
Move like an ocean to the watery war.
The host, securely raised, no dangers harm,
They sit unclouded and o'erlook the storm;
While far beneath, the sky-borne waters ride,
Veil the dark deep and sheet the mountain's side;
The lightning's glancing fires, in fury curl'd,
Bend their long forky foldings o'er the world;
Torrents and broken crags and floods of rain
From steep to steep roll down their force amain,
In dreadful cataracts; the bolts confound
The tumbling clouds, and rock the solid ground.

The blasts unburden'd take their upward course,
And o'er the mountain top resume their force.
Swift thro the long white ridges from the north
The rapid whirlwinds lead their terrors forth;
High walks the storm, the circling surges rise,
And wild gyrations wheel the hovering skies;
Vast hills of snow, in sweeping columns driven,
Deluge the air and choke the void of heaven;
Floods burst their bounds, the rocks forget their place,
And the firm Andes tremble to their base.
Long gazed the host; when thus the stubborn chief,
With eyes on fire, and fill'd with sullen grief:
Behold thy careless god, secure on high,
Laughs at our woes and peaceful walks the sky,
Drives all his evils on these seats sublime,
And wafts his favors to a happier clime;
Sire of the dastard race thy words disclose,
There glads his children, here afflicts his foes.
Hence! speed thy flight! pursue him where he leads;
Lest vengeance seize thee for thy father's deeds,
Thy immolated limbs assuage the fire
Of those curst Powers, who now a gift require.
The youth in haste collects his scanty train,
And, with the sun, flies o'er the western plain;

The fading orb with plaintive voice he plies,
To guide his steps and light him down the skies.
So when the moon and all the host of even
Hang pale and trembling on the verge of heaven,
While storms ascending threat their nightly reign,
They seek their absent sire, and sink below the main.
Now to the south he turns; where one vast plain
Calls from a hundred hordes the warrior train;
Of various dress and various form they show'd;
Each wore the ensign of his local god.
From eastern hills a grisly troop descends,
Whose war song wild the shuddering concave rends;
Cloak'd in a tiger's hide their grim chief towers,
And apes the brinded god his tribe adores.
The tusky jaws grin o'er the sachem's brow,
The bald eyes glare, the paws depend below,
From his bored ears contorted serpents hung,
And drops of gore seem'd rolling on his tongue.
The northern glens pour forth the Vulture-race;
Brown tufts of quills their shaded foreheads grace;
The claws branch wide, the beak expands for blood,
And all the armor imitates the god.
The Condor, frowning from a southern plain,
Borne on a standard, leads a numerous train:

Clench'd in his talons hangs an infant dead,
His long bill pointing where the sachems tread,
His wings, tho lifeless, frighten still the wind,
And his broad tail o'ershades the file behind.
From other plains and other hills afar,
The tribes throng dreadful to the promised war;
Some twine their forelock with a crested snake,
Some wear the emblems of a stream or lake;
All from the Power they serve assume their mode,
And foam and yell to taste the Incan blood.
  The prince incautious with his men drew near,
Known for an Inca by his dress and air;
Till coop'd and caught amid the warrior trains,
They bow in silence to the victor's chains.
When now the gather'd thousands throng the plain,
And echoing skies the rending shouts retain;
Zamor, the chieftain of the Tiger-band,
By choice appointed to the first command,
Shrugg'd up his brinded spoils above the rest,
And grimly frowning thus the crowd addrest:
  Warriors, attend! tomorrow leads abroad
Our sacred vengeance for our brothers' blood.
On those scorch'd plains for ever must they lie,
Their bones still naked to the burning sky?

Left in the field for foreign hawks to tear,
Nor our own vultures can the banquet share.
But soon, ye mountain gods, yon dreary west
Shall sate your hunger with an ampler feast;
When the proud Sun, that terror of the plain,
Shall grieve in heaven for all his children slain,
As o'er his realm our slaughtering armies roam,
And give to your sad Powers a happier home.
Meanwhile, ye tribes, these men of solar race,
Food for the flames, your bloody rites shall grace;
Each to a different god his panting breath
Resigns in fire; this night demands their death:
All but the Inca; him reserved in state
These conquering hands ere long shall immolate
To all the Powers at once that storm the skies,
A grateful gift, before his mother's eyes.
  The sachem ceased; the chiefs of every race
Lead the bold captives to their destined place;
The sun descends, the parting day expires,
And earth and heaven display their sparkling fires.
Soon the raised altars kindle round the gloom,
And call the victims to their vengeful doom;
Led to their pyres, in sullen pomp they tread,
And sing by turns the triumphs of the dead.

Amid the crowd beside his altar stood
The youth devoted to the Tiger-god;
A beauteous form he rose, of noble grace,
The only hope of his illustrious race.
His aged sire, for numerous years, had shone
The first supporter of the Incan throne;
Wise Capac loved the youth, and graced his hand
With a fair virgin from a neighboring band;
And him the legate prince, in equal prime,
Had chose to share his mission round the clime.
He mounts the pyre, the flames approach his breath,
And thus he wakes the dauntless song of death:
  Dark vault of heaven, that greet his daily throne,
Where flee the glories of your absent Sun?
Ye starry hosts, who kindle from his eye,
Can you behold him in the western sky?
Or if unseen beneath his watery bed,
The wearied God reclines his radiant head,
When next his morning steps your courts inflame,
And seek on earth for young Azonto's name,
Then point these ashes, mark the smoky pile,
And say the hero suffer'd with a smile.
So shall the Power in vengeance view the place,
In crimson clothe his terror-beaming face,

Pour swift destruction on these curst abodes,
Whelm the grim tribes and all their savage gods.
But ah, forbear to tell my stooping sire
His darling hopes have fed a coward fire;
Why should he know the tortures of the brave?
Why fruitless sorrows bend him to the grave?
Nor shalt thou e'er be told, my bridal fair,
What silent pangs these panting vitals tear;
But blooming still the patient hours employ
On the blind hope of future scenes of joy.
Now haste, ye fiends of death; the Sire of day
In absent slumber gives your malice way;
While fainter light these livid flames supply,
And short-lived thousands learn of me to die.
He ceased not speaking; when the yell of war
Drowns all their death songs in a hideous jar;
The cries rebounding from the hillsides pour,
And wolves and tigers catch the distant roar.
Now more concordant all their voices join,
And round the plain they form the festive line;
When, to the music of the dismal din,
Indignant Zamor bids the dance begin.
Dim thro the shadowy fires each changing form
Moves like a cloud before an evening storm,

When o'er the moon's pale face and starry plain
The shifting shades lead on their broken train;
The mingling tribes their mazy gambols tread,
Till the last groan proclaims the victims dead,
Then part the smoky flesh, enjoy the feast,
And lose their labors in oblivious rest.

Soon as the western hills announced the morn,
And falling fires were scarcely seen to burn,
Grimm'd by the horrors of the dreadful night,
The hosts woke fiercer for the promised fight;
And dark and silent thro the frowning grove
The different tribes beneath their standards move.

Meantime the solar king collects from far
His martial bands, to meet the expected war,
Camps on the confines of an eastern plain
That skirts the steep rough limit of his reign;
He trains their ranks, their pliant force combines,
To close in columns or extend in lines,
To wheel, change front, in broken files dispart,
And draw new strength from all the warrior's art.

But now the rising sun relumes the plain,
And calls to arms the well-accustom'd train.
High in the front imperial Capac strode,
In fair effulgence like the beaming God;

A golden girdle bound his snowy vest,
A mimic sun hung sparkling on his breast;
The lautu's horned wreath his temples twined,
The bow, the quiver shade his waist behind;
Raised high in air his golden sceptre burn'd,
And hosts surrounding trembled as he turn'd.

O'er eastern hills he cast his watchful eye,
Thro the broad breaks that lengthen down the sky;
In whose blue clefts the sloping pathways bend,
Where annual floods from melting snows descend.
Now dry and deep, they lead from every height
The savage files that headlong rush to fight;
They throng and thicken thro the smoky air,
And every breach pours down the dusky war.
So when a hundred streams explore their way,
Down the same slopes, convolving to the sea,
They boil, they bend, they force their floods amain,
Swell o'er obstructing crags, and sweep the plain.

Capac beholds and waits the coming shock,
As for the billows waits the storm-beat rock;
And while for fight his ardent troops prepare,
Thus thro the ranks he breathes the soul of war:
Ye tribes that flourish in the Sun's mild reign,
Long have your flocks adorn'd the peaceful plain,

As o'er the realm his smiles persuasive flow'd,
And conquer'd all without the stain of blood;
But lo, at last that wild infuriate band
With savage war demands your happy land.
Beneath the dark immeasurable host,
Descending, swarming, how the crags are lost!
Already now their ravening eyes behold
Your star-bright temples and your gates of gold;
And to their gods in fancied goblets pour
The warm libation of your children's gore.
Move then to vengeance, meet the sons of blood,
Led by this arm and lighted by that God;
The strife is fierce, your fanes and fields the prize,
The warrior conquers or the infant dies.

Fill'd with his fire, the troops in squared array
Wait the wild hordes loose huddling to the fray;
Their pointed arrows, rising on the bow,
Look up the sky and chide the lagging foe.

Dread Zamor leads the homicidious train,
Moves from the clefts and stretches o'er the plain.
He gives the shriek; the deep convulsing sound
The hosts reecho, and the hills around
Retain the rending tumult; all the air
Clangs in the conflict of the clashing war.

But firm undaunted as a shelvy strand
That meets the surge, the bold Peruvians stand,
With steady aim the sounding bowstring ply,
And showers of arrows thicken thro the sky;
When each grim host, in closer conflict join'd,
Clench the dire ax and cast the bow behind;
Thro broken ranks sweep wide their slaughtering course,
Now struggle back, now sidelong sway the force.
Here from grim chiefs is lopt the grisly head;
All gride the dying, all deface the dead;
There scattering o'er the field in thin array,
Man tugs with man, and clubs with axes play;
With broken shafts they follow and they fly,
And yells and groans and shouts invade the sky;
Round all the shatter'd groves the ground is strow'd
With sever'd limbs and corses bathed in blood.
Long raged the strife; and where, on either side,
A friend, a father or a brother died,
No trace remain'd of what he was before,
Mangled with horrid wounds and black with gore.

Now the Peruvians, in collected might,
With one wide stroke had wing'd the savage flight;
But their bright Godhead, in his midday race,
With glooms unusual veil'd his radiant face,

Quench'd all his beams, tho cloudless, in affright,
As loth to view from heaven the finish'd fight.
A trembling twilight o'er the welkin moves,
Browns the dim void, and darkens deep the groves;
The waking stars, embolden'd at the sight,
Peep out and gem the anticipated night;
Day-birds, and beasts of light to covert fly,
And owls and wolves begin their evening cry.
The astonish'd Inca marks, with wild surprise,
Dead chills on earth, no cloud in all the skies,
His host o'ershaded in the field of blood,
Gored by his foes, deserted by his God.
Mute with amaze, they cease the war to wage,
Gaze on their leaders and forget their rage;
When pious Capac to the listening crowd
Raised high his wand and pour'd his voice aloud:
Ye chiefs and warriors of Peruvian race,
Some sore offence obscures my father's face;
What moves the Numen to desert the plain,
Nor save his children, nor behold them slain?
Fly! speed your course, regain the guardian town,
Ere darkness shroud you in a deeper frown;
The faithful walls your squadrons shall defend,
While my sad steps the sacred dome ascend,

To learn the cause, and ward the woes we fear:
Haste, haste, my sons! I guard the flying rear.
  The hero spoke; the trembling tribes obey,
While deeper glooms obscure the source of day.
Sudden the savage bands collect amain,
Hang on the rear and sweep them o'er the plain;
Their shouts, redoubling with the flying war,
Drown the loud groans and torture all the air.
The hawks of heaven, that o'er the field had stood,
Scared by the tumult from the scent of blood,
Cleave the far gloom; the beasts forget their prey,
And scour the waste, and give the war its way.
  Zamor elate with horrid joy beheld
The Sun depart, his children fly the field,
And raised his rending voice: Thou darkening sky,
Deepen thy damps, the fiend of death is nigh;
Behold him rising from his shadowy throne,
To veil this heaven and drive the conquer'd Sun;
The glaring Godhead yields to sacred night,
And his foil'd armies imitate his flight.
Confirm, infernal Power, thy rightful reign,
Give deadlier shades and heap the piles of slain;
Soon the young captive prince shall roll in fire,
And all his race accumulate the pyre.

Ye mountain vultures, here your food explore,
Tigers and condors, all ye gods of gore,
In these rich fields, beneath your frowning sky,
A plenteous feast shall every god supply.
Rush forward, warriors, hide the plains with dead;
Twas here our friends in former combat bled;
Strow'd thro the waste their naked bones demand
This tardy vengeance from our conquering hand.

He said; and high before the Tiger-train
With longer strides hangs forward o'er the slain,
Bends like a falling tree to reach the foe,
And o'er tall Capac aims a forceful blow.
The king beheld the ax, and with his wand
Struck the raised weapon from the sachem's hand;
Then clench'd the falling helve, and whirling round,
Fell'd a close file of heroes to the ground;
Nor stay'd, but follow'd where his people run,
Fearing to fight, forsaken by the Sun;
Till Cusco's walls salute their longing sight,
And the wide gates receive their rapid flight.
The folds are barr'd, the foes in shade conceal'd,
Like howling wolves, rave round the frighted field.

The monarch now ascends the sacred dome;
The Sun's fixt image there partakes the gloom;

Thro all the shrines, where erst on new-moon days
Swell'd the full quires of consecrated praise,
A tomb-like silence reigns; till female cries
Burst forth at last, and these sad accents rise:
Was it for this, my son to distant lands
Must trace the wilds, and tempt those lawless bands?
And does the God obscure his golden throne
In mournful darkness for my slaughter'd son?
Oh, had his beam, ere that disastrous day
That call'd the youth from these fond arms away,
Received my spirit to its native sky,
That sad Oella might have seen him die!
  Where slept thy shaft of vengeance, O my God,
When those fell tigers drank his sacred blood?
Did not the pious prince, with rites divine,
Feed the pure flame in this thy hallow'd shrine;
And early learn, beneath his father's hand,
To shed thy blessings round the favor'd land?
Form'd by thy laws the royal seat to grace,
Son of thy son, and glory of his race.
Where, my lost Rocha, rests thy lovely head?
Where the rent robes thy hapless mother made?
I see thee, mid those hideous hills of snow,
Pursued and slaughter'd by the wildman foe;

Or, doom'd a feast for some pretended god,
Drench his black altar with celestial blood.
Snatch me, O Sun, to happier worlds of light—
No: shroud me, shroud me with thyself in night.
Thou hear'st me not, thou dread departed Power,
Thy face is dark, and Rocha lives no more.
  Thus heard the silent king; his equal heart
Caught all her grief, and bore a father's part.
The cause, suggested by her tender moan,
The cause perchance that veil'd the midday sun,
And shouts that spoke the still approaching foe,
Fixt him suspense, in all the strength of woe.
A doubtful moment held his changing choice;
Now would he sooth her, half assumes his voice;
But greater cares the rising wish control,
And call forth all his energy of soul.
Why should he cease to ward the coming fate?
Or she be told the foes besiege the gate?
He turn'd in haste; and now their image-god
High on the spire with newborn lustre glow'd;
Swift thro the portal flew the hero's eye,
And hail'd the growing splendor in the sky.
  The troops courageous at return of light
Throng round the dome, impatient for the fight;

The king descending in the portal stood,
And thus addrest the all-delighting God:
O sovereign Soul of heaven, thy changing face
Makes or destroys the glory of thy race.
If from this mortal life my child be fled,
First of thy line that ever graced the dead;
If thy bright splendor ceased on high to burn
For that loved youth who never must return,
Forgive thine armies, when in fields of blood
They lose their strength and fear the frowning God.
As now thy glory, with superior day,
Glows thro the field and leads the warrior's way,
May our exalted souls, to vengeance driven,
Burn with new brightness in the cause of heaven!
For thy slain son the murderous horde shall bleed;
We mourn the hero, but avenge the deed.
He said; and from the battlement on high
A watchful warrior raised a sudden cry:
" An Inca white on yonder altar tied—
Tis Rocha's self—the flame ascends his side."
In sweeping haste the bursting gates unbar,
And flood the champaign with a tide of war;
A cloud of arrows leads the rapid train,
They shout, they swarm, they hide the dusty plain;

Bows, quivers, girdles strow the field behind,
And the raised axes cleave the passing wind.
The prince, confest to every warrior's sight,
Inspires each soul and centres all the fight;
Each hopes to snatch him from the kindling pyre,
Each fears his breath already flits in fire.
Here Zamor ranged his ax-men deep and wide,
Wedged like a wall, and thus the king defied:
Haste, son of Light, pour fast the winged war,
The prince, the dying prince demands your care;
Hear how his death song chides your dull delay,
Lift longer strides, bend forward to the fray,
Ere flames infolding suffocate his groan,
Child of your beaming God, a victim to our own.

This said, he raised his shaggy shoulders high,
And bade the shafts glide thicker thro the sky.
Like the broad billows of the lifted main,
Rolls into sight the long Peruvian train;
A white sail bounding, on the billows tost,
Is Capac towering o'er the furious host.

Now meet the dreadful chiefs, with eyes on fire;
Beneath their blows the parting ranks retire;
In whirlwind-sweep their meeting axes bound,
Wheel, crash in air, and plow the trembling ground;

Their sinewy limbs in fierce contortions bend,
And mutual strokes with equal force descend,
Parried with equal art, now gyring prest
High at the head, now plunging for the breast.
The king starts backward from the struggling foe,
Collects new strength, and with a circling blow
Rush'd furious on; his flinty edge, whirl'd wide,
Met Zamor's helve, and glancing grazed his side
And settled in his groin; so plunged it lay,
That scarce the king could tear his ax away.
The savage fell; when thro the Tiger-train
The driving Inca turns his force amain;
Where still compact they hem the murderous pyre,
And Rocha's voice seems faltering to expire.
The phrensied father rages, thunders wild,
Hews armies down, to save the sinking child;
The ranks fall staggering where he lifts his arm,
Or roll before him like a billowy storm;
Behind his steps collecting warriors close;
Deep centred in a circling ridge of foes
He cleaves his wasting way; the prince unties,
And thus his voice: Dread Sovereign of the skies,
Accept my living son, again bestow'd
To grace with rites the temple of his God.

Move, heroes, move; complete the work begun,
Crush the grim race, avenge your injured Sun.
The savage host, that view'd the daring deed,
And saw their nations with their leader bleed,
Raised high the shriek of horror; all the plain
Is trod with flight and cover'd with the slain.
The bold Peruvians compass round the field,
Confine their flight, and force the rest to yield;
When Capac raised his placid voice again;
Ye conquering troops, collect the vanquish'd train;
The Sun commands to stay the rage of war,
He knows to conquer, but he loves to spare.
He ceased; and where the savage leader lay
Weltering in gore, directs his eager way,
Unwraps the tiger's hide, and strives in vain
To close the wound, and mitigate the pain;
And while compassion for a foe distrest
Mixt with reproach, he thus the chief addrest:
Too long, proud prince, thy fearless heart with-
stood
Our sacred arms, and braved the living God;
His sovereign will commands all feuds to cease,
His realm is concord and his pleasure peace;

This copious carnage, spreading far the plain,
Insults his bounties, but confirms his reign.
Enough! tis past; thy parting breath demands
The last sad office from my yielding hands.
To share thy pains and feel thy hopeless woe,
Are rites ungrateful to a fallen foe:
Yet rest in peace; and know, a chief so brave,
When life departs, shall find an honor'd grave;
Myself in princely pomp thy tomb shall rear,
And tribes unborn thy hapless fate declare.
Insult me not with tombs! the monster cried,
Let closing clods thy coward carcase hide;
But these brave bones, unburied on the plain,
Touch not with dust, nor dare with rites profane;
Let no curst earth conceal this gory head,
Nor songs proclaim the dreadful Zamor dead.
Me, whom the hungry gods from plain to plain
Have follow'd, feasting on thy slaughter'd train,
Me wouldst thou cover? No! from yonder sky,
The wide-beak'd hawk, that now beholds me die,
Soon with his cowering train my flesh shall tear,
And wolves and tigers vindicate their share.
Receive, dread Powers (since I can slay no more),
My last glad victim, this devoved gore.

Thus pour'd the vengeful chief his fainting breath,
And lost his utterance in the gasp of death.
The sad remaining tribes confess the Power,
That sheds his bounties round Peruvia's shore;
All bow obedient to the Incan throne,
And blest Oella hails her living son.

THE

COLUMBIAD.

BOOK IV.

ARGUMENT.

Destruction of Peru foretold. Grief of Columbus. He is comforted by the promise of a vision of future ages. All Europe appears in vision. Effect of the discovery of America upon the affairs of Europe. Improvement in commerce; government. Revival of letters. Order of the Jesuits. Religious persecution. Inquisition. Rise and progress of more liberal principles. Character of Raleigh; who plans the settlement of North America. Formation of the coast by the gulph stream. Nature of the colonial establishments, the first great asylum and infant empire of Liberty. Liberty the necessary foundation of morals. Delaware arrives with a reinforcement of new settlers, to consolidate the colony of Virginia. Night scene, as contemplated by these patriarchs, while they are sailing up the Chesapeak, and are saluted by the river gods. Prophetic speech of Potowmak. Fleets of settlers from several parts of Europe steering for America.

THE

COLUMBIAD.

BOOK IV.

In one dark age, beneath a single hand,
Thus rose an empire in the savage land.
Its wealth and power with following years increase,
Its growing nations spread the walks of peace;
Religion here, that universal name,
Man's proudest passion, most ungovern'd flame,
Erects her altars on the same bright base,
That dazzled erst, and still deludes the race;
Sun, moon, all powers that forceful strike his eyes,
Earth-shaking storms and constellated skies.
  Yet all the pomp his labors here unfold,
The vales of verdure and the towers of gold,
Those infant arts and sovereign seats of state,
In short-lived glory hasten to their fate.

Thy followers, rushing like an angry flood,
Too soon shall drench them in the nation's blood;
Nor thou, Las Casas, best of men, shalt stay
The ravening legions from their guardless prey.
O hapless prelate! hero, saint and sage,
Foredoom'd with crimes a fruitless war to wage,
To see at last (thy life of virtue run)
A realm unpeopled and a world undone!
While pious Valverde mock of priesthood stands,
Guilt in his heart, the gospel in his hands,
Bids, in one field, their unarm'd thousands bleed,
Smiles o'er the scene and sanctifies the deed.
And thou, brave Gasca, with persuasive strain,
Shalt lift thy voice and urge thy power in vain;
Vain are thy hopes the sinking land to save,
Or call her slaughter'd millions from the grave.
Here Hesper paused. Columbus with a sigh
Cast o'er the continent his moisten'd eye,
And thus replied: Ah, hide me in the tomb;
Why should I live to see the impending doom?
If such foul deeds the scheme of heaven compose,
And virtue's toils induce redoubled woes,
Unfold no more; but grant a kind release;
Give me, tis all I ask, to rest in peace.

And thou shalt rest in peace, the Saint rejoin'd,
Ere these conflicting shades involve mankind.
But broader views shall first thy mind engage,
Years far advanced beyond this darksome age
Shall feast thee here; the fruits of thy long care
A grateful world beneath thy ken shall share.
Europe's contending kings shall soon behold
These fertile plains and hills of treasured gold;
And in the path of thy adventurous sail
Their countless navies float on every gale,
For wealth and commerce search the western shore,
And load each ocean with the shining ore.

As up the orient heaven the dawning ray
Smiles o'er the hills and gives the promised day,
Drives fraud and rapine from their nightly spoil,
And social nature wakes to various toil;
So from the blazing mine the golden store
Mid rival states shall spread from shore to shore,
Unite their force, its opulence to share,
Extend the pomp but sooth the rage of war;
Wide thro the world while genius unconfined
Tempts loftier flights, and opens all the mind,
Dissolves the slavish bands of monkish lore,
Wakes the bold arts and bids the Muses soar.

Then shall thy northern climes their seats display,
United nations there commence their sway;
O'er earth and ocean spread their peerless fame,
And send thro time thy patriarchal name.
 Now turn thy view to Europe; see the rage
Of feudal faction every court engage;
All honest labor, all commercial ties
Their kings discountenance, their lords despise.
The naked harbors, looking to the main,
Rear their kind cliffs and break the storms in vain,
The willing wave no foreign treasures lade,
Nor sails nor cities cast a watery shade;
Save, where yon opening gulph the strand divides,
Proud Venice bathes her in the broken tides,
Weds her tamed sea, shakes every distant throne,
And deems by right the naval world her own.
 Yet must we mark, the bondage of the mind
Spreads deeper glooms, and subjugates mankind;
The zealots fierce, whom local creeds enrage,
In holy feuds perpetual combat wage,
Support all crimes by full indulgence given,
Usurp the power and wield the sword of heaven.
 But lo, where future years their scenes unrol,
The rising arts inspire the venturous soul.

From all the ports that cleave the coast of Spain,
New fleets ascending streak the western main;
From Tago's bank, from Albion's rocky round,
Commercing squadrons o'er the billows bound;
Thro Afric's isles observe the sweeping sails,
Full pinions tossing in Arabian gales,
Indus and Ganges deep in canvass lost,
And navies crowding round Cambodia's coast;
New nations rise, all climes and oceans brave,
And shade with sheets the immeasurable wave.

See lofty Ximenes with solemn gait
Move from the cloister to the walks of state,
And thro the factious monarchies of Spain,
Curb the fierce lords and fix one royal reign.
Behold dread Charles the imperial seat ascends,
O'er Europe's thrones his conquering arm extends;
While wealthier shores, beneath the western day,
Unfold their treasures to confirm his sway.

Roused at false glory's fascinating call,
See Francis train the gallant youths of Gaul,
O'erstrain the strength of her extended states,
Scale the proud Alps, or burst their granite gates,
On Pavia's plain for Cesar's crown contend,
Of arms the votary, but of arts the friend.

And see proud Wolsey rise, securely great,
Kings at his call and mitres round him wait;
From monkish walls the hoarded wealth he draws
To aid the tyrant and restrain the laws,
Wakes Albion's genius, neighboring princes braves,
And shares with them the commonwealth of waves.
Behold dark Solyman, from eastern skies,
With his grim host magnificently rise,
Wave his broad crescent o'er the Midland sea,
Thro vast Hungaria drive his conquering way,
Crowd close the Christian powers, and carry far
The rules of homicide, the lore of war.
The Tuscan dukes excite a nobler strife;
Lorenzo calls the Fine Arts forth to life,
Fair nature's mimic maids; whose powers divine
Her charms develop and her laws define;
From sire to son the splendid labors spread,
And Leo follows where good Cosmo led.
Waked from the ground that Gothic rovers trod,
Starts the bronze hero and the marble god;
Monks, prelates, pontiffs pay the reverence due
To that bold taste their Grecian masters knew;
Resurgent temples throng the Latian shore,
The Pencil triumphs and the Muses soar.

O'er the dark world Erasmus rears his eye,
In schoolman lore sees kings and nations lie,
With strength of judgment and with fancy warm,
Derides their follies and dissolves the charm,
Tears the deep veil that bigot zeal has thrown
On pagan books and science long unknown,
From faith in senseless rites relieves mankind,
And seats bold virtue in the conscious mind.
But still the frightful task, to face alone
The jealous vengeance of the papal throne,
Restrains his hand: he gives the contest o'er,
And leaves his hardier sons to curb that power.

Luther walks forth in yon majestic frame,
Bright beam of heaven, and heir of endless fame,
Born, like thyself, thro toils and griefs to wind,
From slavery's chains to free the captive mind,
Brave adverse crowns, control the pontiff sway,
And bring benighted nations into day.

Remark what crowds his name around him brings,
Schools, synods, prelates, potentates and kings,
All gaining knowledge from his boundless store,
And join'd to shield him from the papal power.
First of his friends, see Frederic's princely form
Ward from the sage divine the gathering storm,

In learned Wittemburgh secure his seat,
High throne of thought, religion's safe retreat.
There sits Melancthon, mild as morning light,
And feuds, tho sacred, soften in his sight;
In terms so gentle flows his tuneful tongue,
Even cloister'd bigots join the pupil throng;
By all sectarian chiefs he lives approved,
By monarchs courted and by men beloved.
And lo, where Europe's utmost limits bend,
From this new source what various lights ascend!
See haughty Henry from the papal tie
His realms dissever, and the priest defy;
While Albion's sons disdain a foreign throne,
And learn to bound the oppressions of their own.
Then rises Loyola, a strange new name,
By paths unseen to reach the goal of fame;
Thro courts and camps he teaches how to wind,
To mine whole states and overreach mankind.
Train'd in his school, a bold and artful race
Range o'er the world, and every sect embrace,
All creeds and powers and policies explore,
New seats of science raise on every shore;
Till their wide empire gains a wondrous birth,
Built in all empires o'er this ancient earth.

Our wildmen too, the tribes of Paraguay,
Receive their rites and bow beneath their sway.
  The world of men thus moving in thy view
Improve their state, more useful works pursue;
Unwonted deeds in rival greatness shine,
Call'd into life, and first inspired by thine.
So while imperial Homer tunes the lyre,
His living lays unnumber'd bards inspire;
From age to age the kindling spirit flies,
Sounds thro the earth and echoes to the skies.
  Now roll the years, when Europe's ample space
By peace and culture rears a wiser race,
Men bred to labor, school'd in freedom's lore,
And form'd to colonize our favorite shore.
To speed their course, the sons of bigot rage
In persecution whelm the inquiring age;
Myriads of martyr'd heroes mount the pyre,
And blind devotion lights the sacred fire.
  Led by the dark Dominicans of Spain,
A newborn Fury walks the wide domain,
Gaunt INQUISITION; mark her giant stride,
Her blood-nursed vulture screaming at her side.
Her priestly train the tools of torment brings,
Racks, wheels and crosses, faggots, stakes and strings;

Scaffolds and cages round her altar stand,
And, tipt with sulphur, waves her flaming brand.
Her imps of inquest round the Fiend advance,
Suspectors grave, and spies with eye askance,
Pretended heretics who worm the soul,
And sly confessors with their secret scroll,
Accusers hired, for each conviction paid,
Judges retain'd and witnesses by trade.

Dragg'd from a thousand jails her victim trains,
Jews, Moors and Christians, clank alike their chains,
Read their known sentence in her fiery eyes,
And breathe to heaven their unavailing cries;
Lash'd on the pile their writhing bodies turn,
And, veil'd in doubling smoke, begin to burn.
Where the flames open, lo! their limbs in vain
Reach out for help, distorted by the pain;
Till folded in the fires they disappear,
Aud not a sound invades the startled ear.

See Philip, throned in insolence and pride,
Enjoy their wailings and their pangs deride;
While o'er the same dread scenes, on Albion's isles,
His well-taught spouse, the cruel Mary, smiles.
What clouds of smoke hang heavy round the shore!
What altars hecatomb'd with Christian gore!

Her sire's best friends, the wise, the brave, the good,
Roll in the flames or fly the land of blood.
To Gallia's plains the maddening phrensy turns,
Religion raves and civil discord burns;
Leaguers and Huguenots their vengeance pour,
They swell Bartholemy's wide feast of gore,
Alternate victors bid their gibbets rise,
And the foul stench of victims chokes the skies.
Now cease the factions with the Valois line,
And Bourbon's virtues every voice combine.
Quell'd by his fame, the furious sects accord,
Europe respires beneath his guardian sword;
Batavia's states to independence soar,
And curb the cohorts of Iberian power.
From Albion's ports her infant navies heave,
Stretch forth and thunder on the Flandrian wave;
Her Howard there first foils the force of Spain,
And there begins her mastery of the main.
The Seraph spoke; when full beneath their eye
A new-form'd squadron rose along the sky.
High on the tallest deck majestic shone
Sage Raleigh, pointing to the western sun;
His eye, bent forward, ardent and sublime,
Seem'd piercing nature and evolving time;

Beside him stood a globe, whose figures traced
A future empire in each present waste;
All former works of men behind him shone
Graved by his hand in ever-during stone;
On his calm brow a various crown displays
The hero's laurel and the scholar's bays;
His graceful limbs in steely mail were drest,
The bright star burning on his lofty breast;
His sword, high waving, flash'd the solar ray,
Illumed the shrouds and rainbow'd far the spray;
The smiling crew rose resolute and brave,
And the glad sails hung bounding o'er the wave.
  Storms of wild Hatteras, suspend your roar,
Ye tumbling billows, cease to shake the shore;
Look thro the doubling clouds, thou lamp of day,
Teach the bold Argonauts their chartless way;
Your viewless capes, broad Chesapeak, unfold,
And show your promised Colchis fleeced with gold.
No plundering squadron your new Jason brings;
No pirate demigods nor hordes of kings
From shore to shore a faithless miscreant steers,
To steal a maid and leave a sire in tears.
But yon wise chief conducts with careful ken
The queen of colonies, the best of men,

To wake to fruitful life your slumbering soil,
And rear an empire with the hand of toil.
Your fond Medea too, whose dauntless breast
All danger braves to screen her hunted guest,
Shall quit her native tribe, but never share
The crimes and sufferings of the Colchian fair.
Blest Pocahontas! fear no lurking guile;
Thy hero's love shall well reward thy smile.
Ah sooth the wanderer in his desperate plight,
Hide him by day and calm his cares by night;
Tho savage nations with thy vengeful sire
Pursue their victim with unceasing ire,
And tho their threats thy startled ear assail,
Let virtue's voice o'er filial fears prevail.
Fly with the faithful youth, his steps to guide,
Pierce the known thicket, breast the fordless tide,
Illude the scout, avoid the ambush'd line,
And lead him safely to his friends and thine;
For thine shall be his friends, his heart, his name;
His camp shall shout, his nation boast thy fame.
But now the Bay unfolds a passage wide,
And leads the squadron up the freshening tide;
Where Pohatan spreads deep her sylvan soil,
And grassy lawns allure the steps of toil.

Here, lodged in peace, they tread the welcome land,
An instant harvest waves beneath their hand,
Spontaneous fruits their easy cares beguile,
And opening fields in living culture smile.
With joy Columbus view'd; when thus his voice:
Ye grove-clad shores, ye generous hosts, rejoice!
Exchange your benefits, your gifts combine;
What nature fashions, let her sons refine.
Be thou, my Seer, the people's guardian friend,
Protect their virtues and their lives defend;
May wealth and wisdom with their arts unfold,
Yet save, oh, save them from the thirst of gold!
Let the poor guardless natives never feel
The flamen's fraud, the soldier's fateful steel;
But learn the blessings that alone attend
On civil rights where social virtues blend,
In these brave leaders find a welcome guide,
And rear their fanes and empires by their side.
Smile, great Hesperia, smile; the star of morn
Illumes thy heavens and bids thy day be born;
Thy opening forests show the work begun,
Thy plains unshaded drink a purer sun;
Yield now thy bounties, load the laboring main,
Give birth to nations, and begin thy reign.

The Hero spoke; when thus the Saint rejoin'd,
Approved his joy, and feasted still his mind:
Well may thy voice, with patriarch pride elate,
Burst forth triumphant at a scene so great;
Here springs indeed the day, since time began,
The brightest, broadest, happiest morn of man.
In these prime settlements thy raptures trace
The germ, the genius of a sapient race,
Predestined here to methodise and mould
New codes of empire to reform the old.

A work so vast a second world required,
By oceans bourn'd, from elder states retired;
Where, uncontaminated, unconfined,
Free contemplation might expand the mind,
To form, fix, prove the well-adjusted plan,
And base and build the commonwealth of man.

This arm, that leads the stellar host of even,
That stretch'd o'er yon rude ridge the western heaven,
That heal'd the wounded earth, when from her side
The moon burst forth, and left the South Sea tide,
That calm'd these elements, and taught them where
To mould their mass and rib the crusted sphere,
Line the closed continent with wrecks of life,
And recommence their generating strife,

That rear'd the mountain, spread the subject plain,
Led the long stream and roll'd the billowy main,
Stole from retiring tides the growing strand,
Heaved the green banks, the shadowy inlets plann'd,
Strow'd the wild fruitage, gave the beast his place,
And form'd the region for thy filial race,—
This arm prepared their future seats of state,
Design'd their limits and prescribed their date.

When first the staggering globe its breach repair'd,
And this bold hemisphere its shoulders rear'd,
Back to those heights, whose hovering vapor shrouds
My rock-raised world in Alleganian clouds,
The Atlantic waste its coral kingdom spread,
And scaly nations here their gambols led;
Till by degrees, thro following tracts of time,
From laboring ocean rose the sedgy clime,
As from unloaded waves the rising sand
Swell'd into light and gently drew to land.
For, moved by trade winds o'er the flaming zone,
The waves roll westward with the constant sun,
Meet my firm isthmus, scoop that gulphy bed,
Wheel to the north, and here their current spread.
Those ravaged banks, that move beneath their force,
Borne on the tide and lost along their course,

Create the shore, consolidate the soil,
And hither lead the enlighten'd steps of toil.
  Think not the lust of gold shall here annoy,
Enslave the nation and its nerve destroy.
No useles mine these northern hills enclose,
No ruby ripens and no diamond glows;
But richer stores and rocks of useful mould
Repay in wealth the penury of gold.
Freedom's unconquer'd race, with healthy toil,
Shall lop the grove and warm the furrow'd soil,
From iron ridges break the rugged ore,
And plant with men the man-ennobling shore;
Sails, villas, towers and temples round them heave,
Shine o'er the realms and light the distant wave.
Nor think the native tribes shall rue the day
That leads our heroes o'er the watery way.
A cause like theirs no mean device can mar,
Nor bigot rage nor sacerdotal war.
From eastern tyrants driven, resolved and brave,
To build new states or seek a distant grave,
Our sons shall try a new colonial plan,
To tame the soil, but spare their kindred man.
  Thro Europe's wilds when feudal nations spread,
The pride of conquest every legion led.

Each fur-clad chief, by servile crowds adored,
O'er conquer'd realms assumed the name of lord,
Built the proud castle, ranged the savage wood,
Fired his grim host to frequent fields of blood,
With new-made honors lured his subject bands,
Price of their lives, and purchase of their lands;
For names and titles bade the world resign
Their faith, their freedom and their rights divine.
  Contending baronies their terrors spread,
And slavery follow'd where the standard led;
Till, little tyrants by the great o'erthrown,
The spoils of nobles build the regal crown;
Wealth, wisdom, virtue, every claim of man
Unguarded fall to consummate the plan.
Ambitious cares, that nature never gave,
Torment alike the monarch and the slave,
Thro all degrees in gradual pomp ascend,
Honor the name, but tyranny the end.
  Far different honors here the heart shall claim,
Sublimer objects, deeds of happier fame;
A new creation waits the western shore,
And moral triumphs o'er monarchic power.
Thy freeborn sons, with genius unconfined,
Nor sloth can slacken nor a tyrant bind;

With self-wrought fame and worth internal blest,
No venal star shall brighten on their breast,
Nor king-created name nor courtly art
Damp the bold thought or desiccate the heart.
Above all fraud, beyond all titles great,
Truth in their voice and sceptres at their feet,
Like sires of unborn states they move sublime,
Look empires thro and span the breadth of time,
Hold o'er the world, that men may choose from far,
The palm of peace, or scourge of barbarous war;
Till their example every nation charms,
Commands its friendship and its rage disarms.

Here social man a second birth shall find,
And a new range of reason lift his mind,
Feed his strong intellect with purer light,
A nobler sense of duty and of right,
The sense of liberty; whose holy fire
His life shall temper and his laws inspire,
Purge from all shades the world-embracing scope
That prompts his genius and expands his hope.

When first his form arose erect on earth,
Parturient nature hail'd the wondrous birth,
With fairest limbs and finest fibres wrought,
And framed for vast and various toils of thought.

To aid his promised powers with loftier flight,
And stretch his views beyond corporeal sight,
Prometheus came, and from the floods of day
Sunn'd his clear soul with heaven's internal ray,
The expanding spark divine; that round him springs,
And leads and lights him thro the immense of things,
Probes the dense earth, explores the soundless main,
Remoulds their mass thro all its threefold reign,
O'er great, o'er small extends his physic laws,
Empalms the empyrean or dissects a gaz,
Weighs the vast orbs of heaven, bestrides the sky,
Walks on the windows of an insect's eye;
Turns then to self, more curious still to trace
The whirls of passion that involve the race,
That cloud with mist the visual lamp of God,
And plunge the poniard in fraternal blood.
Here fails his light. The proud Titanian ray
O'er physic nature sheds indeed its day;
Yet leaves the moral in chaotic jars,
The spoil of violence, the sport of wars,
Presents contrasted parts of one great plan,
Earth, heaven subdued, but man at swords with man;
His wars, his errors into science grown,
And the great cause of all his ills unknown.

But when he steps on these regenerate shores,
His mind unfolding for superior powers,
Freedom, his new Prometheus, here shall rise,
Light her new torch in my refulgent skies,
Touch with a stronger life his opening soul,
Of moral systems fix the central goal,
Her own resplendent essence. Thence expand
The rays of reason that illume the land;
Thence equal rights proceed, and equal laws,
Thence holy Justice all her reverence draws;
Truth with untarnish'd beam descending thence,
Strikes every eye, and quickens every sense,
Bids bright Instruction spread her ample page,
To drive dark dogmas from the inquiring age,
Ope the true treasures of the earth and skies,
And teach the student where his object lies.
Sun of the moral world! effulgent source
Of man's best wisdom and his steadiest force,
Soul-searching Freedom! here assume thy stand,
And radiate hence to every distant land;
Point out and prove how all the scenes of strife,
The shock of states, the impassion'd broils of life,
Spring from unequal sway; and how they fly
Before the splendor of thy peaceful eye;

Unfold at last the genuine social plan,
The mind's full scope, the dignity of man,
Bold nature bursting thro her long disguise,
And nations daring to be just and wise.
Yes! righteous Freedom, heaven and earth and sea
Yield or withold their various gifts for thee;
Protected Industry beneath thy reign
Leads all the virtues in her filial train;
Courageous Probity with brow serene,
And Temperance calm presents her placid mien;
Contentment, Moderation, Labor, Art,
Mould the new man and humanize his heart;
To public plenty private ease dilates,
Domestic peace to harmony of states.
Protected Industry, careering far,
Detects the cause and cures the rage of war,
And sweeps, with forceful arm, to their last graves,
Kings from the earth and pirates from the waves.
But slow proceeds the work. Long toils, my son,
Must base the fabric of so vast a throne;
Where Freedom founds her everlasting reign,
And earth's whole empires form the fair domain.
That great coloniarch, whose exalted soul
Pervades all scenes that future years unrol,

Must yield the palm, and at a courtier's shrine
His plans relinquish and his life resign;
His life that brightens, as his death shall stain,
The fair, foul annals of his master's reign.

That feeble band, the lonely wilds who tread,
Their sire, their genius in their Raleigh dead,
Shall pine and perish in the savage gloom,
Or mount the wave and seek their ancient home.
Others in vain the generous task pursue,
The dangers tempt and all the strife renew;
While kings and ministers obstruct the plan,
Unfaithful guardians of the weal of man.

At last brave Delaware, with his blithe host,
Sails in full triumph to the well-known coast,
Aids with a liberal hand the patriot cause,
Reforms their policy, designs their laws;
Till o'er Virginia's plains they spread their sway,
And push their hamlets tow'rd the setting day.
He comes, my Delaware! how mild and bland
My zephyrs greet him from the long-sought land!
From fluvial glades that thro my cantons run,
From those rich mounds that mask the falling sun.

Borne up my Chesapeak, as first he hails
The flowery banks that scent his slackening sails,

Descending twilight mellows down the gleam
That spreads far forward on the broad blue stream;
The moonbeam dancing, as the pendants glide,
Silvers with trembling tints the ripply tide;
The sand-sown beach, the rocky bluff repays
The faint effulgence with their amber'd rays;
O'er greenwood glens a browner lustre flies,
And bright-hair'd hills walk shadowy round the skies.
Profound solicitude and strong delight
Absorb the chief, as thro the waste of night
He walks the lonely deck, and skirts the lands
That wait their nations from his guiding hands.
Tall thro the tide the river Sires by turns
Rise round the bark and blend their social urns;
Majestic brotherhood! each feels the power
To feed an empire from his future store.
They stand stupendous, flooding full the bay,
And pointing each thro different climes the way.
Resplendent o'er the rest, the regent god
Potowmak towers, and sways the swelling flood;
Vines clothe his arms, wild fruits o'erfill his horn,
Wreaths of green maize his reverend brows adorn,
His silver beard reflects the lunar day,
And round his loins the scaly nations play.

The breeze falls calm, the sails in silence rest,
While thus his greetings cheer the stranger guest:
  Blest be the bark that seized the promised hour
To waft thee welcome to this friendly shore!
Long have we learnt the fame that here awaits
The future sires of our unplanted states;
We all salute thee with our mingling tides,
Our high-fenced havens and our fruitful sides.
The hundred realms our myriad fountains drain
Shall lose their limits in the vast domain;
But my bold banks with proud impatience wait
The palm of glory in a work so great;
On me thy sons their central seat shall raise,
And crown my labors with distinguish'd praise.
For this, from rock-ribb'd lakes I forced my birth,
And climb'd and sunder'd many a mound of earth,
Rent the huge hills that yonder heave on high
And with their tenfold ridges rake the sky,
Removed whole mountains in my headlong way,
Strow'd a strong soil around this branching Bay,
Scoop'd wide his basins to the distant main,
And hung with headlands every marsh they drain.
  Haste then, my heroes, tempt the fearless toil,
Enrich your nations with the nurturing spoil;

O'er my vast vales let yellow harvests wave,
Quay the calm ports and dike the lawns I lave,
Win from the waters every stagnant fen,
Where truant rills escape my conscious ken;
And break those remnant rocks that still impede
My current crowding thro the gaps I made.
  So shall your barks pursue my branching bed,
Slope after slope, to every fountain's head,
Seat your contiguous towns on all my shores,
And charge my channel with their seaward stores.
Freedom and Peace shall well reward your care,
My guardian mounds protect the friendly pair;
Or if delirious War shall dare draw nigh,
And eastern storms o'ercast the western sky,
My soil shall rear the chief to guide your host,
And drive the demon cringing from the coast;
Yon verdant hill his sylvan seat shall claim,
And grow immortal from his deathless fame.
  Then shall your federal towers my bank adorn,
And hail with me the great millennial morn
That gilds your capitol. Thence earth shall draw
Her first clear codes of liberty and law;
There public right a settled form shall find,
Truth trim her lamp to lighten humankind,

Old Afric's sons their shameful fetters cast,
Our wild Hesperians humanize at last,
All men participate, all time expand
The source of good my liberal sages plann'd.
  This said, he plunges in the sacred flood;
That closes calm and lulls the cradled god.
Exulting at his words, the gallant crew
Brace the broad canvass and their course pursue:
For now the breathing airs, from ocean born,
Breeze up the bay, and lead the lively morn
That lights them to their port. Tis here they join
Their bold precursors in the work divine;
And here their followers, yet a numerous train,
Wind o'er the wave and swell the new domain.
For impious Laud, on England's wasted shore,
Renews the flames that Mary fed before;
Contristed sects his sullen fury fly,
To seek new seats beneath a safer sky;
Where faith and freedom yield a forceful charm,
And toils and dangers every bosom warm.
  Amid the tried unconquerable train,
Whom tyrants press and seas oppose in vain,
See Plymouth colons stretch their standards o'er,
Face the dark wildmen and the wintry shore;

See virtuous Baltimore ascend the wave,
See peaceful Penn its unknown terrors brave;
Swedes, Belgians, Gauls their various flags display,
Full pinions crowding on the watery way;
All from their different ports, their sails unfurl'd,
Point their glad streamers to the western world.

THE

COLUMBIAD.

BOOK V.

ARGUMENT.

Vision confined to North America. Progress of the colonies. Troubles with the natives. Settlement of Canada. Spirit of the English and French colonies compared. Hostilities between France and England extended to America. Braddock's defeat. Washington saves the relics of the English army. Actions of Abercrombie, Amherst, Wolfe. Peace. Darkness overspreads the continent. Apprehensions of Columbus from that appearance. Cause explained. Cloud bursts away in the centre. View of congress, and of the differeut regions from which its members are delegated. Their endeavors to arrest the violence of England compared with those of the Genius of Rome to dissuade Cesar from passing the Rubicon. The demon War stalking over the ocean and leading on the English invasion. Conflagration of towns from Falmouth to Norfolk. Battle of Bunker Hill seen thro the smoke. Death of Warren. American army assembles. Review of its chiefs. Speech of Washington. Actions and death of Montgomery. Loss of Newyork.

THE

COLUMBIAD.

BOOK V.

COLUMBUS hail'd them with a father's smile,
Fruits of his cares and children of his toil;
While still his eyes, thro tears of joy, descried
Their course adventurous on the distant tide.
Thus, when o'er deluged earth her Numen stood,
The tost ark bounding on the shoreless flood,
The sacred treasure fixt his guardian view,
While climes unnoticed in the wave withdrew.
The Hero saw them reach the rising strand,
Leap from their ships and share the joyous land;
Receding forests yield the laborers room,
And opening wilds with fields and gardens bloom.
Fill'd with the glance ecstatic, all his soul
Now seems unbounded with the scene to roll,

And now impatient, with retorted eye,
Perceives his station in another sky:
Waft me, indulgent Angel, waft me o'er,
With those blest heroes, to the happy shore;
There let me live and die. But all appears
A fleeting vision! these are future years.
Yet grant the illusion still may nearer spread,
And my glad steps may seem their walks to tread;
While Europe, wrapt in momentary night,
Shall rise no more to intercept the sight.

Columbus thus; when Hesper's potent hand
Moves brightening o'er the visionary land;
The height that bore them still sublimer grew,
And earth's whole circuit settled from their view.
A dusky deep, serene as breathless even,
Seem'd vaulting downward like another heaven;
The sun, rejoicing on his western way,
Stampt his fair image in the inverted day:
When now Hesperia's coast arose more nigh,
And life and action fill'd the dancing eye.

Between the gulphs, where Laurence drains the world
And where Floridia's farthest floods are curl'd,

Where midlands broad their swelling mountains heave
And slope their champaigns to the Atlantic wave,
The sandy streambank and the woodgreen plain
Raise into sight the new-made seats of man.
The placid ports, that break the seaborn gales,
Shoot forth their quays and stretch aloft their sails,
Full harvests wave, new groves with fruitage bend,
Gay villas smile, defensive towers ascend;
All the rich works of art their charms display,
To court the planter and his cares repay:
Till war invades; when soon the dales disclose
Their meadows path'd with files of savage foes;
High tufted quills their painted foreheads press,
Dark spoils of beasts their shaggy shoulders dress,
The bow bent forward for the combat strung,
Ax, quiver, scalpknife on the girdle hung;
Discordant yells, convulsing long the air,
Tone forth at last the war whoop's hideous blare.
  The Patriarch look'd; and every frontier height
Pours down the swarthy nations to the fight.
Where Kennebec's high source forsakes the sky,
Where long Champlain's yet unkeel'd waters lie,
Where Hudson crowds his hill-dissundering tide,
Where Kaatskill dares the starry vault divide,

Where the dim Alleganies sit sublime
And give their streams to every neighboring clime,
The swarms descended like an evening shade,
And wolves and vultures follow'd where they spread.
Thus when a storm, on eastern pinions driven,
Meets the firm Andes in the midst of heaven,
The clouds convulse, the torrents pour amain,
And the black waters sweep the subject plain.

Thro harvest fields the bloody myriads tread,
Sack the lone village, strow the streets with dead;
The flames in spiry volumes round them rise,
And shrieks and shouts redoubling rend the skies.
Fair babes and matrons in their domes expire,
Or bursting frantic thro the folding fire
They scream, fly, fall; promiscuous rave along
The yelling victors and the driven throng;
The streams run purple; all the peopled shore
Is wrapt in flames and trod with steps of gore.
Till colons, gathering from the shorelands far,
Stretch their new standards and oppose the war,
With muskets match the many-shafted bow,
With loud artillery stun the astonish'd foe.
When, like a broken wave, the barbarous train
Lead back the flight and scatter from the plain

Slay their weak captives, drop their shafts in haste,
Forget their spoils and scour the trackless waste;
From wood to wood in wild confusion hurl'd,
They hurry o'er the hills far thro the savage world.
  Now move secure the cheerful works of peace,
New temples rise and fruitful fields increase.
Where Delaware's wide waves behold with pride
Penn's beauteous town ascending on their side,
The crossing streets in just allinement run,
The walls and pavements sparkle to the sun,
Like that famed city rose the checker'd plan,
Whose spacious towers Semiramis began;
Long ages finish'd what her hand design'd,
The pride of kings and wonder of mankind.
  Newyork ascends o'er Hudson's seaward isles,
And flings the sunbeams from her glittering tiles;
Albania, opening thro the distant wood,
Rolls her rich treasures on her parent flood;
Amid a thousand sails young Boston laves,
High looms majestic Newport o'er the waves,
Patapsco's bay contracts his yielding side,
As spreading Baltimore invades his tide;
Aspiring Richmond tops the bank of James,
And Charleston sways her two contending streams.

Thro each colonial realm, for wisdom great,
Elected sires assume the cares of state;
Nursed in equality, to freedom bred,
Firm is their step and straight the paths they tread;
Dispensing justice with paternal hand,
By laws of peace they rule the happy land;
While reason's page their statute codes unfold,
And rites and charters flame in figured gold.
All rights that Britons know they here transfuse,
Their sense invigorate and expand their views,
Dare every height of human soul to scan,
Find, fathom, scope the moral breadth of man,
Learn how his social powers may still dilate,
And tone their tension to a stronger state.

Round the long glade where lordly Laurence strays,
Gaul's migrant sons their forts and villas raise,
Stretch over Canada their colon sway,
And circling far beneath the western day
Plant sylvan Wabash with a watchful post,
O'er Missisippi spread a mantling host,
Bid Louisiana's lovely clime prepare
New arts to prove and infant states to rear;
While the bright lakes, that wide behind them spread,
Unfold their channels to the paths of trade,

Ohio's waves their destined honors claim,
And smile, as conscious of approaching fame.
  But Gallic planters still their trammels wear,
Their feudal genius still attends them here;
Dependent feelings for a distant throne
Gyve the crampt soul that fears to think alone,
Demand their rulers from the parent land,
Laws ready made, and generals to command.
Judge, priest and pedagogue, and all the slaves
Of foreign masters, crowding o'er the waves,
Spread thick the shades of vassalage and sloth,
Absorb their labors and prevent their growth,
Damp every thought that might their tyrants brave,
And keep the vast domain a desert and a grave.
  Too soon the mother states, with jealous fear,
Transport their feuds and homebred quarrels here.
Now Gallia's war-built barks ascend in sight,
White flags unfold, and armies robed in white
On all the frontier streams their forts prepare,
And coop our cantons with surrounding war.
Quebec, as proud she rears her rocky seat,
Feeds their full camp and shades their anchor'd fleet;
Oswego's rampart frowns athwart his flood,
And wild Ontario swells beneath his load.

And now a friendly host from Albion's strand
Arrives to aid her young colonial band.
They join their force, and tow'rd the falling day
Impetuous Braddock leads their hasty way;
O'er Allegany heights, like streams of fire,
The red flags wave and glittering arms aspire
To meet the savage hordes, who there advance
Their skulking files to join the arms of France.

Where, old as earth, yet still unstain'd with blood,
Monongahela roll'd his careless flood,
Flankt with his mantling groves the fountful hills,
Drain'd the vast region thro his thousand rills,
Lured o'er his lawns the buffle herds, and spread
For all his fowls his piscatory glade;
But now perceives, with hostile flag unfurl'd,
A Gallic fortress awe the western world;
There Braddock bends his march; the troops within
Behold their danger and the fire begin.
Forth bursting from the gates they rush amain,
Front, flank and charge the fast approaching train;
The batteries blaze, the leaden volleys pour,
The vales, the streams, the solid mountains roar;
Clouds of convolving smoke the welkin spread,
The champaign shrouding in sulphureous shade.

Lost in the rocking thunder's loud career,
No shouts nor groans invade the Patriarch's ear,
Nor valorous feats are seen, nor flight nor fall,
But one broad burst of darkness buries all;
Till chased by rising winds the smoke withdrew,
And the wide slaughter open'd on his view.
He saw the British leader borne afar,
In dust and gore, beyond the wings of war;
And while delirious panic seized his host,
Their flags, their arms in wild confusion tost,
Bold in the midst a youthful warrior strode,
And tower'd undaunted o'er the field of blood;
He checks the shameful rout, with vengeance burns,
And the pale Britons brighten where he turns.
So, when thick vapors veil the nightly sky,
The starry host in half-seen lustre fly,
Till Phosphor rises o'er the twinkling crowd,
And gives new splendor thro his parting cloud.
Swift on a fiery steed the stripling rose,
Form'd the light files to pierce the line of foes;
Then waved his gleamy sword that flash'd the day,
And thro the Gallic legions hew'd his way:
His troops press forward like a loose-broke flood,
Sweep ranks away and smear their paths in blood;

The hovering foes pursue the combat far,
And shower their balls along the flying war;
When the new leader turns his single force,
Points the flight forward, speeds his backward course;
The French recoiling half their victory yield,
And the glad Britons quit the fatal field.
These deathful deeds as great Columbus eyed,
With anxious tone he thus addrest the Guide:
Why combat here these transatlantic bands,
And strow their corses thro thy pathless lands?
Can Europe's realms, the seat of endless strife,
Afford no trophies for the waste of life?
Can monarchs there no proud applauses gain,
No living laurel for their people slain?
Nor Belgia's plains, so fertile made with gore,
Hide heroes' bones nor feast the vultures more?
Will Rhine no longer cleanse the crimson stain,
Nor Danube bear their bodies to the main,
That infant empires here the shock must feel,
And these pure streams with foreign carnage swell?
But who that chief? his name, his nation say,
Whose lifeblood seems his follies to repay;
And who the youth, that from the combat lost
Springs up and saves the remnant of his host?

The Power replied: Each age successive brings
Their varying views to earth's contentious kings;
Here roll the years when Albion's parent hand,
In aid of thy brave children, guards the land;
That growing states their veteran force may train,
A nobler prize in later fields to gain;
In fields where Albion's self shall turn their foe,
Spread broader sails and aim a deadlier blow,
Recross, in evil hour, the astonish'd wave,
Her own brave sons to ravage and enslave.
But here she combats with the powers of Gaul;
Here her bold Braddock finds his destined fall;
Thy Washington, in that young martial frame,
From yon lost field begins a life of fame.
Tis he, in future straits, with loftier stride,
The colon states to sovereign rule shall guide;
When, prest by wrongs, their own full force they find,
To wield the sword for man, and bulwark humankind.

The Seraph spoke; when thro the purpled air
The northern armies spread the flames of war.
Swift o'er the lake, to Crownpoint's fortful strand,
Rash Abercrombie leads his headlong band
To fierce unequal fight; the batteries roar,
Shield the strong foes and rake the banner'd shore;

Britannia's sons again the contest yield,
Again proud Gaul triumphant sweeps the field.
But Amherst quick renews the raging toil,
And drives wide hosting o'er Acadia's isle;
Young Wolfe beside him points the lifted lance,
The boast of Britain and the scourge of France.
The tide of victory here the heroes turn,
And Gallic navies in their harbors burn;
High flame the ships, the billows swell with gore,
And the red standard shades the conquer'd shore.
Wolfe, now detacht and bent on bolder deeds,
A sail-borne host up sealike Laurence leads,
Stems the long lessening tide; till Abraham's height
And famed Quebec rise frowning into sight.
Swift bounding on the bank, the foe they claim,
Climb the tall mountain like a rolling flame,
Push wide their wings, high bannering bright the air,
And move to fight as comets cope in war.
The smoke falls folding thro the downward sky,
And shrouds the mountain from the Patriarch's eye,
While on the towering top, in glare of day,
The flashing swords in fiery arches play.
As on a side-seen storm, adistance driven,
The flames fork round the semivault of heaven,

Thick thunders roll, descending torrents flow,
Dash down the clouds and whelm the hills below;
Or as on plains of light when Michael strove,
The swords of cherubim to combat move,
Ten thousand fiery forms together fray,
And flash new lightning on empyreal day.
Long raged promiscuous combat, half conceal'd,
When sudden parle suspended all the field;
Then roar the shouts, the smoke forsakes the plain
And the huge hill is topt with heaps of slain.
Stretch'd high in air Britannia's standard waved,
And good Columbus hail'd his country saved;
While calm and silent, where the ranks retire,
He saw brave Wolfe in victory's arms expire.
So the pale moon, when morning beams arise,
Veils her lone visage in her midway skies;
She needs no longer drive the shades away,
Nor waits to view the glories of the day.
Again the towns aspire; the cultured field
And crowded mart their copious treasures yield;
Back to his plough the colon soldier moves,
And songs of triumph fill the warbling groves,
The conscious flocks, returning joys that share,
Spread thro the grassland o'er the walks of war,

Streams, freed of gore, their crystal course regain,
Serener sunbeams gild the tentless plain;
A general jubilee, o'er earth and heaven,
Leads the gay morn and lights the lambent even.
  Rejoicing, confident of long repose,
(Their friends triumphant, far retired their foes,)
The British colonies now feel their sway
Span the whole north and crowd the western day.
Acadia, Canada, earth's total side,
From Slave's long lake to Pensacola's tide,
Expand their soils for them; and here unfold
A range of highest hope, a promised age of gold.
  But soon from eastern seas dark vapors rise,
Sweep the vast Occident and shroud the skies,
Snatch all the vision from the Hero's sight,
And wrap the coast in sudden shades of night.
He turn'd, and sorrowful besought the Power:
Why sinks the scene, or must I view no more?
Must here the fame of that young world descend?
Shall our brave children find so quick their end?
Where then the promised grace? "Thou soon shalt see
That half mankind shall owe their seats to thee."
  The Saint replied: Ere long, beneath thy view
The scene shall brighten and thy joys renew.

Here march the troublous years, when goaded sore
Thy sons shall rise to change the ruling power;
When Albion's prince, who sways the happy land,
To lawless rule extends his tyrant hand,
To bind in slavery's bands the peaceful host,
Their rights unguarded and their charters lost.
Now raise thine eye; from this delusive claim
What nations leap to life, what deeds adorn their fame!

Columbus look'd; and still around them spread,
From south to north, the immeasurable shade;
At last the central darkness burst away,
And rising regions open'd on the day.
Once more bright Delaware's commercial stream
And Penn's throng'd city cast a cheerful gleam;
The dome of state, as conscious of his eye,
Now seem'd to silver in a loftier sky,
Unfolding fair its gates; when lo, within
The assembled states in solemn Congress shine.

The sires elect from every province came,
Where wide Columbia bore the British name,
Where Freedom's sons their highborn lineage trace,
And homebred bravery still exalts the race:
Her sons who plant each various vast domain
That Chesapeak's uncounted currents drain;

The race who Roanoke's clear stream bestride,
Who fell the pine on Apalachia's side,
To Albemarle's wide wave who trust their store,
Who dike proud Pamlico's unstable shore,
Whose groaning barks o'erload the long Santee,
Wind thro the realms and labor to the sea,
(Their cumbrous cargoes, to the sail consign'd,
Seek distant worlds, and feed and clothe mankind;)
The race whose rice-fields suck Savanna's urn,
Whose verdant vines Oconee's bank adorn;
Who freight the Delaware with golden grain,
Who tame their steeds on Monmouth's flowery plain,
From huge Toconnok hills who drag their ore,
And sledge their corn to Hudson's quay-built shore,
Who keel Connecticut's long meadowy tide,
With patient plough his fallow plains divide,
Spread their white flocks o'er Narraganset's vale,
Or chase to each chill pole the monstrous whale;
Whose venturous prows have borne their fame afar,
Tamed all the seas and steer'd by every star,
Dispensed to earth's whole habitants their store,
And with their biting flukes have harrow'd every shore.

The virtuous delegates behold with pain
The hostile Britons hovering o'er the main,

Lament the strife that bids two worlds engage,
And blot their annals with fraternal rage;
Two worlds in one broad state! whose bounds bestride,
Like heaven's blue arch, the vast Atlantic tide,
By language, laws and liberty combined,
Great nurse of thought, example to mankind.
Columbia rears her warning voice in vain,
Brothers to brothers call across the main;
Britannia's patriots lend a listening ear,
But kings and courtiers push their mad career;
Dissension raves, the sheathless falchions glare,
And earth and ocean tremble at the war.
  Thus with stern brow, as worn by cares of state,
His bosom big with dark unfolding fate,
High o'er his lance the sacred Eagle spread,
And earth's whole crown still resting on his head,
Rome's hoary Genius rose, and mournful stood
On roaring Rubicon's forbidden flood,
When Cesar's ensigns swept the Alpine air,
Led their long legions from the Gallic war,
Paused on the opposing bank with wings unfurl'd,
And waved portentous o'er the shuddering world.
The god, with outstretch'd arm and awful look,
Call'd the proud victor and prophetic spoke:

Arrest, my son, thy parricidious hate,
Pass not the stream nor stab my filial state,
Stab not thyself, thy friends, thy total kind,
And worlds and ages in one state combined.
The chief, regardless of the warning god,
Rein'd his rude steed and headlong past the flood,
Cried, Farewel, Peace! took Fortune for his guide,
And o'er his country pour'd the slaughtering tide.
  High on the foremost seat, in living light,
Resplendent Randolph caught the world's full sight.
He opes the cause, and points in prospect far
Thro all the toils that wait impending war:
But, reverend sage! thy race must soon be o'er,
To lend thy lustre and to shine no more.
So the mild morning star, from shades of even,
Leads up the dawn and lights the front of heaven,
Points to the waking world the sun's broad way,
Then veils his own, and vaults above the day.
And see bright Washington behind thee rise,
Thy following sun, to gild our morning skies,
O'er shadowy climes to pour enlivening flame,
The charms of freedom and the fire of fame.
For him the patriot bay beheld with pride
The hero's laurel springing by its side;

His sword still sleeping rested on his thigh,
On Britain still he cast a filial eye;
But sovereign fortitude his visage bore,
To meet her legions on the invaded shore.
Sage Franklin next arose with cheerful mien,
And smiled unruffled o'er the solemn scene;
His locks of age a various wreath embraced,
Palm of all arts that e'er a mortal graced;
Beneath him lay the sceptre kings had borne,
And the tame thunder from the tempest torn.
Wythe, Mason, Pendleton with Henry join'd,
Rush, Rodney, Langdon, friends of humankind,
Persuasive Dickinson, the farmer's boast,
Recording Thomson, pride of all the host,
Nash, Jay, the Livingstons, in council great,
Rutledge and Laurens held the rolls of fate,
O'er wide creation turn'd their ardent eyes,
And bade the opprest to selfexistence rise;
All powers of state, in their extended plan,
Spring from consent, to shield the rights of man.
Undaunted Wolcott urged the holy cause,
With steady hand the solemn scene he draws;
Stern thoughtful temperance with his ardor join'd,
Nor kings nor worlds could warp his steadfast mind.

With graceful ease but energetic tones,
And eloquence that shook a thousand thrones,
Majestic Hosmer stood; the expanding soul
Darts from his eyebeams while his accents roll.
But lo! the shaft of death untimely flew,
And fell'd the patriot from the Hero's view;
Wrapt in the funeral shroud he sees descend
The guide of nations and the Muse's friend.
Columbus dropt a tear; while Hesper's eye
Traced the freed spirit mounting thro the sky.
Each generous Adams, freedom's favorite pair,
And Hancock rose the tyrant's rage to dare,
Groupt with firm Jefferson, her steadiest hope,
Of modest mien but vast unclouded scope.
Like four strong pillars of her state they stand,
They clear from doubt her brave but wavering band;
Colonial charters in their hands they bore,
And lawless acts of ministerial power.
Some injured right in every page appears,
A king in terrors and a land in tears;
From all his guileful plots the veil they drew,
With eye retortive look'd creation thro,
Traced moral nature thro her total plan,
Markt all the steps of liberty and man;

Crowds rose to reason while their accents rung,
And INDEPENDENCE thunder'd from their tongue.
  Columbus turn'd; when rolling to the shore
Swells o'er the seas an undulating roar;
Slow, dark, portentous, as the meteors sweep,
And curtain black the illimitable deep,
High stalks, from surge to surge, a demon Form,
That howls thro heaven and breathes a billowing storm.
His head is hung with clouds; his giant hand
Flings a blue flame far flickering to the land;
His blood-stain'd limbs drip carnage as he strides,
And taint with gory grume the staggering tides;
Like two red suns his quivering eyeballs glare,
His mouth disgorges all the stores of war,
Pikes, muskets, mortars, guns and globes of fire,
And lighted bombs that fusing trails exspire.
Percht on his helmet, two twin sisters rode,
The favorite offspring of the murderous god,
Famine and Pestilence; whom whilom bore
His wife, grim Discord, on Trinacria's shore;
When first their Cyclop sons, from Etna's forge,
Fill'd his foul magazine, his gaping gorge:
Then earth convulsive groan'd, high shriek'd the air,
And hell in gratulation call'd him War.

Behind the fiend, swift hovering for the coast,
Hangs o'er the wave Britannia's sail-wing'd host;
They crowd the main, they spread their sheets abroad,
From the wide Laurence to the Georgian flood,
Point their black batteries to the peopled shore,
And spouting flames commence the hideous roar.
Where fortless Falmouth, looking o'er her bay,
In terror saw the approaching thunders play,
The fire begins; the shells o'er arching fly,
And shoot a thousand rainbows thro the sky;
On Charlestown spires, on Bedford roofs they light,
Groton and Fairfield kindle from the flight,
Norwalk expands the blaze; o'er Reading hills
High flaming Danbury the welkin fills;
Esopus burns, Newyork's delightful fanes
And sea-nursed Norfolk light the neighboring plains.
From realm to realm the smoky volumes bend,
Reach round the bays and up the streams extend;
Deep o'er the concave heavy wreaths are roll'd,
And midland towns and distant groves infold.
Thro solid curls of smoke, the bursting fires
Climb in tall pyramids above the spires,
Concentring all the winds; whose forces, driven
With equal rage from every point of heaven,

Whirl into conflict, round the scantling pour
The twisting flames and thro the rafters roar,
Suck up the cinders, send them sailing far,
To warn the nations of the raging war,
Bend high the blazing vortex, swell'd and curl'd,
Careering, brightening o'er the lustred world,
Absorb the reddening clouds that round them run,
Lick the pale stars, and mock their absent sun:
Seas catch the splendor, kindling skies resound,
And falling structures shake the smouldering ground.
 Crowds of wild fugitives, with frantic tread,
Flit thro the flames that pierce the midnight shade,
Back on the burning domes revert their eyes,
Where some lost friend, some perisht infant lies.
Their maim'd, their sick, their age-enfeebled sires
Have sunk sad victims to the sateless fires;
They greet with one last look their tottering walls,
See the blaze thicken, as the ruin falls,
Then o'er the country train their dumb despair,
And far behind them leave the dancing glare;
Their own crusht roofs still lend a trembling light,
Point their long shadows and direct their flight.
Till wandering wide they seek some cottage door,
Ask the vile pittance due the vagrant poor;

Or faint and faltering on the devious road,
They sink at last and yield their mortal load.
But where the sheeted flames thro Charlestown roar,
And lashing waves hiss round the burning shore,
Thro the deep folding fires dread Bunker's height
Thunders o'er all and shows a field of fight.
Like nightly shadows thro a flaming grove,
To the dark fray the closing squadrons move;
They join, they break, they thicken thro the glare,
And blazing batteries burst along the war;
Now wrapt in reddening smoke, now dim in sight,
They rake the hill, or wing the downward flight;
Here, wheel'd and wedged, Britannia's veterans turn,
And the long lightnings from their muskets burn;
There scattering strive the thin colonial train,
Whose broken platoons still the field maintain;
Till Britain's fresh battalions rise the height,
And with increasing vollies give the fight.
When, choked with dust, discolor'd deep in gore,
And gall'd on all sides from the ships and shore,
Hesperia's host moves off the field afar,
And saves, by slow retreat, the sad remains of war.
There strides bold Putnam, and from all the plains
Calls the tired troops, the tardy rear sustains,

And, mid the whizzing balls that skim the lowe,
Waves back his sword, defies the following foe.
  In this prime prelude of the toil that waits
The nascent glories of his infant states,
Columbus mourn'd the slain. A numerous crowd,
Half of each host, had bought their fame with blood;
From the whole hill he saw the lifestream pour,
And sloping pathways trod with tracks of gore.
Here, glorious Warren, thy cold earth was seen,
Here spring thy laurels in immortal green;
Dearest of chiefs that ever prest the plain,
In freedom's cause with early honors slain;
Still dear in death, as when before our sight
You graced the senate, or you led the fight.
The grateful Muse shall tell the world your fame,
And unborn realms resound the deathless name.
  Now from all plains, as settling smokes decay,
The banded freemen rise in open day;
Tall thro the lessening shadows, half conceal'd,
They throng and gather in a central field;
In unskill'd ranks but ardent soul they stand,
Claim quick the foe, and eager strife demand.
  In front firm Washington superior shone,
His eye directed to the half-seen sun;

As thro the cloud the bursting splendors glow,
And light the passage to the distant foe.
His waving steel returns the living day,
And points, thro unfought fields, the warrior's way;
His valorous deeds to be confined no more,
Monongahela, to thy desert shore.
Matured with years, with nobler glory warm,
Fate in his eye and empire on his arm,
He feels his sword the strength of nations wield,
And moves before them with a broader shield.
Greene rose beside him emulous in arms,
His genius brightening as the danger warms,
In counsel great, in every science skill'd,
Pride of the camp and terror of the field.
With eager look, conspicuous o'er the crowd,
And port majestic, brave Montgomery strode,
Bared his tried blade, with honor's call elate,
Claim'd the first field and hasten'd to his fate.
Lincoln, with force unfolding as he rose,
Scoped the whole war and measured well the foes;
Calm, cautious, firm, for frugal counsels known,
Frugal of other's blood but liberal of his own.
Heath for impending toil his falchion draws,
And fearless Wooster aids the sacred cause,

Mercer advanced an early death to prove,
Sinclair and Mifflin swift to combat move;
Here stood stern Putnam, scored with ancient scars,
The living records of his country's wars;
Wayne, like a moving tower, assumes his post,
Fires the whole field, and is himself a host;
Undaunted Stirling, prompt to meet his foes,
And Gates and Sullivan for action rose;
Macdougal, Clinton, guardians of the state,
Stretch the nerved arm to pierce the depth of fate;
Marion with rapture seized the sword of fame,
Young Laurens graced a father's patriot name;
Moultrie and Sumter lead their banded powers,
Morgan in front of his bold riflers towers,
His host of keen-eyed marksmen, skill'd to pour
Their slugs unerring from the twisted bore.
No sword, no bayonet they learn to wield,
They gall the flank, they skirt the battling field,
Cull out the distant foe in full horse speed,
Couch the long tube and eye the silver bead,
Turn as he turns, dismiss the whizzing lead,
And lodge the death-ball in his heedless head.

So toil'd the huntsman Tell. His quivering dart,
Prest by the bended bowstring, fears to part,

Dreads the tremendous task, to graze but shun
The tender temples of his infant son;
As the loved youth (the tyrant's victim led)
Bears the poised apple tottering on his head.
The sullen father, with reverted eye,
Now marks the satrap, now the bright-hair'd boy;
His second shaft impatient lies, athirst
To mend the expected error of the first,
To pierce the monster, mid the insulted crowd,
And steep the pangs of nature in his blood.
Deep doubling tow'rd his breast, well poised and slow,
Curve the strain'd horns of his indignant bow;
His left arm straightens as the dexter bends,
And his nerved knuckle with the gripe distends;
Soft slides the reed back with the stiff drawn strand,
Till the steel point has reacht his steady hand;
Then to his keen fixt eye the shank he brings,
Twangs the loud cord, the feather'd arrow sings,
Picks off the pippin from the smiling boy,
And Uri's rocks resound with shouts of joy.
Soon by an equal dart the tyrant bleeds,
The cantons league, the work of fate proceeds;
Till Austria's titled hordes, with their own gore,
Fat the fair fields they lorded long before;

On Gothard's height while freedom first unfurl'd
Her infant banner o'er the modern world.
Bland, Moylan, Sheldon the long lines enforce
With light-arm'd scouts, with solid squares of horse;
And Knox from his full park to battle brings
His brazen tubes, *the last resort of kings.*
The long black rows in sullen silence wait,
Their grim jaws gaping, soon to utter fate;
When at his word the carbon clouds shall rise,
And well aim'd thunders rock the shores and skies.
Two foreign Youths had caught the splendent flame,
To Fame's hard school the warm disciples came;
To learn sage Liberty's unlesson'd lore,
To brave the tempest on her war-beat shore,
Prometheus like, to snatch a beam of day,
And homeward bear the unscintillating ray,
To pour new life on Europe's languid horde,
Where millions crouch beneath one stupid lord.
Tho Austria's keiser and the Russian czar
To dungeons doom them, and with fetters mar,
Fayette o'er Gaul's vast realm some light shall spread,
Brave Kosciusko rear Sarmatia's head;
From Garonne's bank to Duna's wintry skies,
The morn shall move, and slumbering nations rise.

And tho their despots quake with wild alarms,
And lash and agonize the world to arms,
Whelm for a while the untutor'd race in blood,
And turn against themselves the raging flood;
Yet shall the undying dawn, with silent pace,
Reach over earth and every land embrace;
Till Europe's well taught sons the boon shall share,
And bless the labors of the imprison'd Pair.
So Leda's Twins from Colchis raped the Fleece,
And brought the treasure to their native Greece.
She hail'd her heroes from their finish'd wars,
Assign'd their place amid the cluster'd stars,
Bade round the eternal sky their trophies flame,
And charged the zodiac with their deathless fame.
—Here move the Strangers, here in freedom's cause
His untried blade each stripling hero draws,
On the great chief their eyes in transport roll,
And war and Washington renerve the soul.
Steuben advanced, in veteran armor drest,
For Prussian lore distinguish'd o'er the rest,
The tactic lore; to this he bends his care,
And here transplants the discipline of war.
Other brave chieftains of illustrious name
Rise into sight and equal honors claim;

But who can tell the dew-drops of the morn,
Or count the rays that in the diamond burn?
—Grieve not, my valiant friends; the faithful song
Shall soon redress the momentary wrong;
Your own bright swords have cleaved your course to fame,
And all her hundred tongues recognize every claim.

Now the broad field as untaught warriors shade,
The sun's glad beam their shining arms display'd;
High waved great Washington his glittering steel,
Bade the long train in circling order wheel;
And, while the banner'd youths around him prest,
With voice revered he thus the ranks addrest:
Ye generous bands, behold the task to save,
Or yield whole nations to an instant grave.
See hosted myriads crowding to your shore,
Hear from all ports their vollied thunders roar;
From Boston heights their bloody standards play,
O'er long Champlain they lead their northern way,
Virginian banks behold their streamers glide,
And hostile navies load each southern tide.
Beneath their steps your towns in ashes lie,
Your inland empires feast their greedy eye;
Soon shall your fields to lordly parks be turn'd,
Your children butcher'd and your villas burn'd;

While following millions, thro the reign of time,
Who claim their birth in this indulgent clime,
Bend the weak knee, to servile toils consign'd,
And sloth and slavery still degrade mankind.
Rise then to war, to timely vengeance rise,
Ere the gray sire, the helpless infant dies;
Look thro the world, see endless years descend,
What realms, what ages on your arms depend!
Reverse the fate, avenge the insulted sky,
Move to the work; we conquer or we die.
So spoke Columbia's chief; his guiding hand
Points out their march to every ardent band,
Assigns to each brave leader, as they claim,
His test of valor and his task of fame.
With his young host Montgomery first moves forth,
To crush the vast invasion of the north;
O'er streams and lakes their flags far onward play,
Navies and forts surrendering mark their way;
Rocks, fens and deserts thwart the paths they go,
And hills before them lose their crags in snow.
Loud Laurence, clogg'd with ice, indignant feels
Their sleet-clad oars, choked helms and crusted keels;
They buffet long his tides; when rise in sight
Quebec's dread walls, and Wolfe's unclouded height.

Already there a few brave patriots stood,
Worn down with toil, by famine half subdued;
Untrench'd before the town, they dare oppose
Their fielded cohorts to the forted foes.
Ah gallant troop! deprived of half the praise
That deeds like yours in other times repays,
Since your prime chief (the favorite erst of fame)
Hath sunk so deep his hateful, hideous name,
That every honest Muse with horror flings
The name unsounded from her sacred strings;
Else what high tones of rapture must have told
The first great action of a chief so bold!
Twas his, twas yours, to brave unusual storms,
To tame rude nature in her drearest forms;
Foodless and guideless, thro that waste of earth,
You march'd long months; and, sore reduced by dearth,
Reach'd the proud capital, too feeble far
To tempt unaided such a task of war;
Till now Montgomery's host, with hopes elate,
Joins your scant powers, to try the test of fate.
With skilful glance he views the fortress round,
Bristled with pikes, with dark artillery crown'd;
Resolves with naked steel to scale the towers,
And snatch a realm from Britain's hostile powers.

Now drear December's boreal blasts arise,
A roaring hailstorm sweeps the shuddering skies,
Night with condensing horror mantles all,
And trembling watch-lights glimmer from the wall.
From bombs o'erarching, fusing, bursting high,
The glare scarce wanders thro the loaded sky;
And in the louder shock of meteors drown'd,
The accustom'd ear in vain expects the sound.

He points the assault; and, thro the howling air,
O'er rocky ramparts leads audacious war.
Swift rise the rapid files; the walls are red
With flashing flames, that show the piles of dead;
Till back recoiling from the ranks of slain,
They leave their leader with a feeble train,
Begirt with foes within the sounding wall,
Who thick beneath his single falchion fall.
But short the conflict; others hemm'd him round,
And brave Montgomery prest the gory ground.
A second Wolfe Columbus here beheld,
In youthful charms, a soul undaunted yield;
Forlorn, o'erpower'd, his hardy host remains,
Stretch'd by his side, or led in captive chains.
Macpherson, Cheesman share their general's doom;
Meigs, Morgan, Dearborn, planning deeds to come,

Resign impatient prisoners; soon to wield
Their happier swords in many a broader field.
   Triumphant to Newyork's ill forted post
Britannia turns her vast amphibious host,
That seas and storms, obedient to her hand,
Heave and discharge on every distant land;
Fleets, floating batteries shake Manhattan's shore,
And Hellgate rocks reverberate the roar.
Swift o'er the shuddering isles that line the bay
The red flags wave, and battering engines play;
Howe leads aland the interminable train,
While his bold brother still bestorms the main,
Great Albion's double pride; both famed afar
On each vext element, each world of war;
Where British rapine follows peaceful toil,
And murders nations but to seize their spoil.
   Wide sweep the veteran myriads o'er the strand,
Outnumbering thrice the raw colonial band;
Flatbush and Harlem sink beneath their fires,
Brave Stirling yields, and Sullivan retires.
In vain sage Washington, from hill to hill,
Plays round his foes with more than Fabian skill,
Retreats, advances, lures them to his snare,
To balance numbers by the shifts of war.

For not their swords alone, but fell disease
Thins his chill camp and chokes the neighboring seas.
The baleful malady, from Syrius sent,
Floats in each breeze, impesting every tent,
Strikes the young soldier with the morning ray,
And lays him lifeless ere the close of day,
Far from his father's house, his mother's care,
And all the charities that nursed him there.
Damp'd is the native rage that first impell'd
The insulted colons to the battling field;
When first their high-soul'd sentiment of right
And full-vein'd vigor nerved their arm to fight.
For stript of health, benumb'd thy vital flood,
Thy muscles lax'd and decomposed thy blood,
What is thy courage, man? a foodless flame,
A light unseen, a soul without a frame.
Each day the decimated ranks forgo
Their dying comrades to repulse the foe,
And each damp night, along the slippery trench,
Breathe at their post the suffocating stench;
They sink by hundreds on the vapory soil,
Till a new fight relieves their deadlier toil.

At last from fruitless combat, sore defeat,
To Croton hills they lead a long retreat;
Pale, curbed, exanimate, in dull despair,
Train the scant relics of the twofold war:
The sword, the pestilence press hard behind;
The body both assail, and one beats down the mind.

THE

COLUMBIAD.

BOOK VI.

ARGUMENT.

British cruelty to American prisoners. Prison Ship. Retreat of Washington with the relics of his army, pursued by Howe. Washington recrossing the Delaware in the night, to surprise the British van, is opposed by uncommon obstacles. His success in this audacious enterprise lays the foundation of the American empire. A monument to be erected on the bank of the Delaware. Approach of Burgoyne, sailing up the St. Laurence with an army of Britons and various other nations. Indignant energy of the colonies, compared to that of Greece in opposing the invasion of Xerxes. Formation of an army of citizens, under the command of Gates. Review of the American and British armies, and of the savage tribes who join the British standard. Battle of Saratoga. Story of Lucinda. Second battle, and capture of Burgoyne and his army.

THE

COLUMBIAD.

BOOK VI.

BUT of all tales that war's black annals hold,
The darkest, foulest still remains untold;
New modes of torture wait the shameful strife,
And Britain wantons in the waste of life.
  Cold-blooded Cruelty, first fiend of hell,
Ah think no more with savage hordes to dwell;
Quit the Caribian tribes who eat their slain,
Fly that grim gang, the Inquisitors of Spain,
Boast not thy deeds in Moloch's shrines of old,
Leave Barbary's pirates to their blood-bought gold,
Let Holland steal her victims, force them o'er 11
To toils and death on Java's morbid shore;
Some cloak, some color all these crimes may plead;
Tis avarice, passion, blind religion's deed;

But Britons here, in this fraternal broil,
Grave, cool, deliberate in thy service toil.
Far from the nation's eye, whose nobler soul
Their wars would humanize, their pride control,
They lose the lessons that her laws impart,
And change the British for the brutal heart.
Fired by no passion, madden'd by no zeal,
No priest, no Plutus bids them not to feel;
Unpaid, gratuitous, on torture bent,
Their sport is death, their pastime to torment;
All other gods they scorn, but bow the knee,
And curb, well pleased, O Cruelty, to thee.

Come then, curst goddess, where thy votaries reign,
Inhale their incense from the land and main;
Come to Newyork, their conquering arms to greet,
Brood o'er their camp and breathe along their fleet;
The brother chiefs of Howe's illustrious name
Demand thy labors to complete their fame.
What shrieks of agony thy praises sound!
What grateless dungeons groan beneath the ground!
See the black Prison Ship's expanding womb
Impested thousands, quick and dead, entomb.
Barks after barks the captured seamen bear,
Transboard and lodge thy silent victims there;

A hundred scows, from all the neighboring shore,
Spread the dull sail and ply the constant oar,
Waft wrecks of armies from the well fought field,
And famisht garrisons who bravely yield;
They mount the hulk, and, cramm'd within the cave,
Hail their last house, their living, floating grave.
She comes, the Fiend! her grinning jaws expand,
Her brazen eyes cast lightning o'er the strand,
Her wings like thunder-clouds the welkin sweep,
Brush the tall spires and shade the shuddering deep;
She gains the deck, displays her wonted store,
Her cords and scourges wet with prisoners' gore;
Gripes, pincers, thumb-screws spread beneath her feet,
Slow poisonous drugs and loads of putrid meat;
Disease hangs drizzling from her slimy locks,
And hot contagion issues from her box.
O'er the closed hatches ere she takes her place,
She moves the massy planks a little space,
Opes a small passage to the cries below,
That feast her soul on messages of woe;
There sits with gaping ear and changeless eye,
Drinks every groan and treasures every sigh,
Sustains the faint, their miseries to prolong,
Revives the dying and unnerves the strong.

But as the infected mass resign their breath,
She keeps with joy the register of death.
As tost thro portholes from the encumber'd cave,
Corpse after corpse fall dashing in the wave;
Corpse after corpse, for days and months and years,
The tide bears off, and still its current clears;
At last, o'erloaded with the putrid gore,
The slime-clad waters thicken round the shore.
Green Ocean's self, that oft his wave renews,
That drinks whole fleets with all their battling crews,
That laves, that purifies the earth and sky,
Yet ne'er before resign'd his natural dye,
Here purples, blushes for the race he bore
To rob and ravage this unconquer'd shore;
The scaly nations, as they travel by,
Catch the contagion, sicken, gasp and die.
Now Hesper turns the Hero's tearful eye
To other fields where other standards fly;
For here constrain'd new warfare to disclose,
And show the feats of more than mortal foes,
Where interposing with celestial might,
His own dread labors must decide the fight,
He bids the scene with pomp unusual rise,
To teach Columbus how to read the skies.

He marks the trace of Howe's triumphant course,
And wheels o'er Jersey plains his gathering force;
Where dauntless Washington, begirt with foes,
Still greater rises as the danger grows,
And wearied troops, o'er kindred warriors slain,
Attend his march thro many a sanguine plain.

From Hudson's bank to Trenton's wintry strand,
He guards in firm retreat his feeble band;
Britons by thousands on his flanks advance,
Bend o'er his rear and point the lifted lance.
Past Delaware's frozen stream, with scanty force,
He checks retreat; then turning back his course,
Remounts the wave, and thro the mingled roar
Of ice and storm reseeks the hostile shore,
Wrapt in the gloom of night. The offended Flood
Starts from his cave, assumes the indignant god,
Rears thro the parting tide his foamy form,
And with his fiery eyeballs lights the storm.
He stares around him on the host he heard,
Clears his choked urn and smooths his icy beard,
And thus: Audacious chief, this troubled wave
Tempt not; or tempting, here shall gape thy grave.
Is nothing sacred to thy venturous might?
The howling storm, the holy truce of night,

High tossing ice-isles crashing round thy side,
Insidious rocks that pierce the tumbling tide?
Fear then this forceful arm, and hear once more,
Death stands between thee and that shelvy shore.
The chief beholds the god, and notes his cry,
But onward drives, nor pauses to reply;
Calls to each bark, and spirits every host
To toil, gain, tempt the interdicted coast.
The crews, regardless of the doubling roar,
Breast the strong helm, and wrestle with the oar,
Stem with resurgent prow the struggling spray,
And with phosphoric lanterns shape their way.
The god perceived his warning words were vain,
And rose more furious to assert his reign,
Lash'd up a loftier surge, and heaved on high
A ridge of billows that obstruct the sky;
And, as the accumulated mass he rolls,
Bares the sharp rocks and lifts the gaping shoals.
Forward the fearless barges plunge and bound,
Top the curl'd wave, or grind the flinty ground,
Careen, whirl, right, and sidelong dasht and tost,
Now seem to reach and now to lose the coast.
Still unsubdued the sea-drench'd army toils,
Each buoyant skiff the flouncing godhead foils;

He raves and roars, and in delirious woe
Calls to his aid his ancient hoary foe,
Almighty Frost; when thus the vanquish'd Flood
Bespeaks in haste the great earth-rending god:
Father of storms! behold this mortal race
Confound my force and brave me to my face.
Not all my waves by all my tempests driven,
Nor black night brooding o'er the starless heaven,
Can check their course; they toss and plunge amain,
And lo, my guardian rocks project their points in vain.
Come to my help, and with thy stiffening breath
Clog their strain'd helms, distend their limbs in death.
Tho ancient enmity our realms divide,
And oft thy chains arrest my laboring tide,
Let strong necessity our cause combine,
Thy own disgrace anticipate in mine;
Even now their oars thy sleet in vain congeals,
Thy crumbling ice-cakes crash beneath their keels;
Their impious arms already cope with ours,
And mortal man defies immortal Powers.
Roused at the call, the Monarch mounts the storm;
In muriat flakes he robes his nitrous form,

Glares thro the compound, all its blast inhales,
And seas turn crystal where he breathes his gales.
He comes careering o'er his bleak domain,
But comes untended by his usual train;
Hail, sleet and snow-rack far behind him fly,
Too weak to wade thro this petrific sky,
Whose air consolidates and cuts and stings,
And shakes hoar tinsel from its flickering wings.
Earth heaves and cracks beneath the alighting god;
He gains the pass, bestrides the roaring flood,
Shoots from his nostrils one wide withering sheet
Of treasured meteors on the struggling fleet;
The waves conglaciate instant, fix in air,
Stand like a ridge of rocks, and shiver there.
The barks, confounded in their headlong surge,
Or wedged in crystal, cease their oars to urge;
Some with prone prow, as plunging down the deep,
And some remounting o'er the slippery steep
Seem laboring still, but moveless, lifeless all;
And the chill'd army here awaits its fall.
But Hesper, guardian of Hesperia's right,
From his far heaven looks thro the rayless night;
And, stung to vengeance at the unequal strife,
To save her host, in jeopardy of life,

Starts from his throne, ascends his flamy car,
And turns tremendous to the field of war.
His wheels, resurging from the depth of even,
Roll back the night, streak wide the startled heaven,
Rgain their easting with reverted gyres,
And stud their path with scintillating fires.
He cleaves the clouds; and, swift as beams of day,
O'er California sweeps his splendid way;
Missouri's mountains at his passage nod,
And now sad Delaware feels the present god,
And trembles at his tread. For here to fight
Rush two dread Powers of such unmeasured might,
As threats to annihilate his doubtful reign,
Convulse the heaven and mingle earth and main.
  Frost views his brilliant foe with scornful eye,
And whirls a tenfold tempest thro the sky;
Where each fine atom of the immense of air,
Steel'd, pointed, barb'd for unexampled war,
Sings o'er the shuddering ground; when thus he broke
Contemptuous silence, and to Hesper spoke:
Thou comest in time to share their last disgrace,
To change to crystal with thy rebel race,
Stretch thy huge corse o'er Delaware's bank afar,
And learn the force of elemental war.

Or if undying life thy lamp inspire,
Take that one blast and to thy sky retire;
There, roll'd eternal round the heavens, proclaim
Thy own disaster and my deathless fame.
  I come, said Hesper, not to insult the brave,
But break thy sceptre and let loose my wave,
Teach the proud Stream more peaceful tides to roll,
And send thee howling to thy stormy pole;
That drear dominion shall thy rage confine;
This land, these waters and those troops are mine.
  He added not; and now the sable storm,
Pierced by strong splendor, burst before his form;
His visage stern an awful lustre shed,
His pearly planet play'd around his head.
He seized a lofty pine, whose roots of yore
Struck deep in earth, to guard the sandy shore
From hostile ravage of the mining tide,
That rakes with spoils of earth its crumbling side.
He wrencht it from the soil, and o'er the foe
Whirl'd the strong trunk, and aim'd a sweeping blow,
That sung thro air, but miss'd the moving god,
And fell wide crashing on the frozen flood.
For many a rood the shivering ice it tore,
Loosed every bark and shook the sounding shore;

Stroke after stroke with doubling force he plied,
Foil'd the hoar Fiend and pulverized the tide.
The baffled tyrant quits the desperate cause;
From Hesper's heat the river swells and thaws,
The fleet rolls gently to the Jersey coast,
And morning splendors greet the landing host.

Tis here dread Washington, when first the day
O'er Trenton beam'd to light his rapid way,
Pour'd the rude shock on Britain's vanguard train,
And led whole squadrons in his captive chain;
Where veteran troops to half their numbers yield,
Tread back their steps, or press the sanguine field,
To Princeton plains precipitate their flight,
Thro new disasters and unfinish'd fight,
Resign their conquests by one sad surprise,
Sink in their pride and see their rivals rise.

Here dawn'd the daystar of Hesperia's fame,
Here herald glory first emblazed her name;
On Delaware's bank her base of empire stands,
The work of Washington's immortal hands;
Prompt at his side while gallant Mercer trod,
And seal'd the firm foundation with his blood.

In future years, if right the Muse divine,
Some great memorial on this bank shall shine;

A column bold its granite shaft shall rear,
Swell o'er the strand and check the passing air,
Cast its broad image on the watery glade,
And Bristol greet the monumental shade;
Eternal emblem of that gloomy hour,
When the great general left her storm-beat shore,
To tempest, night and his own sword consign'd
His country's fates, the fortunes of mankind.

Where sealike Laurence, rolling in his pride,
With Ocean's self disputes the tossing tide,
From shore to shore, thro dim distending skies,
Beneath full sails imbanded nations rise.
Britain and Brunswick here their flags unfold,
Here Hessia's hordes, for toils of slaughter sold,
Anspach and Darmstadt swell the hireling train,
Proud Caledonia crowds the masted main,
Hibernian kerns and Hanoverian slaves
Move o'er the decks and darken wide the waves.

Tall on the boldest bark superior shone
A warrior ensign'd with a various crown;
Myrtles and laurels equal honors join'd,
Which arms had purchased and the Muses twined;
His sword waved forward, and his ardent eye
Seem'd sharing empires in the southern sky.

Beside him rose a herald to proclaim
His various honors, titles, feats and fame;
Who raised an opening scroll, where proudly shone
Burgoyne and vengeance from the British throne.
Champlain receives the congregated host,
And his husht waves beneath the sails are lost;
Ticonderoga rears his rocks in vain,
Nor Edward's walls the weighty shock sustain;
Deep George's loaded lake reluctant guides
Their bounding barges o'er his sacred tides.
State after state the splendid pomp appalls,
Each town surrenders, every fortress falls;
Sinclair retires; and with his feeble train,
In slow retreat o'er many a fatal plain,
Allures their march; wide moves their furious force,
And flaming hamlets mark their wasting course;
Thro fortless realms their spreading ranks are wheel'd,
On Mohawk's western wave, on Bennington's dread field.

At last where Hudson, with majestic pace,
Swells at the sight, and checks his rapid race,
Thro dark Stillwater slow and silent moves,
And flying troops with sullen pause reproves,

A few firm bands their starry standard rear,
Wheel, front and face the desolating war.
Sudden the patriot flame each province warms,
Deep danger calls, the freemen quit their farms,
Seize their tried muskets, name their chiefs to lead,
Endorse their knapsacks and to vengeance speed.
O'er all the land the kindling ardor flies,
Troop follows troop, and flags on flags arise,
Concentred, train'd, their forming files unite,
Swell into squadrons and demand the fight.

When Xerxes, raving at his sire's disgrace,
Pour'd his dark millions on the coast of Thrace,
O'er groaning Hellespont his broad bridge hurl'd,
Hew'd ponderous Athos from the trembling world,
Still'd with his weight of ships the struggling main,
And bound the billows in his boasted chain,
Wide o'er proud Macedon he wheel'd his course,
Thrace, Thebes, Thessalia join'd his furious force.
Thro six torn states his hovering swarms increase,
And hang tremendous on the skirts of Greece;
Deep groan the shrines of all her guardian gods,
Sad Pelion shakes, divine Olympus nods,
Shock'd Ossa sheds his hundred hills of snow,
And Tempe swells her murmuring brook below;

Wild in her starts of rage the Pythian shrieks,
Dodona's Oak the pangs of nature speaks,
Eleusis quakes thro all her mystic caves,
And black Trophonius gapes a thousand graves.
But soon the freeborn Greeks to vengeance rise,
Brave Sparta springs where first the danger lies,
Her self-devoted Band, in one steel'd mass,
Plunge in the gorge of death, and choke the Pass.
Athenian youths, the unwieldy war to meet,
Couch the stiff lance, or mount the well arm'd fleet;
They sweep the incumber'd seas of their vast load,
And fat their fields with lakes of Asian blood.

So leapt our youths to meet the invading hordes,
Fame fired their courage, freedom edged their swords.
Gates in their van on high-hill'd Bemus rose,
Waved his blue steel and dared the headlong foes;
Undaunted Lincoln, laboring on his right,
Urged every arm, and gave them hearts to fight;
Starke, at the dexter flank, the onset claims,
Indignant Herkimer the left inflames;
He bounds exulting to commence the strife,
And buy the victory with his barter'd life.

And why, sweet Minstrel, from the harp of fame
Withhold so long that once resounding name?

The chief who, steering by the boreal star,
O'er wild Canadia led our infant war,
In desperate straits superior powers display'd,
Burgoyne's dread scourge, Montgomery's ablest aid;
Ridgefield and Compo saw his valorous might
With ill-arm'd swains put veteran troops to flight.
Tho treason foul hath since absorb'd his soul,
Bade waves of dark oblivion round him roll,
Sunk his proud heart abhorrent and abhorr'd,
Effaced his memory and defiled his sword;
Yet then untarnisht roll'd his conquering car;
Then famed and foremost in the ranks of war
Brave Arnold trod; high valor warm'd his breast,
And beams of glory play'd around his crest.
Here toils the chief; whole armies from his eye
Resume their souls, and swift to combat fly.

Camp'd on a hundred hills, and trench'd in form,
Burgoyne's long legions view the gathering storm;
Uncounted nations round their general stand,
And wait the signal from his guiding hand.
Canadia crowds her Gallic colons there,
Ontario's yelling tribes torment the air,
Wild Huron sends his lurking hordes from far,
Insidious Mohawk swells the woodland war;

Scalpers and ax-men rush from Erie's shore,
And Iroquois augments the war whoop roar;
While all his ancient troops his train supply,
Half Europe's banners waving thro the sky;
Deep squadron'd horse support his endless flanks,
And park'd artillery frowns behind the ranks.
Flush'd with the conquest of a thousand fields,
And rich with spoils that all the region yields,
They burn with zeal to close the long campaign,
And crush Columbia on this final plain.

His fellow chiefs inhale the hero's flame,
Nerves of his arm and partners in his fame:
Phillips, with treasured thunders poised and wheel'd
In brazen tubes, prepares to rake the field;
The trench-tops darken with the sable rows,
And, tipt with fire, the waving match-rope glows.
There gallant Reidesel in German guise,
And Specht and Breyman, prompt for action, rise;
His savage hordes the murderous Johnson leads,
Files thro the woods and treads the tangled weeds,
Shuns open combat, teaches where to run,
Skulk, couch the ambush, aim the hunter's gun,
Whirl the sly tomahawk, the war whoop sing,
Divide the spoils and pack the scalps they bring.

Frazer in quest of glory seeks the field;—
False glare of glory, what hast thou to yield?
How long, deluding phantom, wilt thou blind,
Mislead, debase, unhumanize mankind?
Bid the bold youth, his headlong sword who draws,
Heed not the object, nor inquire the cause;
But seek adventuring, like an errant knight,
Wars not his own, gratuitous in fight,
Greet the gored field, then plunging thro the fire,
Mow down his men, with stupid pride expire,
Shed from his closing eyes the finish'd flame,
And ask, for all his crimes, a deathless name?
And when shall solid glory, pure and bright,
Alone inspire us, and our deeds requite?
When shall the applause of men their chiefs pursue
In just proportion to the good they do,
On virtue's base erect the shrine of fame,
Define her empire, and her code proclaim?
Unhappy Frazer! little hast thou weigh'd
The crimeful cause thy valor comes to aid.
Far from thy native land, thy sire, thy wife,
Love's lisping race that cling about thy life,
Thy soul beats high, thy thoughts expanding roam
On battles past, and laurels yet to come:

Alas, what laurels? where the lasting gain?
A pompous funeral on a desert plain!
The cannon's roar, the muffled drums proclaim,
In one short blast, thy momentary fame,
And some war minister per-hazard reads
In what far field the tool of placemen bleeds.
   Brave Heartly strode in youth's o'erweening pride;
Housed in the camp he left his blooming bride,
The sweet Lucinda; whom her sire from far,
On steeds high bounding o'er the waste of war,
Had guided thro the lines, and hither led,
That fateful morn, the plighted chief to wed.
He deem'd, deluded sire! the contest o'er,
That routed rebels dared the fight no more;
And came to mingle, as the tumult ceased,
The victor's triumph with the nuptial feast.
They reach'd his tent; when now with loud alarms
The morn burst forth and roused the camp to arms;
Conflicting passions seized the lover's breast,
Bright honor call'd, and bright Lucinda prest:—
And wilt thou leave me for that clangorous call?
Traced I these deserts but to see thee fall?
I know thy valorous heart, thy zeal that speeds
Where dangers press and boldest battle bleeds.

My father said blest Hymen here should join
With sacred Love to make Lucinda thine;
But other union these dire drums foredoom,
The dark dead union of the eternal tomb.
On yonder plain, soon sheeted o'er with blood,
Our nuptial couch shall prove a crimson clod;
For there this night thy livid corse must lie,
I'll seek it there, and on that bosom die.
Yet go; tis duty calls; but o'er thy head
Let this white plume its floating foliage spread;
That from the rampart, thro the troubled air,
These eyes may trace thee toiling in the war.
She fixt the feather on his crest above,
Bound with the mystic knot, the knot of love;
He parted silent, but in silent prayer
Bade Love and Hymen guard the timorous fair.
Where Saratoga show'd her champaign side,
That Hudson bathed with still untainted tide,
The opposing pickets push'd their scouting files,
Wheel'd, skirmisht, halted, practised all their wiles;
Each to mislead, insnare, exhaust their foes,
And court the conquest ere the armies close.
Now roll like winged storms the solid lines,
The clarion thunders and the battle joins,

Thick flames in vollied flashes load the air,
And echoing mountains give the noise of war;
Sulphureous clouds rise reddening round the height,
And veil the skies, and wrap the sounding fight.
Soon from the skirts of smoke, where thousands toil,
Ranks roll away and into light recoil;
Starke pours upon them in a storm of lead;
His hosted swains bestrew the field with dead,
Pierce with strong bayonets the German reins,
Whelm two battalions in their captive chains,
Bid Baum, with wounds enfeebled, quit the field,
And Breyman next his gushing lifeblood yield.
This Frazer sees, and thither turns his course,
Bears down before them with Britannia's force,
Wheels a broad column on the victor flank,
And springs to vengeance thro the foremost rank.
Lincoln, to meet the hero, sweeps the plain;
His ready bands the laboring Starke sustain;
Host matching host, the doubtful battle burns,
And now the Britons, now their foes by turns
Regain the ground; till Frazer feels the force
Of a rude grapeshot in his flouncing horse;
Nor knew the chief, till struggling from the fall,
That his gored thigh had first received the ball.

He sinks expiring on the slippery soil;
Shock'd at the sight, his baffled troops recoil;
Where Lincoln, pressing with redoubled might,
Broke thro their squadrons and confirm'd the flight;
When this brave leader met a stunning blow,
That stopt his progress and avenged the foe.
He left the field; but prodigal of life,
Unwearied Francis still prolong'd the strife;
Till a chance carabine attain'd his head,
And stretch'd the hero mid the vulgar dead.
His near companions rush with ardent gait,
Swift to revenge, but soon to share his fate;
Brown, Adams, Coburn, falling side by side,
Drench the chill sod with all their vital tide.

Firm on the west bold Herkimer sustains
The gather'd shock of all Canadia's trains;
Colons and wildmen post their skulkers there,
Outflank his pickets and assail his rear,
Drive in his distant scouts with hideous blare,
And press, on three sides close, the hovering war.
Johnson's own shrieks commence the deafening din,
Rouse every ambush and the storm begin.
A thousand thickets, thro each opening glen,
Pour forth their hunters to the chase of men;

Trunks of huge trees, and rocks and ravines lend
Unnumber'd batteries and their files defend;
They fire, they squat, they rise, advance and fly,
And yells and groans alternate rend the sky.
The well aim'd hatchet cleaves the helmless head,
Mute showers of arrows and loud storms of lead
Rain thick from hands unseen, and sudden fling
A deep confusion thro the laboring wing.
  But Herkimer undaunted quits the stand,
Breaks in loose files his disencumber'd band,
Wheels on the howling glens each light-arm'd troop,
And leads himself where Johnson tones his whoop,
Pours thro his copse a well directed fire;
The semisavage sees his tribes retire,
Then follows thro the brush in full horse speed,
And gains the hilltop where the Hurons lead;
Here turns his courser; when a grateful sight
Recals his stragglers, and restrains his flight.
For Herkimer no longer now sustains
The loss of blood that his faint vitals drains:
A ball had pierced him ere he changed his field;
The slow sure death his prudence had conceal'd,
Till dark derouted foes should yield to flight,
And his firm friends could finish well the fight.

Lopt from his horse the hero sinks at last;
The Hurons ken him, and with hallooing blast
Shake the vast wilderness; the tribes around
Drink with broad ears and swell the rending sound,
Rush back to vengeance with tempestuous might,
Sweep the long slopes from every neighboring height,
Full on their check'd pursuers; who regain,
From all their woods, the first contested plain.
Here open fight begins; and sure defeat
Had forced that column to a swift retreat,
But Arnold, toiling thro the distant smoke,
Beheld their plight, a small detachment took,
Bore down behind them with his field-park loud,
And hail'd his grapeshot thro the savage crowd;
Strow'd every copse with dead, and chased afar
The affrighted relics from the skirts of war.
But on the centre swells the heaviest charge,
The squares develop and the lines enlarge.
Here Kosciusko's mantling works conceal'd
His batteries mute, but soon to scour the field;
Morgan with all his marksmen flanks the foe,
Hull, Brooks and Courtlandt in the vanguard glow;
Here gallant Dearborn leads his light-arm'd train,
Here Scammel towers, here Silly shakes the plain.

Gates guides the onset with his waving brand,
Assigns their task to each unfolding band,
Sustains, inspirits, prompts the warrior's rage,
Now bids the flank and now the front engage,
Points the stern riflers where their slugs to pour,
And tells the unmasking batteries when to roar.
For here impetuous Powell wheels and veers
His royal guards, his British grenadiers;
His Highland broadswords cut their wasting course,
His horse-artillery whirls its furious force.
Here Specht and Reidesel to battle bring
Their scattering yagers from each folding wing;
And here, concentred in tremendous might,
Britain's whole park, descending to the fight,
Roars thro the ranks; tis Phillips leads the train,
And toils and thunders o'er the shuddering plain.

Burgoyne, secure of victory, from his height,
Eyes the whole field and orders all the fight,
Marks where his veterans plunge their fiercest fire,
And where his foes seem halting to retire,
Already sees the starry staff give way,
And British ensigns gaining on the day;
When from the western wing, in steely glare,
All-conquering Arnold surged the tide of war.

Columbia kindles as her hero comes;
Her trump's shrill clangor and her deafening drums
Redoubling sound the charge; they rage, they burn,
And hosted Europe trembles in her turn.
So when Pelides' absence check'd her fate,
All Ilion issued from her guardian gate;
Her huddling squadrons like a tempest pour'd,
Each man a hero and each dart a sword,
Full on retiring Greece tumultuous fall,
And Greece reluctant seeks her sheltering wall;
But Pelius' son rebounding o'er the plain,
Troy backward starts and seeks her towers again.
  Arnold's dread falchion, with terrific sway,
Rolls on the ranks and rules the doubtful day,
Confounds with one wide sweep the astonish'd foes,
And bids at last the scene of slaughter close.
Pale rout begins, Britannia's broken train
Tread back their steps and scatter from the plain,
To their strong camp precipitate retire,
And wide behind them streams the roaring fire.
  Meantime, the skirts of war as Johnson gored,
His kindred cannibals desert their lord;
They scour the waste for undistinguish'd prey,
Howl thro the night the horrors of the day,

Scalp every straggler from all parties stray'd,
Each wounded wanderer thro the moonlight glade;
And while the absent armies give them place,
Each camp they plunder and each world disgrace.
One deed shall tell what fame great Albion draws
From these auxiliars in her barbarous cause,
Lucinda's fate; the tale, ye nations, hear;
Eternal ages, trace it with a tear.
Long from the rampart, thro the imbattled field,
She spied her Heartly where his column wheel'd,
Traced him with steadfast eye and tortured breast,
That heaved in concert with his dancing crest;
And oft, with head advanced and hand outspread,
Seem'd from her Love to ward the flying lead;
Till, dimm'd by distance and the gathering cloud;
At last he vanish'd in the warrior crowd.
She thought he fell; and wild with fearless air,
She left the camp to brave the woodland war,
Made a long circuit, all her friends to shun,
And wander'd wide beneath the falling sun;
Then veering to the field, the pickets past,
To gain the hillock where she miss'd him last.
Fond maid, he rests not there; from finish'd fight
He sought the camp, and closed the rear of flight.

He hurries to his tent;—oh rage! despair!
No glimpse, no tidings of the frantic fair;
Save that some carmen, as acamp they drove,
Had seen her coursing for the western grove.
Faint with fatigue and choked with burning thirst,
Forth from his friends with bounding leap he burst,
Vaults o'er the palisade with eyes on flame,
And fills the welkin with Lucinda's name,
Swift thro the wild wood paths phrenetic springs,—
Lucind! Lucinda! thro the wild wood rings.
All night he wanders; barking wolves alone
And screaming night-birds answer to his moan;
For war had roused them from their savage den;
They scent the field, they snuff the walks of men.
The fair one too, of every aid forlorn,
Had raved and wander'd, till officious morn
Awaked the Mohawks from their short repose,
To glean the plunder, ere their comrades rose.
Two Mohawks met the maid,—historian, hold!—
Poor Human Nature! must thy shame be told?
Where then that proud preeminence of birth,
Thy Moral Sense? the brightest boast of earth.
Had but the tiger changed his heart for thine,
Could rocks their bowels with that heart combine,

Thy tear had gusht, thy hand relieved her pain,
And led Lucinda to her lord again.

She starts, with eyes upturn'd and fleeting breath,
In their raised axes views her instant death,
Spreads her white hands to heaven in frantic prayer,
Then runs to grasp their knees, and crouches there.
Her hair, half lost along the shrubs she past,
Rolls in loose tangles round her lovely waist;
Her kerchief torn betrays the globes of snow
That heave responsive to her weight of woe.
Does all this eloquence suspend the knife?
Does no superior bribe contest her life?
There does: the scalps by British gold are paid;
A long-hair'd scalp adorns that heavenly head;
And comes the sacred spoil from friend or foe,
No marks distinguish, and no man can know.

With calculating pause and demon grin,
They seize her hands, and thro her face divine
Drive the descending ax; the shriek she sent
Attain'd her lover's ear; he thither bent
With all the speed his wearied limbs could yield,
Whirl'd his keen blade, and stretch'd upon the field
The yelling fiends; who there disputing stood
Her gory scalp, their horrid prize of blood.

He sunk delirious on her lifeless clay,
And past, in starts of sense, the dreadful day.
Are these thy trophies, Carleton! these the swords
Thy hand unsheath'd and gave the savage hordes,
Thy boasted friends, by treaties brought from far,
To aid thy master in his murderous war?
But now Britannia's chief, with proud disdain
Coop'd in his camp, demands the field again.
Back to their fate his splendid host he drew,
Swell'd high their rage, and led the charge anew;
Again the batteries roar, the lightnings play,
Again they fall, again they roll away;
For now Columbia, with rebounding might,
Foil'd quick their columns, but confined their flight.
Her wings, like fierce tornados, gyring ran,
Crusht their wide flanks and gain'd their flying van;
Here Arnold charged; the hero storm'd and pour'd
A thousand thunders where he turn'
No pause, no parley; onward far he fray'd,
Dispersed whole squadrons every bound he made,
Broke thro their rampart, seized their camp and stores
And pluck'd the standard from their broken towers.
Aghast, confounded in the midway field,
They drop their arms; the banded nations yield.

When sad Burgoyne, in one disastrous day,
Sees future crowns and former wreaths decay,
His banners furl'd, his long battalions wheel'd
To pile their muskets on the battle field;
While two pacific armies shade one plain,
The mighty victors and the captive train.

THE

COLUMBIAD.

BOOK VII.

ARGUMENT.

Coast of France rises in vision. Louis, to humble the British power, forms an alliance with the American states. This brings France, Spain and Holland into the war, and rouses Hyder Ally to attack the English in India. The vision returns to America, where the military operations continue with various success. Battle of Monmouth. Storming of Stonypoint by Wayne. Actions of Lincoln, and surrender of Charleston. Movements of Cornwallis. Actions of Greene, and battle of Eutaw. French army arrives, and joins the American. They march to besiege the English army of Cornwallis in York and Gloster. Naval battle of Degrasse and Graves. Two of their ships grappled and blown up. Progress of the siege. A citadel mined and blown up. Capture of Cornwallis and his army. Their banners furled and muskets piled on the field of battle.

THE

COLUMBIAD.

BOOK VII.

Thus view'd the Pair; when lo, in eastern skies,
From glooms unfolding, Gallia's coasts arise.
Bright o'er the scenes of state a golden throne,
Instarr'd with gems and hung with purple, shone;
Young Bourbon there in royal splendor sat,
And fleets and moving armies round him wait.
For now the contest, with increased alarms,
Fill'd every court and roused the world to arms;
As Hesper's hand, that light from darkness brings,
And good to nations from the scourge of kings,
In this dread hour bade broader beams unfold,
And the new world illuminate the old.
  In Europe's realms a school of sages trace
The expanding dawn that waits the Reasoning Race;

On the bright Occident they fix their eyes,
Thro glorious toils where struggling nations rise;
Where each firm deed, each new illustrious name
Calls into light a field of nobler fame:
A field that feeds their hope, confirms the plan
Of well poized freedom and the weal of man.
They scheme, they theorize, expand their scope,
Glance o'er Hesperia to her utmost cope;
Where streams unknown for other oceans stray,
Where suns unseen their waste of beams display,
Where sires of unborn nations claim their birth,
And ask their empires in those wilds of earth.
While round all eastern climes, with painful eye,
In slavery sunk they see the kingdoms lie,
Whole states exhausted to enrich a throne,
Their fruits untasted and their rights unknown;
Thro tears of grief that speak the well taught mind,
They hail the æra that relieves mankind.

Of these the first, the Gallic sages stand,
And urge their king to lift an aiding hand.
The cause of humankind their souls inspired,
Columbia's wrongs their indignation fired;
To share her fateful deeds their counsel moved,
To base in practice what in theme they proved:

That no proud privilege from birth can spring,
No right divine, nor compact form a king;
That in the people dwells the sovereign sway,
Who rule by proxy, by themselves obey;
That virtues, talents are the test of awe,
And Equal Rights the only source of law.
Surrounding heroes wait the monarch's word,
In foreign fields to draw the patriot sword,
Prepared with joy to join those infant powers,
Who build republics on the western shores.
By honest guile the royal ear they bend,
And lure him on, blest Freedom to defend;
That, once recognised, once establisht there,
The world might learn her profer'd boon to share.
But artful arguments their plan disguise,
Garb'd in the gloss that suits a monarch's eyes.
By arms to humble Britain's haughty power,
From her to sever that extended shore,
Contents his utmost wish. For this he lends
His powerful aid, and calls the opprest his friends.
The league proposed, he lifts his arm to save,
And speaks the borrow'd language of the brave:
Ye states of France, and ye of rising name
Who work those distant miracles of fame,

Hear and attend; let heaven the witness bear,
We wed the cause, we join the righteous war.
Let leagues eternal bind each friendly land,
Given by our voice, and stablisht by our hand;
Let that brave people fix their infant sway,
And spread their blessings with the bounds of day.
Yet know, ye nations; hear, ye Powers above,
Our purposed aid no views of conquest move;
In that young world revives no ancient claim
Of regions peopled by the Gallic name;
Our envied bounds, already stretch'd afar,
Nor ask the sword, nor fear encroaching war;
But virtue, coping with the tyrant power
That drenches earth in her best children's gore,
With nature's foes bids former compact cease;
We war reluctant, and our wish is peace;
For man's whole race the sword of France we draw;
Such is our will, and let our will be law.

He spoke; his moving armies veil'd the plain,
His fleets rode bounding on the western main;
O'er lands and seas the loud applauses rung,
And war and union dwelt on every tongue.

The other Bourbon caught the splendid strain,
To Gallia's arms he joins the powers of Spain;

Their sails assemble; Crillon lifts the sword,
Minorca bows and owns her ancient lord.
But while dread Elliott shakes the Midland wave,
They strive in vain the Calpian rock to brave.
Batavia's states with equal speed prepare
Thro western isles to meet the naval war;
For Albion there rakes rude the tortured main,
And foils the force of Holland, France and Spain.
Where old Indostan still perfumes the skies,
To furious strife his ardent myriads rise;
Fierce Hyder there, unconquerably bold,
Bids a new flag its horned moons unfold,
Spreads o'er Carnatic kings his splendid force,
And checks the Britons in their wasting course.
Europe's pacific powers their counsels join,
The laws of trade to settle and define.
The imperial Moscovite around him draws
Each Baltic state to join the righteous cause;
Whose arm'd Neutrality the way prepares
To check the ravages of future wars;
Till by degrees the wasting sword shall cease,
And commerce lead to universal peace.
Thus all the ancient world with anxious eyes
Enjoy the lights that gild Atlantic skies,

Wake to new life, assume a borrow'd flame,
Enlarge the lustre and partake the fame.
So mounts of ice, that polar heavens invade,
Tho piled unseen thro night's long wintry shade,
When morn at last illumes their glaring throne,
Give back the day and imitate the sun.
  But still Columbus, on his war-beat shore,
Sees Albion's fleets her new battalions pour;
The states unconquer'd still their terrors wield,
And stain with mingled gore the embattled field.
On Pennsylvania's various plains they move,
And adverse armies equal slaughter prove;
Columbia mourns her Nash in combat slain,
Britons around him press the gory plain;
Skirmish and cannonade and distant fire
Each power diminish and each nation tire.
Till Howe from fruitless toil demands repose,
And leaves despairing in a land of foes
His wearied host; who now, to reach their fleet,
O'er Jersey hills commence their long retreat,
Tread back the steps their chief had led before,
And ask in vain the late abandon'd shore,
Where Hudson meets the main; for on their rear
Columbia moves, and checks their swift career.

But where green Monmouth lifts his grassy height,
They halt, they face, they dare the coming fight.
Howe's proud successor, Clinton, hosting there,
To tempt once more the desperate chance of war,
Towers at their head, in hopes to work relief,
And mend the errors of his former chief.
Here shines his day; and here with loud acclaim
Begins and ends his little task of fame.
He vaults before them with his balanced blade,
Wheels the bright van, and forms the long parade;
Where Britons, Hessians crowd the glittering field,
And all their powers for ready combat wield.
As the dim sun, beneath the skirts of even,
Crimsons the clouds that sail the western heaven;
So, in red wavy rows, where spread the train
Of men and standards, shone the fateful plain.

They shone, till Washington obscured their light,
And his long ranks roll'd forward to the fight.
He points the charge; the mounted thunders roar,
And rake the champaign to the distant shore.
Above the folds of smoke that veil the war,
His guiding sword illumes the fields of air;
And vollied flames, bright bursting o'er the plain,
Break the brown clouds, discovering far the slain:

Till flight begins; the smoke is roll'd away,
And the red standards open into day.
Britons and Germans hurry from the field,
Now wrapt in dust, and now to sight reveal'd;
Behind, swift Washington his falchion drives,
Thins the pale ranks, but saves submissive lives.
Hosts captive bow and move behind his arm,
And hosts before him wing the sounding storm;
When the glad sea salutes their fainting sight,
And Albion's fleet wide thundering aids their flight;
They steer to sad Newyork their hasty way,
And rue the toils of Monmouth's mournful day.

But Hudson still, with his interior tide,
Laves a rude rock that bears Britannia's pride,
Swells round the headland with indignant roar,
And mocks her thunders from his murmuring shore;
When a firm cohort starts from Peekskill plain,
To crush the invaders and the post regain.
Here, gallant Hull, again thy sword is tried,
Meigs, Fleury, Butler, laboring side by side,
Wayne takes the guidance, culls the vigorous band,
Strikes out the flint, and bids the nervous hand
Trust the mute bayonet and midnight skies,
To stretch o'er craggy walls the dark surprise.

With axes, handspikes on the shoulder hung,
And the sly watchword whisper'd from the tongue,
Thro different paths the silent march they take,
Plunge, climb the ditch, the palisado break,
Secure each sentinel, each picket shun,
Grope the dim postern where the byways run.
Soon the roused garrison perceives its plight;
Small time to rally and no means of flight,
They spring confused to every post they know,
Point their poized cannon where they hear the foe,
Streak the dark welkin with the flames they pour,
And rock the mountain with convulsive roar.
  The swift assailants still no fire return,
But, tow'rd the batteries that above them burn,
Climb hard from crag to crag; and scaling higher
They pierce the long dense canopy of fire
That sheeted all the sky; then rush amain,
Storm every outwork, each dread summit gain,
Hew timber'd gates, the sullen drawbridge fall,
File thro and form within the sounding wall.
The Britons strike their flag, the fort forgo,
Descend sad prisoners to the plain below.
A thousand veterans, ere the morning rose,
Received their handcuffs from five hundred foes;

And Stonypoint beheld, with dawning day,
His own starr'd standard on his rampart play.
From sack'd Savanna, whelm'd in hostile fires,
A few raw troops brave Lincoln now retires;
With rapid march to suffering Charleston goes,
To meet the myriads of concentring foes,
Who shade the pointed strand. Each fluvial flood
Their gathering fleets and floating batteries load,
Close their black sails, debark the amphibious host,
And with their moony anchors fang the coast.
The bold beleaguer'd post the hero gains,
And the hard siege with various fate sustains.
Cornwallis, towering at the British van,
In these fierce toils his wild career began;
He mounts the forky streams, and soon bestrides
The narrow neck that parts converging tides,
Sinks the deep trench, erects the mantling tower,
Lines with strong forts the desolated shore,
Hems on all sides the long unsuccour'd place,
With mines and parallels contracts the space;
Then bids the battering floats his labors crown,
And pour their bombard on the shuddering town.
High from the decks the mortar's bursting fires
Sweep the full streets, and splinter down the spires.

Blaze-trailing fuses vault the night's dim round,
And shells and langrage lacerate the ground;
Till all the tented plain, where heroes tread,
Is torn with crags and cover'd with the dead.
Each shower of flames renews the townsmen's woe,
They wail the fight, they dread the cruel foe.
Matrons in crowds, while tears bedew their charms,
Babes at their sides and infants in their arms,
Press round their Lincoln and his hand implore,
To save them trembling from the tyrant's power.
He shares their anguish with a moistening eye,
And bids the balls rain thicker thro the sky;
Tries every aid that art and valor yield,
The sap, the countermine, the battling field,
The bold sortie, by famine urged afar,
That dreadful daughter of earth-wasting War.
But vain the conflict now; on all the shore
The foes in fresh brigades around him pour;
He yields at last the well contested prize,
And freedom's banners quit the southern skies.
The victor Britons soon the champaign tread,
And far anorth their fire and slaughter spread;
Thro fortless realms, where unarm'd peasants fly,
Cornwallis bears his bloody standard high;

O'er Carolina rolls his growing force,
And thousands fall and thousands aid his course;
While in his march athwart the wide domain,
Colonial dastards join his splendid train.
So mountain streams thro slopes of melting snow
Swell their foul waves and flood the world below.

Awhile the Patriarch saw, with heaving sighs,
These crimson flags insult the saddening skies,
Saw desolation whelm his favorite coast,
His children scatter'd and their vigor lost,
Dekalb in furious combat press the plain,
Morgan and Smallwood every shock sustain,
Gates, now no more triumphant, quit the field,
Indignant Davidson his lifeblood yield,
Blount, Gregory, Williamson, with souls of fire
But slender force, from hill to hill retire;
When Greene in lonely greatness takes the ground,
And bids at last the trump of vengeance sound.

A few firm patriots to the chief repair,
Raise the star standard and demand the war.
But o'er the regions as he turns his eyes,
What foes develop! and what forts arise!
Rawdon with rapid marches leads their course,
From state to state Cornwallis whirls their force,

Impetuous Tarleton like a torrent pours,
And fresh battalions land along the shores;
Where, now resurgent from his captive chain,
Phillips wide storming shakes the field again;
And traitor Arnold, lured by plunder o'er,
Joins the proud powers his valor foil'd before.
  Greene views the tempest with collected soul,
And fates of empires in his bosom roll;
So small his force, where shall he lift the steel?
(Superior hosts o'er every canton wheel)
Or how behold their wanton carnage spread,
Himself stand idle and his country bleed?
Fixt in a moment's pause the general stood,
And held his warriors from the field of blood;
Then points the British legions where to steer,
Marks to their chief a rapid wild career,
Wide o'er Virginia lets him foeless roam,
To search for pillage and to find his doom,
With short-lived glory feeds his sateless flame,
But leaves the victory to a nobler name,
Gives to great Washington to meet his way,
Nor claims the honors of so bright a day.
  Now to the conquer'd south he turns his force,
Renerves the nation by his rapid course;

Forts fall around him, hosts before him fly,
And captive bands his growing train supply;
A hundred leagues of coast, in one campaign,
Return reconquer'd to their lords again.
At last Britannia's vanguard, near the strand,
Veers on her foe to make one vigorous stand.
Her gallant Stuart here amass'd from far
The veteran legions of the Georgian war,
To aid her hard-pusht powers, and quick restore
The British name to that extended shore.
He checks their flight, and chooses well their field,
Flank'd with a marsh, by lofty woods conceal'd;
Where Eutaw's fountains, tinged of old with gore,
Still murmuring swell'd amid the bones they bore,
Destined again to foul their pebbly stream,
The mournful monuments of human fame;
There Albion's columns, ranged in order bright,
Stand like a fiery wall and wait the shock of fight.

Swift on the neighboring hill as Greene arose,
He view'd, with rapid glance, the glittering foes,
Disposed for combat all his ardent train,
To charge, change front, each echelon sustain;
Roused well their rage, superior force to prove,
Waved his bright blade and bade the onset move.

As hovering clouds, when morning beams arise,
Hang their red curtains round our eastern skies,
Unfold a space to hail the promised sun,
And catch their splendors from his rising throne;
Thus glow'd the opposing fronts, whose steely glare
Glanced o'er the shuddering interval of war.

From Albion's left the cannonade began,
And pour'd thick thunders on Hesperia's van,
Forced in her dexter guards, that skirmisht wide
To prove what powers the forest hills might hide;
They break, fall back, with measured quickstep tread,
Form close, and flank the solid squares they led.
Now roll, with kindling haste, the long stark lines,
From wing to wing the sounding battle joins;
Batteries and field-parks and platoons of fire,
In mingled shocks their roaring blasts exspire.
Each front approaching fast, with equal pace,
Devours undaunted their dividing space;
Till, dark beneath the smoke, the meeting ranks
Slope their strong bayonets, with short firm shanks
Protruded from their tubes; each bristling van,
Steel fronting steel, and man encountering man,
In dreadful silence tread. As, wrapt from sight,
The nightly ambush moves to secret fight;

So rush the raging files, and sightless close
In plunging thrust with fierce conflicting foes.
They reach, they strike, they stagger o'er the slain,
Deal doubtful blows, or closing clench their man,
Intwine their twisting limbs, the gun forgo,
Wrench off the bayonet and dirk the foe;
Then struggling back, reseize the musket bare,
Club the broad breech, and headlong whirl to war.
Ranks crush on ranks with equal slaughter gored;
Warm dripping streams from every lifted sword
Stain the thin carnaged corps, who still maintain,
With mutual shocks, the vengeance of the plain.
At last where Williams fought and Campbell fell,
Unwonted strokes the British line repel.
The rout begins; the shatter'd wings afar
Roll back in haste and scatter from the war;
They drop their arms, they scour the marshy field,
Whole squadrons fall and faint battalions yield.
  The great Observer, fixt in his midsky,
View'd the whole combat, saw them fall and fly:
He mark'd where Greene with every onset drove,
Saw death and victory with his presence move,
Beneath his arm saw Marion, Sumter, Gaine,
Pickens and Sumner shake the astonish'd plain;

He saw young Washington, the child of fame,
Preserve in fight the honors of his name.
Lee, Jackson, Hampton, Pinckney, matcht in might,
Roll'd on the storm and hurried fast the flight:
While numerous chiefs, that equal trophies raise,
Wrought, not unseen, the deeds of deathless praise.

As Europe now the newborn states beheld
The shock sustain of many a hard-fought field;
Swift o'er the main, with high-spread sails, advance
Our brave auxiliars from the coast of France.
On the tall decks their curious chiefs explore,
With optic tube, our camp-encumber'd shore;
And, as the lessening wave behind them flies,
Wide scenes of conflict open on their eyes.
Rochambeau foremost with his gleamy brand
Points to each field and singles every band,
Sees Washington the power of nations guide,
And longs to toil and conquer by his side.
Two brother chiefs, Viominil the name,
Brothers in birth but twins in generous fame,
Behold with steadfast eye the plains disclose,
Uncase their arms and claim the promised foes.
Biron, beneath his sail, in armor bright,
Frown'd o'er the wave impatient for the fight;

A fiery steed beside the hero stood,
And his blue blade waved forward o'er the crowd.
  With eager haste descending on the coast,
Thro the glad states they march their veteran host,
From sea-nursed Newport file o'er western roads,
Pitch many a camp, and bridge a hundred floods,
Pass the full towns, where joyful crowds admire
Their foreign speech, gay mien and gilt attire,
Applaud their generous deeds, the zeal that draws
Their swords untried in freedom's doubtful cause.
Thro Hartford plains, on Litchfield hills they gleam,
Wave their white flags o'er Hudson's loaded stream,
Band after band with Delaware's current pour,
Shade Schuylkill's wave and Elk's indented shore,
Join their new friends, where allied banners lead,
Demand the foe and bid the war proceed.
  Again Columbus turn'd his anxious eye
Where Britain's banner waved along the sky;
And, graced with spoils of many fields of blood,
Cornwallis boastful on a bulwark stood.
Where York and Gloster's rocky towers bestride
Their parent stream, Virginia's midmost tide,
He camp'd his hundred nations, to regain
Their force, exhausted in the long campaign;

Paused for a moment on a scene so vast,
To plan the future and review the past.
Thro vanquisht provinces and towns in flame
He mark'd his recent monuments of fame,
His checker'd marches, long and various toils,
And camp well stored with wide collected spoils.
High glittering to the sun his hands unfold
A map new drafted on a sheet of gold;
There in delusive haste his burin graved
A country conquer'd and a race enslaved.
Its middle realm, by fairer figures known
And rich with fruits, lay bounded for his own;
Deep thro the centre spreads a branching bay,
Full sails ascend and golden rivers stray;
Bright palaces arise relieved in gold,
And gates and streets the crossing lines unfold.
James furrows o'er the plate with turgid tide,
Young Richmond roughens on his masted side;
Reviving Norfolk from her ashes springs,
A golden phœnix on refulgent wings;
Potowmak's yellow waves reluctant spread,
And Vernon rears his rich and radiant head.
'Tis here the chief his pointed graver stays,
The bank to burnish with a purer blaze,

Gives all his art, on this bright hill to trace
His future seat and glory of his race;
Deems his long line of lords the realm shall own,
The kings predestined to Columbia's throne.

But while his mind thus quafft its airy food,
And gazing thousands round the rampart stood,
Whom future ease and golden dreams employ,
The songs of triumph and the feast of joy;
Sudden great Washington arose in view,
And allied flags his stately steps pursue;
Gaul's veteran host and young Hesperia's pride
Bend the long march concentring at his side,
Stream over Chesapeak, like sheets of flame,
And drive tempestuous to the field of fame.

Far on the wild expanse, where ocean lies,
And scorns all confines but incumbent skies,
Scorns to retain the imprinted paths of men
To guide their wanderings or direct their ken;
Where warring vagrants, raging as they go,
Ask of the stars their way to find the foe,
Columbus saw two hovering fleets advance,
And rival ensigns o'er their pinions dance.
Graves, on the north, with Albion's flag unfurl'd,
Waves proud defiance to the watery world;

Degrasse, from southern isles, conducts his train,
And shades with Gallic sheets the moving main.
Now Morn, unconscious of the coming fray
That soon shall storm the crystal cope of day,
Glows o'er the heavens, and with her orient breeze
Fans her fair face and curls the summer seas.
The swelling sails, as far as eye can sweep,
Look thro the skies and awe the shadowy deep,
Lead their long bending lines; and, ere they close,
To count, recognise, circumvent their foes,
Each hauls his wind, the weathergage to gain
And master all the movements of the plain;
Or bears before the breeze with loftier gait,
And, beam to beam, begins the work of fate.
As when the warring winds, from each far pole,
Their adverse storms across the concave roll,
Thin fleecy vapors thro the expansion run,
Veil the blue vault and tremble o'er the sun,
Till the dark folding wings together drive,
And, ridged with fire and rock'd with thunder, strive;
So, hazing thro the void, at first appear
White clouds of canvass floating on the air,
Then frown the broad black decks, the sails are stay'd,
The gaping portholes cast a frightful shade,

Flames, triple tier'd, and tides of smoke, arise,
And fulminations rock the seas and skies.
  From van to rear the roaring deluge runs,
The storm disgorging from a thousand guns,
Each like a vast volcano, spouting wide
His hissing hell-dogs o'er the shuddering tide,
Whirls high his chainshot, cleaves the mast and strows
The shiver'd fragments on the staggering foes;
Whose gunwale sides with iron globes are gored,
And a wild storm of splinters sweeps the board.
Husht are the winds of heaven; no more the gale
Breaks the red rolls of smoke nor flaps the sail;
A dark dead calm continuous cloaks the glare,
And holds the clouds of sulphur on the war,
Convolving o'er the space that yawns and shines,
With frequent flash, between the laboring lines.
Nor sun nor sea nor skyborn lightning gleams,
But flaming Phlegethon's asphaltic steams
Streak the long gaping gulph; where varying glow
Carbonic curls above, blue flakes of fire below.
  Hither two hostile ships to contact run,
Both grappling, board to board and gun to gun;
Each thro the adverse ports their contents pour,
Rake the lower decks, the interior timbers bore,

Drive into chinks the illumined wads unseen,
Whose flames approach the unguarded magazine.
Above, with shrouds afoul and gunwales mann'd,
Thick halberds clash; and, closing hand to hand,
The huddling troops, infuriate from despair,
Tug at the toils of death, and perish there;
Grenados, carcasses their fragments spread,
And pikes and pistols strow the decks with dead.
Now on the Gallic board the Britons rush,
The intrepid Gauls the rash adventurers crush;
And now, to vengeance stung, with frantic air,
Back on the British maindeck roll the war.
There swells the carnage; all the tar-beat floor
Is clogg'd with spatter'd brains and glued with gore;
And down the ship's black waist fresh brooks of blood
Course o'er their clots, and tinge the sable flood.
Till War, impatient of the lingering strife
That tires and slackens with the waste of life,
Opes with engulphing gape the astonish'd wave,
And whelms the combat whole, in one vast grave.
For now the imprison'd powder caught the flames,
And into atoms whirl'd the monstrous frames
Of both the entangled ships; the vortex wide
Roars like an Ætna thro the belching tide,

And blazing into heaven, and bursting high,
Shells, carriages and guns obstruct the sky;
Cords, timbers, trunks of men the welkin sweep,
And fall on distant ships, or shower along the deep.
  The matcht armadas still the fight maintain,
But cautious, distant; lest the staggering main
Drive their whole lines afoul, and one dark day
Glut the proud ocean with too rich a prey.
At last, where scattering fires the cloud disclose,
Hulls heave in sight and blood the decks o'erflows;
Here from the field tost navies rise to view,
Drive back to vengeance and the roar renew,
There shatter'd ships commence their flight afar,
Tow'd thro the smoke, hard struggling from the war;
And some, half seen amid the gaping wave,
Plunge in the whirl they make, and gorge their grave.
  Soon the dark smoky volumes roll'd away,
And a long line ascended into day;
The pinions swell'd, Britannia's cross arose
And flew the terrors of triumphing foes;
When to Virginia's bay, new shocks to brave,
The Gallic powers their conquering banners wave.
Glad Chesapeak unfolds his bosom wide,
And leads their prows to York's contracting tide;

Where still dread Washington directs his way,
And seas and continents his voice obey;
While brave Cornwallis, mid the gathering host,
Perceives his glories gone, his promised empire lost.
Columbus here with silent joy beheld
His favorite sons the fates of nations wield.
Here joyous Lincoln rose in arms again,
Nelson and Knox moved ardent o'er the plain;
Scammel alert with force unusual trod,
Prepared to seal their victory with his blood;
Cobb, Dearborn, Laurens, Tilghman, green in years
But ripe in glory, tower'd amid their peers;
Death-daring Hamilton with splendor shone,
And claim'd each post of danger for his own,
Skill'd every arm in war's whole hell to wield,
An Ithacus in camp, an Ajax in the field.
Their Gallic friends an equal ardor fires;
Brisk emulation every troop inspires:
Where Tarleton turns, with hopes of flight elate,
Brave Biron moves and drives him back to fate,
Hems in his host, to wait, on Gloster plains,
Their finish'd labors and their destined chains.
Two British forts the growing siege outflank,
Rake its wide works and awe the tide-beat bank;

Swift from the lines two chosen bands advance,
Our light-arm'd scouts, the grenadiers of France;
These young Viominil conducts to fame,
And those Fayette's unerring guidance claim.
No cramm'd cartouch their belted back attires,
No grains of sleeping thunder wait their fires;
The flint, the ramrod spurn'd, away they cast;
The strong bright bayonet, imbeaded fast,
Stands beaming from the bore; with this they tread,
Nor heed from high-wall'd foes their showers of lead.
Each rival band, tho wide and distant far,
Springs simultaneous to this task of war;
For here a twofold force each hero draws,
His own proud country and the general cause;
And each with twofold energy contends,
His foes to vanquish and outstrip his friends.
They summon all their zeal, and wild and warm
O'er flaming ramparts pour the maddening storm,
The mounted cannons crush, and lead the foe
Two trains of captives to the plain below;
An equal prize each gallant troop ameeds,
Alike their numbers and alike their deeds.
  A strong high citadel still thundering stood,
And stream'd her standard o'er the field of blood,

Check'd long the siege with fulminating blare,
Scorn'd all the steel and every globe of war,
Defied fell famine, heapt her growing store,
And housed in bombproof all the host she bore.
No rude assault can stretch the scale so high,
In vain the battering siege-guns round her ply;
Mortars well poized their deafening deluge rain,
Load the red skies and shake the shores in vain;
Her huge rock battlements rebound the blow,
And roll their loose crags on the men below.
But while the fusing fireballs scorch the sky,
Their mining arts the staunch besiegers ply,
Delve from the bank of York, and gallery far,
Deep subterranean, to the mount of war;
Beneath the ditch, thro rocks and fens they go,
Scoop the dark chamber plumb beneath the foe;
There lodge their tons of powder and retire,
Mure the dread passage, wave the fatal fire,
Send a swift messenger to warn the foe
To seek his safety and the post forgo.
A taunting answer comes; he dares defy
To spring the mine and all its Ætnas try;
When a black miner seized the sulphur'd brand,
Shriek'd high for joy, and with untrembling hand

Touch'd quick the insidious train; lest here the chief
Should change his counsel and afford relief:
For hard the general's task, to speak the doom
That sends a thousand heroes to the tomb;
Heroes who know no wrong; who thoughtless speed
Where kings command or where their captains lead.
—Burst with the blast, the reeling mountain roars,
Heaves, labors, boils, and thro the concave pours
His flaming contents high; he chokes the air
With all his warriors and their works of war;
Guns, bastions, magazines confounded fly,
Vault wide their fresh explosions o'er the sky,
Encumber each far camp, and plough profound
With their rude fragments every neighboring ground.

Britain's brave leader, where he sought repose,
And deem'd his hill-fort still repulsed the foes,
Starts at the astounding earthquake, and descries
His chosen veterans whirling down the skies.
Their mangled members round his balcon fall,
Scorch'd in the flames, and dasht on every wall:
Sad field of contemplation! Here, ye great,
Kings, priests of God, and ministers of state,
Review your system here! behold and scan
Your own fair deeds, your benefits to man!

You will not leave him to his natural toil,
To tame these elements and till the soil,
To reap, share, tithe you what his hand has sown,
Enjoy his treasures and increase your own,
Build up his virtues on the base design'd,
The well-toned harmonies of humankind.
You choose to check his toil, and band his eyes
To all that's honest and to all that's wise;
Lure with false fame, false morals and false lore,
To barter fields of corn for fields of gore,
To take by bands what single thieves would spare,
And methodise his murders into war.

Now the prest garrison fresh danger warms;
They rush impetuous to each post of arms,
Man the long trench, each embrasure sustain,
And pour their langrage on the allied train;
Whose swift approaches, crowding on the line,
Each wing envelop and each front confine.
O'er all sage Washington his arm extends,
Points every movement, every work defends,
Bids closer quarters, bloodier strokes proceed,
New batteries blaze and heavier squadrons bleed.
Line within line fresh parallels enclose;
Here runs a zigzag, there a mantlet grows,

Round the pent foe approaching breastworks rise,
And bombs, like meteors, vault the flaming skies.
Night, with her hovering wings, asserts in vain
The shades, the silence of her rightful reign;
High roars her canopy with fiery flakes,
And War stalks wilder thro the glare he makes.
With dire dismay the British chief beheld
The foe advance, his veterans shun the field,
Despair and slaughter where he turns his eye,
No hope in combat and no power to fly;
Degrasse victorious shakes the shadowy tide,
Imbodied nations all the champaign hide,
Fosses and batteries, growing on the sight,
Still pour new thunders and increase the fight;
Shells rain before him, rending every mound,
Crags, gunstones, balls o'erturn the tented ground,
From post to post his driven ranks retire,
The earth in crimson and the skies on fire.
Death wantons proud in this decisive round,
For here his hand its favorite victim found;
Brave Scammel perisht here. Ah! short, my friend,
Thy bright career, but glorious to its end.
Go join thy Warren's ghost, your fates compare,
His that commenced, with thine that closed the war;

Freedom, with laurel'd brow but tearful eyes,
Bewails her first and last, her twinlike sacrifice.

Now grateful truce suspends the burning war,
And groans and shouts promiscuous load the air;
When the tired Britons, where the smokes decay,
Quit their strong station and resign the day.
Slow files along the immeasurable train,
Thousands on thousands redden all the plain,
Furl their torn bandrols, all their plunder yield,
And pile their muskets on the battle field.
Their wide auxiliar nations swell the crowd,
And the coop'd navies, from the neighboring flood,
Repeat surrendering signals, and obey
The landmen's fate on this concluding day.

Cornwallis first, their late all-conquering lord,
Bears to the victor chief his conquer'd sword,
Presents the burnisht hilt, and yields with pain
The gift of kings, here brandisht long in vain.
Then bow their hundred banners, trailing far
Their wearied wings from all the skirts of war.
Battalion'd infantry and squadron'd horse
Dash the silk tassel and the golden torse;
Flags from the forts and ensigns from the fleet
Roll in the dust, and at Columbia's feet

Prostrate the pride of thrones; they firm the base
Of Freedom's temple, while her arms they grace.
Here Albion's crimson Cross the soil o'erspreads,
Her Lion crouches and her Thistle fades;
Indignant Erin rues her trampled Lyre,
Brunswick's pale Steed forgets his foamy fire,
Proud Hessia's Castle lies in dust o'erthrown,
And venal Anspach quits her broken Crown.

Long trains of wheel'd artillery shade the shore,
Quench their blue matches and forget to roar;
Along the encumber'd plain, thick planted rise
High stacks of muskets glittering to the skies,
Numerous and vast. As when the toiling swains
Heap their whole harvest on the stubbly plains,
Gerb after gerb the bearded shock expands,
Shocks, ranged in rows, hill high the burden'd lands;
The joyous master numbers all the piles,
And o'er his well-earn'd crop complacent smiles:
Such growing heaps this iron harvest yield,
So tread the victors this their final field.

Triumphant Washington, with brow serene,
Regards unmoved the exhilarating scene,
Weighs in his balanced thought the silent grief
That sinks the bosom of the fallen chief,

With all the joy that laurel crowns bestow,
A world reconquer'd and a vanquish'd foe.
Thus thro extremes of life, in every state,
Shines the clear soul, beyond all fortune great;
While smaller minds, the dupes of fickle chance,
Slight woes o'erwhelm and sudden joys entrance.
So the full sun, thro all the changing sky,
Nor blasts nor overpowers the naked eye;
Tho transient splendors, borrow'd from his light,
Glance on the mirror and destroy the sight.

He bids brave Lincoln guide with modest air
The last glad triumph of the finish'd war;
Who sees, once more, two armies shade one plain,
The mighty victors and the captive train.

THE

COLUMBIAD.

BOOK VIII.

ARGUMENT.

Hymn to Peace. Eulogy on the heroes slain in the war; in which the Author finds occasion to mention his Brother. Address to the patriots who have survived the conflict; exhorting them to preserve the liberty they have established. The danger of losing it by inattention illustrated in the rape of the Golden Fleece. Freedom succeeding to Despotism in the moral world, like Order succeeding to Chaos in the physical world. Atlas, the guardian Genius of Africa, denounces to Hesper the crimes of his people in the slavery of the Africans. The Author addresses his countrymen on that subject, and on the principles of their government.

Hesper, recurring to his object of showing Columbus the importance of his discoveries, reverses the order of time, and exhibits the continent again in its savage state. He then displays the progress of arts in America. Fur-trade. Fisheries. Productions. Commerce. Education. Philosophical discoveries. Painting. Poetry.

THE

COLUMBIAD.

BOOK VIII.

HAIL, holy Peace, from thy sublime abode
Mid circling saints that grace the throne of God!
Before his arm around our embryon earth
Stretch'd the dim void, and gave to nature birth,
Ere morning stars his glowing chambers hung,
Or songs of gladness woke an angel's tongue,
Veil'd in the splendors of his beamful mind,
In blest repose thy placid form reclined,
Lived in his life, his inward sapience caught,
And traced and toned his universe of thought.
Borne thro the expanse with his creating voice
Thy presence bade the unfolding worlds rejoice,
Led forth the systems on their bright career,
Shaped all their curves and fashion'd every sphere,

Spaced out their suns, and round each radiant goal,
Orb over orb, compell'd their train to roll,
Bade heaven's own harmony their force combine,
Taught all their host symphonious strains to join,
Gave to seraphic harps their sounding lays,
Their joys to angels, and to men their praise.

From scenes of blood, these verdant shores that stain,
From numerous friends in recent battle slain,
From blazing towns that scorch the purple sky,
From houseless hordes their smoking walls that fly,
From the black prison ships, those groaning graves,
From warring fleets that vex the gory waves,
From a storm'd world, long taught thy flight to mourn,
I rise, delightful Peace, and greet thy glad return.

For now the untuneful trump shall grate no more;
Ye silver streams, no longer swell with gore,
Bear from your war-beat banks the guilty stain
With yon retiring navies to the main.
While other views, unfolding on my eyes,
And happier themes bid bolder numbers rise;
Bring, bounteous Peace, in thy celestial throng,
Life to my soul, and rapture to my song;
Give me to trace, with pure unclouded ray,
The arts and virtues that attend thy sway,

To see thy blissful charms, that here descend,
Thro distant realms and endless years extend.
  Too long the groans of death and battle's bray
Have rung discordant thro my turgid lay:
The drum's rude clang, the war wolf's hideous howl
Convulsed my nerves and agonized my soul,
Untuned the harp for all but misery's pains,
And chased the Muse from corse-encumber'd plains.
Let memory's balm its pious fragrance shed
On heroes' wounds and patriot warriors dead;
Accept, departed Shades, these grateful sighs,
Your fond attendants thro your homeward skies.
  And thou, my earliest friend, my Brother dear,
Thy fall untimely still renews my tear.
In youthful sports, in toils, in taste allied,
My kind companion and my faithful guide,
When death's dread summons, from our infant eyes,
Had call'd our last loved parent to the skies.
Tho young in arms, and still obscure thy name,
Thy bosom panted for the deeds of fame;
Beneath Montgomery's eye, when by thy steel
In northern wilds the frequent savage fell.
Fired by his voice, and foremost at his call,
To mount the breach or scale the flamy wall,

Thy daring hand had many a laurel gain'd,
If years had ripen'd what thy fancy feign'd.
Lamented Youth! when thy great leader bled,
Thro the same wound thy parting spirit fled,
Join'd the long train, the self-devoted band,
The gods, the saviors of their native land.
  On fame's high pinnacle their names shall shine,
Unending ages greet the group divine,
Whose holy hands our banners first unfurl'd,
And conquer'd freedom for the grateful world.
  And you, their peers, whose steel avenged their blood,
Whose breasts with theirs our sacred rampart stood,
Illustrious relics of a thousand fields!
To you at last the foe reluctant yields.
But tho the Muse, too prodigal of praise,
Dares with the dead your living worth to raise,
Think not, my friends, the patriot's task is done,
Or Freedom safe, because the battle's won.
Unnumber'd foes, far different arms that wield,
Wait the weak moment when she quits her shield,
To plunge in her bold breast the insidious dart,
Or pour keen poison round her thoughtless heart.
Perhaps they 'll strive her votaries to divide,
From their own veins to draw the vital tide;

Perhaps, by cooler calculation shown,
Create materials to construct a throne,
Dazzle her guardians with the glare of state,
Corrupt with power, with borrow'd pomp inflate,
Bid thro the land the soft infection creep,
Whelm all her sons in one lethargic sleep,
Crush her vast empire in its brilliant birth,
And chase the goddess from the ravaged earth.

The Dragon thus, that watch'd the Colchian fleece,
Foil'd the fierce warriors of wide-plundering Greece;
Warriors of matchless might and wondrous birth,
Jove's sceptred sons and demigods of earth.
High on the sacred tree, the glittering prize
Hangs o'er its guard, and fires the warriors' eyes;
First their hurl'd spears his spiral folds assail,
Their spears fall pointless from his flaky mail;
Onward with dauntless swords they plunge amain;
He shuns their blows, recoils his twisting train,
Darts forth his forky tongue, heaves high in air
His fiery crest, and sheds a hideous glare,
Champs, churns his poisonous juice, and hissing loud
Spouts thick the stifling tempest o'er the crowd;
Then, with one sweep of convoluted train,
Rolls back all Greece, and besoms wide the plain,

O'erturns the sons of gods, dispersing far
The pirate horde, and closes quick the war.
From his red jaws tremendous triumph roars,
Dark Euxine trembles to its distant shores,
Proud Jason starts, confounded in his might,
Leads back his peers, and dares no more the fight.
But the sly Priestess brings her opiate spell,
Soft charms that hush the triple hound of hell,
Bids Orpheus tune his all-enchanting lyre,
And join to calm the guardian's sleepless ire.
Soon from the tepid ground blue vapors rise,
And sounds melodious move along the skies;
A settling tremor thro his folds extends,
His crest contracts, his rainbow neck unbends,
O'er all his hundred hoops the languor crawls,
Each curve developes, every volute falls,
His broad back flattens as he spreads the plain,
And sleep consigns him to his lifeless reign.
Flusht at the sight the pirates seize the spoil,
And ravaged Colchis rues the insidious toil.

Yes! fellow freemen, sons of high renown,
Chant your loud peans, weave your civic crown;
But know, the goddess you 've so long adored,
Tho now she scabbards your avenging sword,

Calls you to vigilance, to manlier cares,
To prove in peace the men she proved in wars:
Superior task! severer test of soul!
Tis here bold virtue plays her noblest role
And merits most of praise. The warrior's name,
Tho peal'd and chimed on all the tongues of fame,
Sounds less harmonious to the grateful mind
Than his who fashions and improves mankind.
  And what high meed your new vocation waits!
Freedom, parturient with a hundred states,
Confides them to your hand; the nascent prize
Claims all your care, your soundest wisdom tries.
Ah nurture, temper, train your infant charge,
Its force develop and its life enlarge,
Unfold each day some adolescent grace,
Some right recognise or some duty trace;
Mould a fair model for the realms of earth,
Call moral nature to a second birth,
Reach, renovate the world's great social plan,
And here commence the sober sense of man.
  For lo, in other climes and elder states,
What strange inversion all his works awaits!
From age to age, on every peopled shore,
Stalks the fell Demon of despotic power,

Sweeps in his march the mounds of art away,
Blots with his breath the trembling disk of day,
Treads down whole nations every stride he takes,
And wraps their labors in his fiery flakes.
  As Anarch erst around his regions hurl'd
The wrecks, long crush'd, of time's anterior world;
While nature mourn'd, in wild confusion tost,
Her suns extinguisht and her systems lost;
Light, life and instinct shared the dreary trance,
And gravitation fled the field of chance;
No laws remain'd of matter, motion, space;
Time lost his count, the universe his place;
Till Order came, in her cerulean robes,
And launch'd and rein'd the renovated globes,
Stock'd with harmonious worlds the vast Inane,
Archt her new heaven and fixt her boundless reign:
So kings convulse the moral frame, the base
Of all the codes that can accord the race;
And so from their broad grasp, their deadly ban,
Tis yours to snatch this earth, to raise regenerate man.
  My friends, I love your fame, I joy to raise
The high-toned anthem of my country's praise;
To sing her victories, virtues, wisdom, weal,
Boast with loud voice the patriot pride I feel;

Warm wild I sing; and, to her failings blind,
Mislead myself, perhaps mislead mankind.
Land that I love! is this the whole we owe?
Thy pride to pamper, thy fair face to show;
Dwells there no blemish where such glories shine?
And lurks no spot in that bright sun of thine?
Hark! a dread voice, with heaven-astounding strain,
Swells like a thousand thunders o'er the main,
Rolls and reverberates around thy hills,
And Hesper's heart with pangs paternal fills.
Thou hearst him not; tis Atlas, throned sublime,
Great brother guardian of old Afric's clime;
High o'er his coast he rears his frowning form,
O'erlooks and calms his sky-borne fields of storm,
Flings off the clouds that round his shoulders hung,
And breaks from clogs of ice his trembling tongue;
While far thro space with rage and grief he glares,
Heaves his hoar head and shakes the heaven he bears:
—Son of my sire! O latest brightest birth
That sprang from his fair spouse, prolific earth!
Great Hesper, say what sordid ceaseless hate
Impels thee thus to mar my elder state.
Our sire assign'd thee thy more glorious reign,
Secured and bounded by our laboring main;

That main (tho still my birthright name it bear)
Thy sails o'ershadow, thy brave children share;
I grant it thus; while air surrounds the ball,
Let breezes blow, let oceans roll for all.
But thy proud sons, a strange ungenerous race,
Enslave my tribes, and each fair world disgrace,
Provoke wide vengeance on their lawless land,
The bolt ill placed in thy forbearing hand.—
Enslave my tribes! then boast their cantons free,
Preach faith and justice, bend the sainted knee,
Invite all men their liberty to share,
Seek public peace, defy the assaults of war,
Plant, reap, consume, enjoy their fearless toil,
Tame their wild floods, to fatten still their soil,
Enrich all nations with their nurturing store,
And rake with venturous fluke each wondering shore.—
Enslave my tribes! what, half mankind imban,
Then read, expound, enforce the rights of man!
Prove plain and clear how nature's hand of old
Cast all men equal in her human mould!
Their fibres, feelings, reasoning powers the same,
Like wants await them, like desires inflame.
Thro former times with learned book they tread,
Revise past ages and rejudge the dead,

Write, speak, avenge, for ancient sufferings feel,
Impale each tyrant on their pens of steel,
Declare how freemen can a world create,
And slaves and masters ruin every state.—
Enslave my tribes! and think, with dumb disdain,
To scape this arm and prove my vengeance vain!
But look! methinks beneath my foot I ken
A few chain'd things that seem no longer men;
Thy sons perchance! whom Barbary's coast can tell
The sweets of that loved scourge they wield so well.
Link'd in a line, beneath the driver's goad,
See how they stagger with their lifted load;
The shoulder'd rock, just wrencht from off my hill
And wet with drops their straining orbs distil,
Galls, grinds them sore, along the rampart led,
And the chain clanking counts the steps they tread.

By night close bolted in the bagnio's gloom,
Think how they ponder on their dreadful doom,
Recal the tender sire, the weeping bride,
The home, far sunder'd by a waste of tide,
Brood all the ties that once endear'd them there,
But now, strung stronger, edge their keen despair.
Till here a fouler fiend arrests their pace:
Plague, with his burning breath and bloated face,

With saffron eyes that thro the dungeon shine,
And the black tumors bursting from the groin,
Stalks o'er the slave; who, cowering on the sod,
Shrinks from the Demon and invokes his God,
Sucks hot contagion with his quivering breath,
And, rack'd with rending torture, sinks in death.

Nor shall these pangs atone the nation's crime;
Far heavier vengeance, in the march of time,
Attends them still; if still they dare debase
And hold inthrall'd the millions of my race;
A vengeance that shall shake the world's deep frame,
That heaven abhors, and hell might shrink to name.
Nature, long outraged, delves the crusted sphere,
And moulds the mining mischief dark and drear;
Europa too the penal shock shall find,
The rude soul-selling monsters of mankind:

Where Alps and Andes at their bases meet,
In earth's mid caves to lock their granite feet,
Heave their broad spines, expand each breathing lobe,
And with their massy members rib the globe,
Her cauldron'd floods of fire their blast prepare;
Her wallowing womb of subterranean war
Waits but the fissure that my wave shall find,
To force the foldings of the rocky rind,

Crash your curst continent, and whirl on high
The vast avulsion vaulting thro the sky,
Fling far the bursting fragments, scattering wide
Rocks, mountains, nations o'er the swallowing tide.
Plunging and surging with alternate sweep,
They storm the day-vault and lay bare the deep,
Toss, tumble, plough their place, then slow subside,
And swell each ocean as their bulk they hide;
Two oceans dasht in one! that climbs and roars,
And seeks in vain the exterminated shores,
The deep drencht hemisphere. Far sunk from day,
It crumbles, rolls, it churns the settling sea,
Turns up each prominence, heaves every side,
To pierce once more the landless length of tide:
Till some poized Pambamarca looms at last
A dim lone island in the watery waste,
Mourns all his minor mountains wreck'd and hurl'd,
Stands the sad relic of a ruin'd world,
Attests the wrath our mother kept in store,
And rues her judgments on the race she bore.
No saving Ark around him rides the main,
Nor Dove weak-wing'd her footing finds again;
His own bald Eagle skims alone the sky,
Darts from all points of heaven her searching eye,

Kens, thro the gloom, her ancient rock of rest,
And finds her cavern'd crag, her solitary nest.
  Thus toned the Titan his tremendous knell,
And lash'd his ocean to a loftier swell;
Earth groans responsive, and with laboring woes
Leans o'er the surge and stills the storm he throws.
  Fathers and friends, I know the boding fears
Of angry genii and of rending spheres
Assail not souls like yours; whom Science bright
Thro shadowy nature leads with surer light;
For whom she strips the heavens of love and hate,
Strikes from Jove's hand the brandisht bolt of fate,
Gives each effect its own indubious cause,
Divides her moral from her physic laws,
Shows where the virtues find their nurturing food,
And men their motives to be just and good.
  You scorn the Titan's threat; nor shall I strain
The powers of pathos in a task so vain
As Afric's wrongs to sing; for what avails
To harp for you these known familiar tales?
To tongue mute misery, and re-rack the soul
With crimes oft copied from that bloody scroll
Where Slavery pens her woes; tho tis but there
We learn the weight that mortal life can be.

The tale might startle still the accustom'd ear,
Still shake the nerve that pumps the pearly tear,
Melt every heart, and thro the nation gain
Full many a voice to break the barbarous chain.
But why to sympathy for guidance fly,
(Her aids uncertain and of scant supply)
When your own self-excited sense affords
A guide more sure, and every sense accords?
Where strong self-interest, join'd with duty, lies,
Where doing right demands no sacrifice,
Where profit, pleasure, life-expanding fame
League their allurements to support the claim,
Tis safest there the impleaded cause to trust;
Men well instructed will be always just.

From slavery then your rising realms to save,
Regard the master, notice not the slave;
Consult alone for freemen, and bestow
Your best, your only cares, to keep them so.
Tyrants are never free; and, small and great,
All masters must be tyrants soon or late;
So nature works; and oft the lordling knave
Turns out at once a tyrant and a slave,
Struts, cringes, bullies, begs, as courtiers must,
Makes one a god, another treads in dust,

Fears all alike, and filches whom he can,
But knows no equal, finds no friend in man.
 Ah! would you not be slaves, with lords and kings,
Then be not masters; there the danger springs.
The whole crude system that torments this earth,
Of rank, privation, privilege of birth,
False honor, fraud, corruption, civil jars,
The rage of conquest and the curse of wars,
Pandora's total shower, all ills combined
That erst o'erwhelm'd and still distress mankind,
Box'd up secure in your deliberate hand,
Wait your behest, to fix or fly this land.
 Equality of Right is nature's plan;
And following nature is the march of man.
Whene'er he deviates in the least degree,
When, free himself, he would be more than free,
The baseless column, rear'd to bear his bust,
Falls as he mounts, and whelms him in the dust.
 See Rome's rude sires, with autocratic gait,
Tread down their tyrant and erect their state;
Their state secured, they deem it wise and brave
That every freeman should command a slave,
And, flusht with franchise of his camp and town,
Rove thro the world and hunt the nations down;

Master and man the same vile spirit gains,
Rome chains the world, and wears herself the chains.
  Mark modern Europe with her feudal codes,
Serfs, villains, vassals, nobles, kings and gods,
All slaves of different grades, corrupt and curst
With high and low, for senseless rank athirst,
Wage endless wars; not fighting to be free,
But *cujum pecus*, whose base herd they 'll be.
  Too much of Europe, here transplanted o'er,
Nursed feudal feelings on your tented shore,
Brought sable serfs from Afric, call'd it gain,
And urged your sires to forge the fatal chain.
But now, the tents o'erturn'd, the war dogs fled,
Now fearless Freedom rears at last her head
Matcht with celestial Peace,—my friends, beware
To shade the splendors of so bright a pair;
Complete their triumph, fix their firm abode,
Purge all privations from your liberal code,
Restore their souls to men, give earth repose,
And save your sons from slavery, wars and woes.
  Based on its rock of Right your empire lies,
On walls of wisdom let the fabric rise;
Preserve your principles, their force unfold,
Let nations prove them and let kings behold.

EQUALITY, your first firm-grounded stand;
Then FREE ELECTION; then your FEDERAL BAND;
This holy Triad should forever shine
The great compendium of all rights divine,
Creed of all schools, whence youths by millions draw
Their themes of right, their decalogues of law;
Till men shall wonder (in these codes inured)
How wars were made, how tyrants were endured.

Then shall your works of art superior rise,
Your fruits perfume a larger length of skies,
Canals careering climb your sunbright hills,
Vein the green slopes and strow their nurturing rills,
Thro tunnel'd heights and sundering ridges glide,
Rob the rich west of half Kenhawa's tide,
Mix your wide climates, all their stores confound,
And plant new ports in every midland mound.
Your lawless Missisippi, now who slimes
And drowns and desolates his waste of climes,
Ribb'd with your dikes, his torrent shall restrain,
And ask your leave to travel to the main;
Won from his wave while rising cantons smile,
Rear their glad nations and reward their toil.

Thus Nile's proud flood to human hands of yore
Raised and resign'd his tide-created shore,

Call'd from his Ethiop hills their hardy swains,
And waved their harvests o'er his newborn plains;
Earth's richest realm from his tamed current sprung;
There nascent science toned her infant tongue,
Taught the young arts their tender force to try,
To state the seasons and unfold the sky;
Till o'er the world extended and refined,
They rule the destinies of humankind.

Now had Columbus well enjoy'd the sight
Of armies vanquisht and of fleets in flight,
From all Hesperia's heaven the darkness flown,
And colon crowds to sovereign sages grown.
To cast new glories o'er the changing clime,
The guardian Power reversed the flight of time,
Roll'd back the years that led their course before,
Stretch'd out immense the wild uncultured shore;
Then shifts the total scene, and rears to view
Arts and the men that useful arts pursue.
As o'er the canvass when the painter's mind
Glows with a future landscape well design'd,
While Panorama's wondrous aid he calls,
To crowd whole realms within his circling walls,
Lakes, fields and forests, ports and navies rise,
A new creation to his kindling eyes;

He smiles o'er all; and in delightful strife
The pencil moves and calls the whole to life.
So while Columbia's patriarch stood sublime,
And saw rude nature clothe the trackless clime;
The green banks heave, the winding currents pour,
The bays and harbors cleave the yielding shore,
The champaigns spread, the solemn groves arise,
And the rough mountains lengthen round the skies;
Thro all their bounds he traced, with skilful ken,
The unform'd seats and future walks of men;
Mark'd where the field should bloom, the pennon play,
Great cities grow and empires claim their sway;
When, sudden waked by Hesper's waving hand,
They rose obedient round the cultured land.

In western tracts, where still the wildmen tread,
From sea to sea an inland commerce spread;
On the dim streams and thro the gloomy grove
The trading bands their cumbrous burdens move;
Furs, peltry, drugs, and all the native store
Of midland realms descended to the shore.

Where summer suns, along the northern coast,
With feeble force dissolve the chains of frost,
Prolific waves the scaly nations trace,
And tempt the toils of man's laborious race.

Tho rich Brazilian strands, beneath the tide,
Their shells of pearl and sparkling pebbles hide,
While for the gaudy prize a venturous train
Plunge the dark deep and brave the surging main,
Drag forth the shining gewgaws into air,
To stud a sceptre or emblaze a star;
Far wealthier stores these genial tides display,
And works less dangerous with their spoils repay.
The Hero saw the hardy crews advance,
Cast the long line and aim the barbed lance;
Load the deep floating barks, and bear abroad
To every land the life-sustaining food;
Renascent swarms by nature's care supplied,
Repeople still the shoals and fin the fruitful tide.
Where southern streams thro broad savannas bend,
The rice-clad vales their verdant rounds extend;
Tobago's plant its leaf expanding yields,
The maize luxuriant clothes a thousand fields;
Steeds, herds and flocks o'er northern regions rove,
Embrown the hill and wanton thro the grove.
The woodlands wide their sturdy honors bend,
The pines, the liveoaks to the shores descend,
There couch the keels, the crooked ribs arise,
Hulls heave aloft and mastheads mount the skies;

Launcht on the deep o'er every wave they fly,
Feed tropic isles and Europe's looms supply.
To nurse the arts and fashion freedom's lore
Young schools of science rise along the shore;
Great without pomp their modest walls expand,
Harvard and Yale and Princeton grace the land,
Penn's student halls his youths with gladness greet,
On James's bank Virginian Muses meet,
Manhattan's mart collegiate domes command,
Bosom'd in groves, see growing Dartmouth stand;
Bright o'er its realm reflecting solar fires,
On yon tall hill Rhode Island's seat aspires.
Thousands of humbler name around them rise,
Where homebred freemen seize the solid prize;
Fixt in small spheres, with safer beams to shine,
They reach the useful and refuse the fine,
Found, on its proper base, the social plan,
The broad plain truths, the common sense of man,
His obvious wants, his mutual aids discern,
His rights familiarize, his duties learn,
Feel moral fitness all its force dilate,
Embrace the village and comprise the state.
Each rustic here who turns the furrow'd soil,
The maid, the youth that ply mechanic toil,

In equal rights, in useful arts inured,
Know their just claims, and see their claims secured;
They watch their delegates, each law revise,
Its faults designate and its merits prize,
Obey, but scrutinize; and let the test
Of sage experience prove and fix the best.
  Here, fired by virtue's animating flame,
The preacher's task persuasive sages claim,
To mould religion to the moral mind,
In bands of peace to harmonize mankind,
To life, to light, to promised joys above
The soften'd soul with ardent hope to move.
No dark intolerance blinds the zealous throng,
No arm of power attendant on their tongue;
Vext Inquisition, with her flaming brand,
Shuns their mild march, nor dares approach the land.
Tho different creeds their priestly robes denote,
Their orders various and their rites remote,
Yet one their voice, their labors all combined,
Lights of the world and friends of humankind.
So the bright galaxy o'er heaven displays
Of various stars the same unbounded blaze;
Where great and small their mingling rays unite,
And earth and skies exchange the friendly light.

And lo, my son, that other sapient band,
The torch of science flaming in their hand!
Thro nature's range their searching souls aspire,
Or wake to life the canvass and the lyre.
Fixt in sublimest thought, behold them rise
World after world unfolding to their eyes,
Lead, light, allure them thro the total plan,
And give new guidance to the paths of man.

Yon meteor-mantled hill see Franklin tread,
Heaven's awful thunders rolling o'er his head;
Convolving clouds the billowy skies deform,
And forky flames emblaze the blackening storm.
See the descending streams around him burn,
Glance on his rod and with his finger turn;
He bids conflicting fulminants expire
The guided blast, and holds the imprison'd fire.
No more, when doubling storms the vault o'erspread,
The livid glare shall strike thy race with dread,
Nor towers nor temples, shuddering with the sound,
Sink in the flames and shake the sheeted ground.
His well tried wires, that every tempest wait,
Shall teach mankind to ward the bolts of fate,
With pointed steel o'ertop the trembling spire,
And lead from untouch'd walls the harmless fire;

Fill'd with his fame while distant climes rejoice,
Wherever lightning shines or thunder rears its voice.
  And see sage Rittenhouse, with ardent eye,
Lift the long tube and pierce the starry sky;
Clear in his view the circling planets roll,
And suns and satellites their course control.
He marks what laws the widest wanderers bind,
Copies creation in his forming mind,
Sees in his hall the total semblance rise,
And mimics there the labors of the skies.
There student youths without their tubes behold
The spangled heavens their mystic maze unfold,
And crowded schools their cheerful chambers grace
With all the spheres that cleave the vast of space.
  To guide the sailor in his wandering way,
See Godfrey's glass reverse the beams of day.
His lifted quadrant to the eye displays
From adverse skies the counteracting rays;
And marks, as devious sails bewilder'd roll,
Each nice gradation from the steadfast pole.
  West with his own great soul the canvass warms,
Creates, inspires, impassions human forms,
Spurns critic rules, and seizing safe the heart,
Breaks down the former frightful bounds of Art;

Where ancient manners, with exclusive reign,
From half mankind withheld her fair domain.
He calls to life each patriot, chief or sage,
Garb'd in the dress and drapery of his age.
Again bold Regulus to death returns,
Again her falling Wolfe Britannia mourns;
Lahogue, Boyne, Cressy, Nevilcross demand
And gain fresh lustre from his copious hand;
His Lear stalks wild with woes, the gods defies,
Insults the tempest and outstorms the skies;
Edward in arms to frowning combat moves,
Or, won to pity by the queen he loves,
Spares the devoted *Six*, whose deathless deed
Preserves the town his vengeance doom'd to bleed.

With rival force, see Copley's pencil trace
The air of action and the charms of face.
Fair in his tints unfold the scenes of state,
The senate listens and the peers debate;
Pale consternation every heart appals,
In act to speak, when death-struck Chatham falls.
He bids dread Calpe cease to shake the waves,
While Elliott's arm the host of Bourbon saves;
O'er sail-wing'd batteries sinking in the flood,
Mid flames and darkness, drench'd in hostile blood,

Britannia's sons extend their generous hand
To rescue foes from death, and bear them to the land.
  Fired with the martial deeds that bathed in gore
His brave companions on his native shore,
Trumbull with daring hand their fame recals;
He shades with night Quebec's beleagured walls,
Thro flashing flames, that midnight war supplies,
The assailants yield, their great Montgomery dies.
On Bunker height, thro floods of hostile fire,
His Putnam toils till all the troops retire,
His Warren, pierced with balls, at last lies low,
And leaves a victory to the wasted foe.
Britannia too his glowing tint shall claim,
To pour new splendor on her Calpean fame;
He leads her bold sortie, and from their towers
O'erturns the Gallic and Iberian powers.
  See rural seats of innocence and ease,
High tufted towers and walks of waving trees,
The white waves dashing on the craggy shores,
Meandring streams and meads of mingled flowers,
Where nature's sons their wild excursions tread,
In just design from Taylor's pencil spread.
  Stuart and Brown the moving portrait raise,
Each rival stroke the force of life conveys;

Heroes and beauties round their tablets stand,
And rise unfading from their plastic hand;
Each breathing form preserves its wonted grace,
And all the soul stands speaking in the face.
 Two kindred arts the swelling statue heave,
Wake the dead wax, and teach the stone to live.
While the bold chissel claims the rugged strife,
To rouse the sceptred marble into life,
See Wright's fair hands the livelier fire control,
In waxen forms she breathes impassion'd soul;
The pencil'd tint o'er moulded substance glows,
And different powers the peerless art compose.
Grief, rage and fear beneath her fingers start,
Roll the wild eye and pour the bursting heart;
The world's dead fathers wait her wakening call,
And distant ages fill the storied hall.
 To equal fame ascends thy tuneful throng,
The boast of genius and the pride of song;
Caught from the cast of every age and clime,
Their lays shall triumph o'er the lapse of time.
 With lynx-eyed glance thro nature far to pierce,
With all the powers and every charm of verse,
Each science opening in his ample mind,
His fancy glowing and his taste refined,

See Trumbull lead the train. His skilful hand
Hurls the keen darts of satire round the land.
Pride, knavery, dullness feel his mortal stings,
And listening virtue triumphs while he sings;
Britain's foil'd sons, victorious now no more,
In guilt retiring from the wasted shore,
Strive their curst cruelties to hide in vain;
The world resounds them in his deathless strain.

On wings of faith to elevate the soul
Beyond the bourn of earth's benighted pole,
For Dwight's high harp the epic Muse sublime
Hails her new empire in the western clime.
Tuned from the tones by seers seraphic sung,
Heaven in his eye and rapture on his tongue,
His voice revives old Canaan's promised land,
The long-fought fields of Jacob's chosen band.
In Hanniel's fate, proud faction finds its doom,
Ai's midnight flames light nations to their tomb,
In visions bright supernal joys are given,
And all the dark futurities of heaven.

While freedom's cause his patriot bosom warms,
In counsel sage, nor inexpert in arms,
See Humphreys glorious from the field retire,
Sheathe the glad sword and string the soothing lyre;

That lyre which erst, in hours of dark despair,
Roused the sad realms to finish well the war.
O'er fallen friends, with all the strength of woe,
Fraternal sighs in his strong numbers flow;
His country's wrongs, her duties, dangers, praise,
Fire his full soul and animate his lays:
Wisdom and War with equal joy shall own
So fond a votary and so brave a son.

THE

COLUMBIAD.

BOOK IX.

ARGUMENT.

Vision suspended. Night scene, as contemplated from the mount of vision. Columbus inquires the reason of the slow progress of science, and its frequent interruptions. Hesper answers, that all things in the physical as well as the moral and intellectual world are progressive in like manner. He traces their progress from the birth of the universe to the present state of the earth and its inhabitants; asserts the future advancement of society, till perpetual peace shall be established. Columbus proposes his doubts; alleges in support of them the successive rise and downfal of ancient nations; and infers future and periodical convulsions. Hesper, in answer, exhibits the great distinction between the ancient and modern state of the arts and of society. Crusades. Commerce. Hanseatic League. Copernicus. Kepler. Newton. Galileo. Herschel. Descartes. Bacon. Printing Press. Magnetic Needle. Geographical discoveries. Federal system in America. A similar system to be extended over the whole earth. Columbus desires a view of this.

THE

COLUMBIAD.

BOOK IX.

But now had Hesper from the Hero's sight
Veil'd the vast world with sudden shades of night.
Earth, sea and heaven, where'er he turns his eye,
Arch out immense, like one surrounding sky
Lamp'd with reverberant fires. The starry train
Paint their fresh forms beneath the placid main;
Fair Cynthia here her face reflected laves,
Bright Venus gilds again her natal waves,
The Bear redoubling foams with fiery joles,
And two dire dragons twine two arctic poles.
Lights o'er the land, from cities lost in shade,
New constellations, new galaxies spread,
And each high pharos double flames provides,
One from its fires, one fainter from the tides.

Centred sublime in this bivaulted sphere,
On all sides void, unbounded, calm and clear,
Soft o'er the Pair a lambent lustre plays,
Their seat still cheering with concentred rays;
To converse grave the soothing shades invite,
And on his Guide Columbus fixt his sight:
Kind messenger of heaven, he thus began,
Why this progressive laboring search of man?
If men by slow degrees have power to reach
These opening truths that long dim ages teach,
If, school'd in woes and tortured on to thought,
Passion absorbing what experience taught,
Still thro the devious painful paths they wind,
And to sound wisdom lead at last the mind,
Why did not bounteous nature, at their birth,
Give all their science to these sons of earth,
Pour on their reasoning powers pellucid day,
Their arts, their interests clear as light display?
That error, madness and sectarian strife
Might find no place to havock human life.
To whom the guardian Power: To thee is given
To hold high converse and inquire of heaven,
To mark untraversed ages, and to trace
Whate'er improves and what impedes thy race.

Know then, progressive are the paths we go
In worlds above thee, as in thine below.
Nature herself (whose grasp of time and place
Deals out duration and impalms all space)
Moves in progressive march; but where to tend,
What course to compass, how the march must end,
Her sons decide not; yet her works we greet
Imperfect in their parts, but in their whole complete.

When erst her hand the crust of Chaos thirl'd,
And forced from his black breast the bursting world,
High swell'd the huge existence crude and crass,
A formless dark impermeated mass;
No light nor heat nor cold nor moist nor dry,
But all concocting in their causes lie.
Millions of periods, such as these her spheres
Learn since to measure and to call their years,
She broods the mass; then into motion brings
And seeks and sorts the principles of things,
Pours in the attractive and repulsive force,
Whirls forth her globes in cosmogyral course,
By myriads and by millions, scaled sublime,
To scoop their skies, and curve the rounds of time.

She groups their systems, lots to each his place,
Strow'd thro immensity, and drown'd in space,

All yet unseen; till light at last begun,
And every system found a centred sun,
Call'd to his neighbor and exchanged from far
His infant gleams with every social star;
Rays thwarting rays and skies o'erarching skies
Robed their dim planets with commingling dyes,
Hung o'er each heaven their living lamps serene,
And tinged with blue the frore expanse between:
Then joyous Nature hail'd the golden morn,
Drank the young beam, beheld her empire born.

Lo the majestic movement! there they trace
Their blank infinitudes of time and space,
Vault with careering curves her central goal,
Pour forth her day and stud her evening stole,
Heedless of count; their numbers still unknown,
Unmeasured still their progress round her throne;
For none of all her firstborn sons, endow'd
With heavenly sapience and pretensions proud,
No seraph bright, whose keen considering eye
And sunbeam speed ascend from sky to sky,
Has yet explored or counted all their spheres,
Or fixt or found their past record of years.
Nor can a ray from her remotest sun,
Shot forth when first their splendid morn begun,

Borne straight, continuous thro the void of space,
Doubling each thousand years its rapid pace
And hither posting, yet have reach'd this earth,
To bring the tidings of its master's birth.

And mark thy native orb! tho later born,
Tho still unstored with light her silver horn,
As seen from sister planets, who repay
Far more than she their borrow'd streams of day,
Yet what an age her shell-rock ribs attest!
Her sparry spines, her coal-encumber'd breast!
Millions of generations toil'd and died
To crust with coral and to salt her tide,
And millions more, ere yet her soil began,
Ere yet she form'd or could have nursed her man.

Then rose the proud phenomenon, the birth
Most richly wrought, the favorite child of earth;
But frail at first his frame, with nerves ill strung,
Unform'd his footsteps, long untoned his tongue,
Unhappy, unassociate, unrefined,
Unfledged the pinions of his lofty mind,
He wander'd wild, to every beast a prey,
More prest with wants, and feebler far than they;
For countless ages forced from place to place,
Just reproduced but scarce preserved his race.

At last, a soil more fixt and streams more sweet
Inform the wretched migrant where to seat;
Euphrates' flowery banks begin to smile,
Fruits fringe the Ganges, gardens grace the Nile;
Nile, ribb'd with dikes, a length of coast creates,
And giant Thebes begins her hundred gates,
Mammoth of human works! her grandeur known
These thousand lustres by its wrecks alone;
Wrecks that humiliate still all modern states,
Press the poized earth with their enormous weights,
Refuse to quit their place, dissolve their frame
And trust, like Ilion, to the bards their fame.
Memphis amass'd her piles, that still o'erclimb
The clouds of heaven, and task the tooth of time;
Belus and Brama tame their vagrant throngs,
And Homer, with his monumental songs,
Builds far more durable his splendid throne
Than all the Pharaohs with their hills of stone.

High roll'd the round of years that hung sublime
These wondrous beacons in the night of time;
Studs of renown! that to thine eyes attest
The waste of ages that beyond them rest;
Ages how fill'd with toils! how gloom'd with woes!
Trod with all steps that man's long march compose,

Dim drear disastrous; ere his foot could gain
A height so brilliant o'er the bestial train.
  In those blank periods, where no man can trace
The gleams of thought that first illumed his race,
His errors, twined with science, took their birth,
And forged their fetters for this child of earth.
And when, as oft, he dared expand his view,
And work with nature on the line she drew,
Some monster, gender'd in his fears, unmann'd
His opening soul, and marr'd the works he plann'd.
Fear, the first passion of his helpless state,
Redoubles all the woes that round him wait,
Blocks nature's path and sends him wandering wide,
Without a guardian and without a guide.
  Beat by the storm, refresht by gentle rain,
By sunbeams cheer'd or founder'd in the main,
He bows to every force he can't control,
Indows them all with intellect and soul,
With passions various, turbulent and strong,
Rewarding virtue and avenging wrong,
Gives heaven and earth to their supernal doom,
And swells their sway beyond the closing tomb.
Hence rose his gods, that mystic monstrous lore
Of blood-stain'd altars and of priestly power,

Hence blind credulity on all dark things,
False morals hence, and hence the yoke of kings.
  Yon starry vault that round him rolls the spheres,
And gives to earth her seasons, days and years,
The source designates and the clue imparts
Of all his errors and of all his arts.
There spreads the system that his ardent thought
First into emblems, then to spirits wrought;
Spirits that ruled all matter and all mind,
Nourish'd or famish'd, kill'd or cured mankind,
Bade him neglect the soil whereon he fed,
Work with hard hand for that which was not bread,
Erect the temple, darken deep the shrine,
Yield the full hecatomb with awe divine,
Despise this earth, and claim with lifted eyes
His health and harvest from the meteor'd skies.
  Accustom'd thus to bow the suppliant head,
And reverence powers that shake his heart with dread,
His pliant faith extends with easy ken
From heavenly hosts to heaven-anointed men;
The sword, the tripod join their mutual aids,
To film his eyes with more impervious shades,
Create a sceptred idol, and enshrine
The Robber Chief in attributes divine,

Arm the new phantom with the nation's rod,
And hail the dreadful delegate of God.
Two settled slaveries thus the race control,
Engross their labors and debase their soul;
Till creeds and crimes and feuds and fears compose
The seeds of war and all its kindred woes.
  Unfold, thou Memphian dungeon! there began
The lore of Mystery, the mask of man;
There Fraud with Science leagued, in early times,
Plann'd a resplendent course of holy crimes,
Stalk'd o'er the nations with gigantic pace,
With sacred symbols charm'd the cheated race,
Taught them new grades of ignorance to gain,
And punish truth with more than mortal pain,—
Unfold at last thy cope! that man may see
The mines of mischief he has drawn from thee.
—Wide gapes the porch with hieroglyphics hung,
And mimic zodiacs o'er its arches flung;
Close labyrinth'd here the feign'd Omniscient dwells,
Dupes from all nations seek the sacred cells;
Inquiring strangers, with astonish'd eyes,
Dive deep to read these subterranean skies,
To taste that holiness which faith bestows,
And fear promulgates thro its world of woes.

The bold Initiate takes his awful stand,
A thin pale taper trembling in his hand;
Thro hells of howling monsters lies the road,
To season souls and teach the ways of God.

Down the crampt corridor, far sunk from day,
On hands and bended knees he gropes his way,
Swims roaring streams, thro dens of serpents crawls,
Descends deep wells and clambers flaming walls;
Now thwart his lane a lake of sulphur gleams,
With fiery waves and suffocating steams;
He dares not shun the ford; for full in view
Fierce lions rush behind and force him thro.
Long ladders heaved on end, with banded eyes
He mounts, and mounts, and seems to gain the skies;
Then backward falling, tranced with deadly fright,
Finds his own feet and stands restored to light.
Here all dread sights of torture round him rise;
Lash'd on a wheel, a whirling felon flies;
A wretch, with members chain'd and liver bare,
Writhes and disturbs the vulture feasting there:
One strains to roll his rock, recoiling still;
One, stretch'd recumbent o'er a limpid rill,
Burns with devouring thirst; his starting eyes,
Swell'd veins and frothy lips and piercing cries

Accuse the faithless eddies, as they shrink
And keep him panting still, still bending o'er the brink.
At last Elysium to his ravisht eyes
Spreads flowery fields and opens golden skies;
Breathes Orphean music thro the dancing groves,
Trains the gay troops of Beauties, Graces, Loves,
Lures his delirious sense with sweet decoys,
Fine fancied foretaste of eternal joys,
Fastidious pomp or proud imperial state,—
Illusions all, that pass the Ivory Gate!
Various and vast the fraudful drama grows,
Feign'd are the pleasures, as unfelt the woes;
Where sainted hierophants, with well taught mimes,
Play'd first the role for all succeeding times;
Which, vamp'd and varied as the clime required,
More trist or splendid, open or retired,
Forms local creeds, with multifarious lore,
Creates the God and bids the world adore.
Lo at the Lama's feet, as lord of all,
Age following age in dumb devotion fall;
The youthful god, mid suppliant kings enshrined,
Dispensing fate and ruling half mankind,
Sits with contorted limbs, a silent slave,
An early victim of a secret grave;

His priests by myriads famish every clime
And sell salvation in the tones they chime.
  See India's Triad frame their blood-penn'd codes,
Old Ganges change his gardens for his gods,
Ask his own waves from their celestial hands,
And choke his channel with their sainted sands.
Mad with the mandates of their scriptured word,
And prompt to snatch from hell her dear dead lord,
The wife, still blooming, decks her sacred urns,
Mounts the gay pyre, and with his body burns.
  Shrined in his golden fane the Delphian stands,
Shakes distant thrones and taxes unknown lands.
Kings, consuls, khans from earth's whole regions come,
Pour in their wealth, and then inquire their doom;
Furious and wild the priestess rends her veil,
Sucks, thro the sacred stool, the maddening gale,
Starts reddens foams and screams and mutters loud,
Like a fell fiend, her oracles of God.
The dark enigma, by the pontiff scroll'd
In broken phrase, and close in parchment roll'd,
From his proud pulpit to the suppliant hurl'd,
Shall rive an empire and distract the world.
  And where the mosque's dim arches bend on high,
Mecca's dead prophet mounts the mimic sky;

Pilgrims, imbanded strong for mutual aid,
Thro dangerous deserts that their faith has made,
Train their long caravans, and famish'd come
To kiss the shrine and trembling touch the tomb,
By fire and sword the same fell faith extend,
And howl their homilies to earth's far end.
  Phenician altars reek with human gore,
Gods hiss from caverns or in cages roar,
Nile pours from heaven a tutelary flood,
And gardens grow the vegetable god.
Two rival powers the magian faith inspire,
Primeval Darkness and immortal Fire;
Evil and good in these contending rise,
And each by turns the sovereign of the skies.
Sun, stars and planets round the earth behold
Their fanes of marble and their shrines of gold;
The sea, the grove, the harvest and the vine
Spring from their gods and claim a birth divine;
While heroes, kings and sages of their times,
Those gods on earth, are gods in happier climes;
Minos in judgment sits, and Jove in power,
And Odin's friends are feasted there with gore.
  Man is an infant still; and slow and late
Must form and fix his adolescent state,

Mature his manhood, and at last behold
His reason ripen and his force unfold.
From that bright eminence he then shall cast
A look of wonder on his wanderings past,
Congratulate himself, and o'er the earth
Firm the full reign of peace predestined at his birth.

So Hesper taught; and farther had pursued
A theme so grateful as a world renew'd;
But dubious thoughts disturb'd the Hero's breast,
Who thus with modest mien the Seer addrest:
Say, friend of man, in this unbounded range,
Where error vagrates and illusions change,
What hopes to see his baleful blunders cease,
And earth commence that promised age of peace?
Like a loose pendulum his mind is hung,
From wrong to wrong by ponderous passion swung,
It vibrates wide, and with unceasing flight
Sweeps all extremes and scorns the mean of right.
Tho in the times you trace he seems to gain
A steadier movement and a path more plain,
And tho experience will have taught him then
To mark some dangers, some delusions ken,
Yet who can tell what future shocks may spread
New shades of darkness round his lofty head,

Plunge him again in some broad gulph of woes,
Where long and oft he struggled, wreck'd and rose?
  What strides he took in those gigantic times
That sow'd with cities all his orient climes!
When earth's proud floods he tamed, made many a shore,
And talk'd with heaven from Babel's glittering tower!
Did not his Babylon exulting say,
I sit a queen, for ever stands my sway?
Thebes, Memphis, Nineveh, a countless throng,
Caught the same splendor and return'd the song;
Each boasted, promised o'er the world to rise,
Spouse of the sun, eternal as the skies.
Where shall we find them now? the very shore
Where Ninus rear'd his empire is no more:
The dikes decay'd, a putrid marsh regains
The sunken walls, the tomb-encumber'd plains,
Pursues the dwindling nations where they shrink,
And skirts with slime its deleterious brink.
The fox himself has fled his gilded den,
Nor holds the heritage he won from men;
Lapwing and reptile shun the curst abode,
And the foul dragon, now no more a god,

Trails off his train; the sickly raven flies;
A wide strong-stencht Avernus chokes the skies.
So pride and ignorance fall a certain prey
To the stanch bloodhound of despotic sway.
Then past a long drear night, with here and there
A doubtful glimmering from a single star;
Tyre, Carthage, Syracuse the gleam increase,
Till dawns at last the effulgent morn of Greece.
Here all his Muses meet, all arts combine
To nerve his genius and his works refine;
Morals and laws and arms, and every grace
That e'er adorn'd or could exalt the race,
Wrought into science and arranged in rules,
Swell the proud splendor of her cluster'd schools,
Build and sustain the state with loud acclaim,
And work those deathless miracles of fame
That stand unrivall'd still; for who shall dare
Another field with Marathon compare?
Who speaks of eloquence or sacred song,
But calls on Greece to modulate his tongue?
And where has man's fine form so perfect shone
In tint or mould, in canvass or in stone?
Yet from that splendid height o'erturn'd once more,
He dasht in dust the living lamp he bore.

Dazzled with her own glare, decoy'd and sold
For homebred faction and barbaric gold,
Greece treads on Greece, subduing and subdued,
New crimes inventing, all the old renew'd,
Canton o'er canton climbs; till, crush'd and broke,
All yield the sceptre and resume the yoke.

Where shall we trace him next, the migrant man,
To try once more his meliorating plan?
Shall not the Macedonian, where he strides
O'er Asian worlds and Nile's neglected tides,
Prepare new seats of glory, to repay
The transient shadows with perpetual day?
His heirs erect their empires, and expand
The beams of Greece thro each benighted land;
Seleucia spreads o'er ten broad realms her sway,
And turns on eastern climes the western ray;
Palmyra brightens earth's commercial zone,
And sits an emblem of her god the sun;
While fond returning to that favorite shore
Where Ammon ruled and Hermes taught of yore,
All arts concentrate, force and grace combine
To rear and blend the useful with the fine,
Restore the Egyptian glories, and retain,
Where science dawn'd, her great resurgent reign.

From Egypt chased again, he seeks his home,
More firmly fixt in sage considerate Rome.
Here all the virtues long resplendent shone,
All that was Greek, barbarian and her own;
She school'd him sound, and boasted to extend
Thro time's long course and earth's remotest end
His glorious reign of reason; soon to cease
The clang of arms, and rule the world in peace.
Great was the sense he gain'd, and well defined
The various functions of his tutor'd mind;
Could but his sober sense have proved his guide,
And kind experience pruned the shoots of pride.
A field magnificent before him lay;
Land after land received the spreading ray;
Franchise and friendship travell'd in his train,
Bandits of earth and pirates of the main
Rose into citizens, their rage resign'd,
And hail'd the great republic of mankind.
If ever then state slaughter was to pause,
And man from nature learn to frame his laws,
This was the moment; here the sunbeam rose
To hush the human storm and let the world repose.
But drunk with pomp and sickening at the light,
He stagger'd wild on this delirious height;

Forgot the plainest truths he learnt before,
And barter'd moral for material power.
From Calpe's rock to India's ardent skies,
O'er shuddering earth his talon'd Eagle flies,
To justice blind, and heedless where she drove,
As when she bore the brandisht bolt of Jove.
Rome loads herself with chains, seals fast her eyes,
And tells the insulted nations when to rise;
And rise they do, like sweeping tempests driven,
Swarm following swarm, o'ershading earth and heaven,
Roll back her outrage, and indignant shed
The world's wide vengeance on her sevenfold head.
Then dwindling back to littleness and shade
Man soon forgets the gorgeous glare he made,
Sinks to a savage serf or monkish drone,
Roves in rude hordes or counts his beads alone,
Wars with his arts, obliterates his lore,
And burns the books that rear'd his race before.
Shrouded in deeper darkness now he veers
The vast gyration of a thousand years,
Strikes out each lamp that would illume his way,
Disputes his food with every beast of prey;
Imbands his force to fence his trist abodes,
A wretched robber with his feudal codes.

At length, it seems, some parsimonious rays
Collect from each far heaven a feeble blaze,
Dance o'er his Europe, and again excite
His numerous nations to receive the light.
But faint and slow the niggard dawn expands,
Diffused o'er various far dissunder'd lands,
Dreading, as well it may, to prove once more
The same sad chance so often proved before.

And why not lapse again? Celestial Seer,
Forgive my doubts, and ah remove my fear!
Man is my brother; strong I feel the ties,
From strong solicitude my doubts arise;
My heart, while opening with the boundless scope
That swells before him and expands his hope,
Forebodes another fall; and tho at last
Thy world is planted and with light o'ercast,
Tho two broad continents their beams combine
Round his whole globe to stream his day divine,
Perchance some folly, yet uncured, may spread
A storm proportion'd to the lights they shed,
Veil both his continents, and leave again
Between them stretch'd the impermeable main;
All science buried, sails and cities lost,
Their lands uncultured, as their seas uncrost.

Till on thy coast, some thousand ages hence,
New pilots rise, bold enterprise commence,
Some new Columbus (happier let him be,
More wise and great and virtuous far than me)
Launch on the wave, and tow'rd the rising day
Like a strong eaglet steer his untaught way,
Gird half the globe, and to his age unfold
A strange new world, the world we call the old.
From Finland's glade to Calpe's storm-beat head
He'll find some tribes of scattering wildmen spread;
But one vast wilderness will shade the soil,
No wreck of art, no sign of ancient toil
Tell where a city stood; nor leave one trace
Of all that honors now, and all that shames the race.
 If such the round we run, what hope, my friend,
To see our madness and our miseries end?—
Here paused the Patriarch: mild the Saint return'd,
And as he spoke, fresh glories round him burn'd:
My son, I blame not but applaud thy grief;
Inquiries deep should lead to slow belief.
So small the portion of the range of man
His written stories reach or views can span,
That wild confusion seems to clog his march,
And the dull progress made illudes thy search.

But broad beyond compare, with steadier hand
Traced o'er his earth, his present paths expand.
In sober majesty and matron grace
Sage Science now conducts her filial race;
And if, while all their arts around them shine,
They culture more the solid than the fine,
Tis to correct their fatal faults of old,
When, caught by tinsel, they forgot the gold;
When their strong brilliant imitative lines
Traced nature only in her gay designs,
Rear'd the proud column, toned her chanting lyre,
Warm'd the full senate with her words of fire,
Pour'd on the canvass every pulse of life,
And bade the marble rage with human strife.

These were the arts that nursed unequal sway,
That priests would pamper and that kings would pay,
That spoke to vulgar sense, and often stole
The sense of right and freedom from the soul.
While, circumscribed in some concentred clime,
They reach'd but one small nation at a time,
Dazzled that nation, pufft her local pride,
Proclaim'd her hatred to the world beside,
Drew back returning hatred from afar,
And sunk themselves beneath the storms of war.

As, when the sun moves o'er the flaming zone,
Collecting clouds attend his fervid throne,
Superior splendors, in his morn display'd,
Prepare for noontide but a heavier shade;
Thus where the brilliant arts alone prevail'd,
Their shining course succeeding storms assail'd;
Pride, wrong and insult hemm'd their scanty reign,
A Nile their stream, a Hellespont their main,
Content with Tiber's narrow shores to wind,
They fledged their Eagle but to fang mankind;
Ere great inventions found a tardy birth,
And with their new creations blest the earth.

Now sober'd man a steadier gait assumes,
Broad is the beam that breaks the Gothic glooms.
At once consenting nations lift their eyes,
And hail the holy dawn that streaks the skies;
Arabian caliphs rear the spires of Spain,
The Lombards keel their Adriatic main,
Great Charles, invading and reviving all,
Plants o'er with schools his numerous states of Gaul;
And Alfred opes the mines whence Albion draws
The ore of all her wealth,—her liberty and laws.

Ausonian cities interchange and spread
The lights of learning on the wings of trade;

Bologna's student walls arise to fame,
Germania, thine their rival honors claim;
Halle, Gottinge, Upsal, Kiel and Leyden smile,
Oxonia, Cambridge cheer Britannia's isle;
Where, like her lark, gay Chaucer leads the lay,
The matin carol of his country's day.

Blind War himself, that erst opposed all good,
And whelm'd meek Science in her votaries' blood,
Now smooths, by means unseen, her modest way,
Extends her limits and secures her sway.
From Europe's world his mad crusaders pour
Their banded myriads on the Asian shore;
The mystic Cross, thro famine toil and blood,
Leads their long marches to the tomb of God.
Thro realms of industry their passage lies,
And labor'd affluence feasts their curious eyes;
Till fields of slaughter whelm the broken host,
Their pride appall'd, their warmest zealots lost,
The wise remains to their own shores return,
Transplant all arts that Hagar's race adorn,
Learn from long intercourse their mutual ties,
And find in commerce where their interest lies.

From Drave's long course to Biscay's bending shores,
Where Adria sleeps, to where the Bothnian roars,

In one great Hanse, for earth's whole trafic known,
Free cities rise, and in their golden zone
Bind all the interior states; nor princes dare
Infringe their franchise with voracious war.
All shield them safe, and joy to share the gain
That spreads o'er land from each surrounding main,
Makes Indian stuffs, Arabian gums their own,
Plants Persian gems on every Celtic crown,
Pours thro their opening woodlands milder day,
And gives to genius his expansive play.

This blessed moment, from the towers of Thorn
New splendor rises; there the sage is born!
The sage who starts these planetary spheres,
Deals out their task to wind their own bright years,
Restores his station to the parent Sun,
And leads his duteous daughters round his throne.
Each mounts obedient on her wheels of fire,
Whirls round her sisters, and salutes the sire,
Guides her new car, her youthful coursers tries,
Curves careful paths along her alter'd skies,
Learns all her mazes thro the host of even,
And hails and joins the harmony of heaven.
—Fear not, Copernicus! let loose the rein,
Launch from their goals, and mark the moving train;

Fix at their sun thy calculating eye,
Compare and count their courses round their sky.
Fear no disaster from the slanting force
That warps them staggering in elliptic course;
Thy sons with steadier ken shall aid the search,
And firm and fashion their majestic march,
Kepler prescribe the laws no stars can shun,
And Newton tie them to the eternal sun.

By thee inspired, his tube the Tuscan plies,
And sends new colonies to stock the skies,
Gives Jove his satellites, and first adorns
Effulgent Phosphor with his silver horns.
Herschel ascends himself with venturous wain,
And joins and flanks thy planetary train,
Perceives his distance from their elder spheres,
And guards with numerous moons the lonely round he steers.

Yes, bright Copernicus, thy beams, far hurl'd,
Shall startle well this intellectual world,
Break the delusive dreams of ancient lore,
New floods of light on every subject pour,
Thro Physic Nature many a winding trace,
And seat the Moral on her sister's base.
Descartes with force gigantic toils alone,
Unshrines old errors and propounds his own;

Like a blind Samson, gropes their strong abodes,
Whelms deep in dust their temples and their gods,
Buries himself with those false codes they drew,
And makes his followers frame and fix the true.

Bacon, with every power of genius fraught,
Spreads over worlds his mantling wings of thought,
Draws in firm lines, and tells in nervous tone
All that is yet and all that shall be known,
Withes Proteus Matter in his arms of might,
And drags her tortuous secrets forth to light,
Bids men their unproved systems all forgo,
Informs them what to learn, and how to know,
Waves the first flambeau thro the night that veils
Egyptian fables and Phenician tales,
Strips from all-plundering Greece the cloak she wore,
And shows the blunders of her borrow'd lore.

One vast creation, lately borne abroad,
Cheers the young nations like a nurturing God,
Breathes thro them all the same wide-searching soul,
Forms, feeds, refines and animates the whole,
Guards every ground they gain, and forward brings
Glad Science soaring on cerulean wings,
Trims her gay plumes, directs her upward course,
Props her light pinions and sustains her force,

Instructs all men her golden gifts to prize,
And catch new glories from her beamful eyes,—
Tis the prolific Press; whose tablet, fraught
By graphic Genius with his painted thought,
Flings forth by millions the prodigious birth,
And in a moment stocks the astonish'd earth.
  Genius, enamor'd of his fruitful bride,
Assumes new force and elevates his pride.
No more, recumbent o'er his finger'd style,
He plods whole years each copy to compile,
Leaves to ludibrious winds the priceless page,
Or to chance fires the treasure of an age;
But bold and buoyant, with his sister Fame,
He strides o'er earth, holds high his ardent flame,
Calls up Discovery with her tube and scroll,
And points the trembling magnet to the pole.
Hence the brave Lusitanians stretch the sail,
Scorn guiding stars, and tame the midsea gale;
And hence thy prow deprest the boreal wain,
Rear'd adverse heavens, a second earth to gain,
Ran down old Night, her western curtain thirl'd,
And snatch'd from swaddling shades an infant world.
  Rome, Athens, Memphis, Tyre! had you but known
This glorious triad, now familiar grown,

The Press, the Magnet faithful to its pole,
And earth's own Movement round her steadfast goal,
Ne'er had your science, from that splendid height,
Sunk in her strength, nor seen succeeding night.
Her own utility had forced her sway,
All nations caught the fast-extending ray,
Nature thro all her kingdoms oped the road,
Resign'd her secrets and her wealth bestow'd;
Her moral codes a like dominion rear'd,
Freedom been born and folly disappear'd,
War and his monsters sunk beneath her ban,
And left the world to reason and to man.
   But now behold him bend his broader way,
Lift keener eyes and drink diviner day,
All systems scrutinize, their truths unfold,
Prove well the recent, well revise the old,
Reject all mystery, and define with force
The point he aims at in his laboring course,—
To know these elements, learn how they wind
Their wondrous webs of matter and of mind,
What springs, what guides organic life requires,
To move, rule, rein its ever-changing gyres,
Improve and utilise each opening birth,
And aid the labors of this nurturing earth.

But chief their moral soul he learns to trace,
That stronger chain which links and leads the race;
Which forms and sanctions every social tie,
And blinds or clears their intellectual eye.
He strips that soul from every filmy shade
That schools had caught, that oracles had made,
Relumes her visual nerve, develops strong
The rules of right, the subtle shifts of wrong;
Of civil power draws clear the sacred line,
Gives to just government its right divine,
Forms, varies, fashions, as his lights increase,
Till earth is fill'd with happiness and peace.
Already taught, thou know'st the fame that waits
His rising seat in thy confederate states.
There stands the model, thence he long shall draw
His forms of policy, his traits of law;
Each land shall imitate, each nation join
The well-based brotherhood, the league divine,
Extend its empire with the circling sun,
And band the peopled globe beneath its federal zone.
As thus he spoke, returning tears of joy
Suffused the Hero's cheek and pearl'd his eye:
Unveil, said he, my friend, and stretch once more
Beneath my view that heaven-illumined shore;

Let me behold her silver beams expand,
To lead all nations, lighten every land,
Instruct the total race, and teach at last
Their toils to lessen and their chains to cast,
Trace and attain the purpose of their birth,
And hold in peace this heritage of earth.
The Seraph smiled consent, the Hero's eye
Watch'd for the daybeam round the changing sky.

THE

COLUMBIAD.

BOOK X.

ARGUMENT.

The vision resumed, and extended over the whole earth. Present character of different nations. Future progress of society with respect to commerce; discoveries; inland navigation; philosophical, medical and political knowledge. Science of government. Assimilation and final union of all languages. Its effect on education, and on the advancement of physical and moral science. The physical precedes the moral, as Phosphor precedes the Sun. View of a general Congress from all nations, assembled to establish the political harmony of mankind. Conclusion.

THE

COLUMBIAD.

BOOK X.

HESPER again his heavenly power display'd,
And shook the yielding canopy of shade.
Sudden the stars their trembling fires withdrew,
Returning splendors burst upon the view,
Floods of unfolding light the skies adorn,
And more than midday glories grace the morn.
So shone the earth, as if the sideral train,
Broad as full suns, had sail'd the ethereal plain;
When no distinguisht orb could strike the sight,
But one clear blaze of all-surrounding light
O'erflow'd the vault of heaven. For now in view
Remoter climes and future ages drew;
Whose deeds of happier fame, in long array,
Call'd into vision, fill the newborn day.

Far as seraphic power could lift the eye,
Or earth or ocean bend the yielding sky,
Or circling suns awake the breathing gale,
Drake lead the way, or Cook extend the sail;
Where Behren sever'd, with adventurous prow,
Hesperia's headland from Tartaria's brow;
Where sage Vancouvre's patient leads were hurl'd,
Where Deimen stretch'd his solitary world;
All lands, all seas that boast a present name,
And all that unborn time shall give to fame,
Around the Pair in bright expansion rise,
And earth, in one vast level, bounds the skies.
They saw the nations tread their different shores,
Ply their own toils and wield their local powers,
Their present state in all its views disclose,
Their gleams of happiness, their shades of woes,
Plodding in various stages thro the range
Of man's unheeded but unceasing change.
Columbus traced them with experienced eye,
And class'd and counted all the flags that fly;
He mark'd what tribes still rove the savage waste,
What cultured realms the sweets of plenty taste;
Where arts and virtues fix their golden reign,
Or peace adorns, or slaughter dyes the plain.

He saw the restless Tartar, proud to roam,
Move with his herds and pitch a transient home;
Tibet's long tracts and China's fixt domain,
Dull as their despots, yield their cultured grain;
Cambodia, Siam, Asia's myriad isles
And old Indostan, with their wealthy spoils
Attract adventurous masters, and o'ershade
Their sunbright ocean with the wings of trade.
Arabian robbers, Syrian Kurds combined,
Create their deserts and infest mankind;
The Turk's dim Crescent, like a day-struck star,
As Russia's Eagle shades their haunts of war,
Shrinks from insulted Europe, who divide
The shatter'd empire to the Pontic tide.
He mark'd impervious Afric, where alone
She lies encircled with the verdant zone
That lines her endless coast, and still sustains
Her northern pirates and her eastern swains,
Mourns her interior tribes purloin'd away,
And chain'd and sold beyond Atlantic day.
Brazilla's wilds, Mackensie's savage lands
With bickering strife inflame their furious bands;
Atlantic isles and Europe's cultured shores
Heap their vast wealth, exchange their growing stores,

All arts inculcate, new discoveries plan,
Tease and torment but school the race of man.
While his own federal states, extending far,
Calm their brave sons now breathing from the war,
Unfold their harbors, spread their genial soil,
And welcome freemen to the cheerful toil.
  A sight so solemn, as it varied round,
Fill'd his fond heart with reveries profound;
He felt the infinitude of thoughts that pass
And guide and govern that enormous mass.
The cares that agitate, the creeds that blind,
The woes that waste the many-master'd kind,
The distance great that still remains to trace,
Ere sober sense can harmonize the race,
Held him suspense, imprest with reverence meek,
And choked his utterance as he wish'd to speak:
When Hesper thus: The paths they here pursue,
Wide as they seem unfolding to thy view,
Show but a point in that long circling course
Which cures their weakness and confirms their force,
Lends that experience which alone can close
The scenes of strife, and give the world repose.
Yet here thou seest the same progressive plan
That draws for mutual succour man to man,

From twain to tribe, from tribe to realm dilates,
In federal union groups a hundred states,
Thro all their turns with gradual scale ascends,
Their powers, their passions and their interest blends;
While growing arts their social virtues spread,
Enlarge their compacts and unlock their trade;
Till each remotest clan, by commerce join'd,
Links in the chain that binds all humankind,
Their bloody banners sink in darkness furl'd,
And one white flag of peace triumphant walks the world.

As infant streams, from oozing earth at first
With feeble force and lonely murmurs burst,
From myriad unseen fountains draw the rills
And curl contentious round their hundred hills,
Meet, froth and foam, their dashing currents swell,
O'er crags and rocks their furious course impel,
Impetuous plunging plough the mounds of earth,
And tear the fostering flanks that gave them birth;
Mad with the strength they gain, they thicken deep
Their muddy waves and slow and sullen creep,
O'erspread whole regions in their lawless pride,
Then stagnate long, then shrink and curb their tide;
Anon more tranquil grown, with steadier sway,
Thro broader banks they shape their seaward way,

From different climes converging, join and spread
Their mingled waters in one widening bed,
Profound, transparent; till the liquid zone
Bands half the globe and drinks the golden sun,
Sweeps onward still the still expanding plain,
And moves majestic to the boundless main.
Tis thus Society's small sources rise;
Thro passions wild her infant progress lies;
Fear, with its host of follies, errors, woes,
Creates her obstacles and forms her foes;
Misguided interest, local pride withstand,
Till long-tried ills her growing views expand,
Till tribes and states and empires find their place,
Whose mutual wants her widest walks embrace;
Enlighten'd interest, moral sense at length
Combine their aids to elevate her strength,
Lead o'er the world her peace-commanding sway,
And light her steps with everlasting day.
From that mark'd stage of man we now behold,
More rapid strides his coming paths unfold;
His continents are traced, his islands found,
His well-taught sails on all his billows bound,
His varying wants their new discoveries ply,
And seek in earth's whole range their sure supply.

First of his future stages, thou shalt see
His trade unfetter'd and his ocean free.
From thy young states the code consoling springs,
To strip from vulture War his naval wings;
In views so just all Europe's powers combine,
And earth's full voice approves the vast design.
Tho still her inland realms the combat wage
And hold in lingering broils the unsettled age,
Yet no rude shocks that shake the crimson plain
Shall more disturb the labors of the main;
The main that spread so wide his travell'd way,
Liberal as air, impartial as the day,
That all thy race the common wealth might share,
Exchange their fruits and fill their treasures there,
Their speech assimilate, their counsels blend,
Till mutual interest fix the mutual friend.
Now see, my son, the destined hour advance;
Safe in their leagues commercial navies dance,
Leave their curst cannon on the quay-built strand,
And like the stars of heaven a fearless course command.

The Hero look'd; beneath his wondering eyes
Gay streamers lengthen round the seas and skies;
The countless nations open all their stores,
Load every wave and crowd the lively shores;

Bright sails in mingling mazes streak the air,
And commerce triumphs o'er the rage of war.
From Baltic streams, from Elba's opening side,
From Rhine's long course and Texel's laboring tide,
From Gaul, from Albion, tired of fruitless fight,
From green Hibernia, clothed in recent light,
Hispania's strand that two broad oceans lave,
From Senegal and Gambia's golden wave,
Tago the rich, and Douro's viny shores,
The sweet Canaries and the soft Azores,
Commingling barks their mutual banners hail,
And drink by turns the same distending gale.
Thro Calpe's strait that leads the Midland main,
From Adria, Pontus, Nile's resurgent reign,
The sails look forth and wave their bandrols high
And ask their breezes from a broader sky.
Where Asia's isles and utmost shorelands bend,
Like rising suns the sheeted masts ascend;
Coast after coast their flowing flags unrol,
From Deimen's rocks to Zembla's ice-propt pole,
Where Behren's pass collapsing worlds divides,
Where California breaks the billowy tides,
Peruvian streams their golden margins boast,
Or Chili bluffs or Plata flats the coast.

Where, clothed in splendor, his Atlantic way
Spreads the blue borders of Hesperian day,
From all his havens, with majestic sweep,
The swiftest boldest daughters of the deep
Swarm forth before him; till the cloudlike train
From pole to pole o'ersheet the whitening main.
 So some primeval seraph, placed on high,
From heaven's sublimest point o'erlook'd the sky,
When space unfolding heard the voice of God,
And suns and stars and systems roll'd abroad,
Caught their first splendors from his beamful eye,
Began their years and vaulted round their sky;
Their social spheres in bright confusion play,
Exchange their beams and fill the newborn day.
 Nor seas alone the countless barks behold;
Earth's inland realms their naval paths unfold.
Her plains, long portless, now no more complain
Of useless rills and fountains nursed in vain;
Canals curve thro them many a liquid line,
Prune their wild streams, their lakes and oceans join.
Where Darien hills o'erlook the gulphy tide,
Cleft in his view the enormous banks divide;
Ascending sails their opening pass pursue,
And waft the sparkling treasures of Peru.

Moxoe resigns his stagnant world of fen,
Allures, rewards the cheerful toils of men,
Leads their long new-made rivers round his reign,
Drives off the stench and waves his golden grain,
Feeds a whole nation from his cultured shore,
Where not a bird could skim the skies before.

From Mohawk's mouth, far westing with the sun,
Thro all the midlands recent channels run,
Tap the redundant lakes, the broad hills brave,
And Hudson marry with Missouri's wave.
From dim Superior, whose uncounted sails
Shade his full seas and bosom all his gales,
New paths unfolding seek Mackensie's tide,
And towns and empires rise along their side;
Slave's crystal highways all his north adorn,
Like coruscations from the boreal morn.
Proud Missisippi, tamed and taught his road,
Flings forth irriguous from his generous flood
Ten thousand watery glades; that, round him curl'd,
Vein the broad bosom of the western world.

From the red banks of Arab's odorous tide
Their Isthmus opens, and strange waters glide;
Europe from all her shores, with crowded sails,
Looks thro the pass and calls the Asian gales.

Volga and Obi distant oceans join,
Delighted Danube weds the wasting Rhine;
Elbe, Oder, Neister channel many a plain,
Exchange their barks and try each other's main.
All infant streams and every mountain rill
Choose their new paths, some useful task to fill,
Each acre irrigate, re-road the earth,
And serve at last the purpose of their birth.
  Earth, garden'd all, a tenfold burden brings;
Her fruits, her odors, her salubrious springs
Swell, breathe and bubble from the soil they grace,
String with strong nerves the renovating race,
Their numbers multiply in every land,
Their toils diminish and their powers expand;
And while she rears them with a statelier frame
Their soul she kindles with diviner flame,
Leads their bright intellect with fervid glow
Thro all the mass of things that still remains to know.
  He saw the aspiring genius of the age
Soar in the Bard and strengthen in the Sage:
The Bard with bolder hand assumes the lyre,
Warms the glad nations with unwonted fire,
Attunes to virtue all the tones that roll
Their tides of transport thro the expanding soul.

For him no more, beneath their furious gods,
Old ocean crimsons and Olympus nods,
Uprooted mountains sweep the dark profound,
Or Titans groan beneath the rending ground.
No more his clangor maddens up the mind
To crush, to conquer and enslave mankind,
To build on ruin'd realms the shrines of fame,
And load his numbers with a tyrant's name.
Far nobler objects animate his tongue,
And give new energies to epic song;
To moral charms he bids the world attend,
Fraternal states their mutual ties extend,
O'er cultured earth the rage of conquest cease,
War sink in night and nature smile in peace.
Soaring with science then he learns to string
Her highest harp, and brace her broadest wing,
With her own force to fray the paths untrod,
With her own glance to ken the total God,
Thro heavens o'ercanopied by heavens behold
New suns ascend and other skies unfold,
Social and system'd worlds around him shine,
And lift his living strains to harmony divine.
  The Sage with steadier lights directs his ken,
Thro twofold nature leads the walks of men,

Remoulds her moral and material frames,
Their mutual aids, their sister laws proclaims.
Disease before him with its causes flies,
And boasts no more of sickly soils and skies;
His well-proved codes the healing science aid,
Its base establish and its blessing spread,
With long-wrought life to teach the race to glow,
And vigorous nerves to grace the locks of snow.
From every shape that varying matter gives,
That rests or ripens, vegetates or lives,
His chymic powers new combinations plan,
Yield new creations, finer forms to man,
High springs of health for mind and body trace,
Add force and beauty to the joyous race,
Arm with new engines his adventurous hand,
Stretch o'er these elements his wide command,
Lay the proud storm submissive at his feet,
Change, temper, tame all subterranean heat,
Probe laboring earth and drag from her dark side
The mute volcano, ere its force be tried;
Walk under ocean, ride the buoyant air,
Brew the soft shower, the labor'd land repair,
A fruitful soil o'er sandy deserts spread,
And clothe with culture every mountain's head.

Where system'd realms their mutual glories lend,
And well-taught sires the cares of state attend,
Thro every maze of man they learn to wind,
Note each device that prompts the Proteus mind,
What soft restraints the temper'd breast requires,
To taste new joys and cherish new desires,
Expand the selfish to the social flame,
And rear the soul to deeds of nobler fame.

They mark, in all the past records of praise,
What partial views heroic zeal could raise;
What mighty states on others' ruins stood,
And built unsafe their haughty seats in blood;
How public virtue's ever borrow'd name
With proud applauses graced the deeds of shame,
Bade each imperial standard wave sublime,
And wild ambition havoc every clime;
From chief to chief the kindling spirit ran,
Heirs of false fame and enemies of man.

Where Grecian states in even balance hung,
And warm'd with jealous fires the patriot's tongue,
The exclusive ardor cherish'd in the breast
Love to one land and hatred to the rest.
And where the flames of civil discord rage,
And Roman arms with Roman arms engage,

The mime of virtue rises still the same,
To build a Cesar's as a Pompey's name.
But now no more the patriotic mind,
To narrow views and local laws confined,
Gainst neighboring lands directs the public rage,
Plods for a clan or counsels for an age;
But soars to loftier thoughts, and reaches far
Beyond the power, beyond the wish of war;
For realms and ages forms the general aim,
Makes patriot views and moral views the same,
Works with enlighten'd zeal, to see combined
The strength and happiness of humankind.
Long had Columbus with delighted eyes
Mark'd all the changes that around him rise,
Lived thro descending ages as they roll,
And feasted still the still expanding soul;
When now the peopled regions swell more near,
And a mixt noise tumultuous stuns his ear.
At first, like heavy thunders roll'd in air,
Or the rude shock of cannonading war,
Or waves resounding on the craggy shore,
Hoarse roll'd the loud-toned undulating roar.
But soon the sounds like human voices rise,
All nations pouring undistinguisht cries;

Till more distinct the wide concussion grown
Rolls forth at times an accent like his own.
By turns the tongues assimilating blend,
And smoother idioms over earth ascend;
Mingling and softening still in every gale,
O'er discord's din harmonious tones prevail.
At last a simple universal sound
Winds thro the welkin, sooths the world around,
From echoing shores in swelling strain replies,
And moves melodious o'er the warbling skies.

Such wild commotions as he heard and view'd,
In fixt astonishment the Hero stood,
And thus besought the Guide: Celestial friend,
What good to man can these dread scenes intend?
Some sore distress attends that boding sound
That breathed hoarse thunder and convulsed the ground.
War sure hath ceased; or have my erring eyes
Misread the glorious visions of the skies?
Tell then, my Seer, if future earthquakes sleep,
Closed in the conscious caverns of the deep,
Waiting the day of vengeance, when to roll
And rock the rending pillars of the pole.
Or tell if aught more dreadful to my race
In these dark signs thy heavenly wisdom trace;

And why the loud discordance melts again
In the smooth glidings of a tuneful strain.
The guardian god replied: Thy fears give o'er;
War's hosted hounds shall havoc earth no more;
No sore distress these signal sounds foredoom,
But give the pledge of peaceful years to come;
The tongues of nations here their accents blend,
Till one pure language thro the world extend.
Thou know'st the tale of Babel; how the skies
Fear'd for their safety as they felt him rise,
Sent unknown jargons mid the laboring bands,
Confused their converse and unnerved their hands,
Dispersed the bickering tribes and drove them far,
From peaceful toil to violence and war;
Bade kings arise with bloody flags unfurl'd,
Bade pride and conquest wander o'er the world,
Taught adverse creeds, commutual hatreds bred,
Till holy homicide the climes o'erspread.
—For that fine apologue, with mystic strain,
Gave like the rest a golden age to man,
Ascribed perfection to his infant state,
Science unsought and all his arts innate;
Supposed the experience of the growing race
Must lead him retrograde and cramp his pace,

Obscure his vision as his lights increast,
And sink him from an angel to a beast.
Tis thus the teachers of despotic sway
Strive in all times to blot the beams of day,
To keep him curb'd, nor let him lift his eyes
To see where happiness, where misery lies.
They lead him blind, and thro the world's broad waste
Perpetual feuds, unceasing shadows cast,
Crush every art that might the mind expand,
And plant with demons every desert land;
That, fixt in straiten'd bounds, the lust of power
May ravage still and still the race devour,
An easy prey the hoodwink'd hordes remain,
And oceans roll and shores extend in vain.
Long have they reign'd; till now the race at last
Shake off their manacles, their blinders cast,
O'errule the crimes their fraudful foes produce,
By ways unseen to serve the happiest use,
Tempt the wide wave, probe every yielding soil,
Fill with their fruits the hardy hand of toil,
Unite their forces, wheel the conquering car,
Deal mutual death, but civilize by war.
Dear-bought the experiment and hard the strife
Of social man, that rear'd his arts to life.

His Passions wild that agitate the mind,
His Reason calm, their watchful guide design'd,
While yet unreconciled, his march restrain,
Mislead the judgment and betray the man.
Fear, his first passion, long maintain'd the sway,
Long shrouded in its glooms the mental ray,
Shook, curb'd, controll'd his intellectual force,
And bore him wild thro many a devious course.
Long had his Reason, with experienced eye,
Perused the book of earth and scaled the sky,
Led fancy, memory, foresight in her train,
And o'er creation stretch'd her vast domain;
Yet would that rival Fear her strength appal;
In that one conflict always sure to fall,
Mild Reason shunn'd the foe she could not brave,
Renounced her empire and remain'd a slave.
  But deathless, tho debased, she still could find
Some beams of truth to pour upon the mind;
And tho she dared no moral code to scan,
Thro physic forms she learnt to lead the man;
To strengthen thus his opening orbs of sight,
And nerve and clear them for a stronger light.
That stronger light, from nature's double codes,
Now springs expanding and his doubts explodes;

All nations catch it, all their tongues combine
To hail the human morn and speak the day divine.
At this blest period, when the total race
Shall speak one language and all truths embrace,
Instruction clear a speedier course shall find,
And open earlier on the infant mind.
No foreign terms shall crowd with barbarous rules
The dull unmeaning pageantry of schools;
Nor dark authorities nor names unknown
Fill the learnt head with ignorance not its own;
But wisdom's eye with beams unclouded shine,
And simplest rules her native charms define;
One living language, one unborrow'd dress
Her boldest flights with fullest force express;
Triumphant virtue, in the garb of truth,
Win a pure passage to the heart of youth,
Pervade all climes where suns or oceans roll,
And warm the world with one great moral soul,
To see, facilitate, attain the scope
Of all their labor and of all their hope.
As early Phosphor, on his silver throne,
Fair type of truth and promise of the sun,
Smiles up the orient in his dew-dipt ray,
Illumes the front of heaven and leads the day;

Thus Physic Science, with exploring eyes,
First o'er the nations bids her beauties rise,
Prepares the glorious way to pour abroad
Her Sister's brighter beams, the purest light of God.
Then Moral Science leads the lively mind
Thro broader fields and pleasures more refined;
Teaches the temper'd soul, at one vast view,
To glance o'er time and look existence thro,
See worlds and worlds, to being's formless end,
With all their hosts on her prime power depend,
Seraphs and suns and systems, as they rise,
Live in her life and kindle from her eyes,
Her cloudless ken, her all-pervading soul
Illume, sublime and harmonize the whole;
Teaches the pride of man its breadth to bound
In one small point of this amazing round,
To shrink and rest where nature fixt its fate,
A line its space, a moment for its date;
Instructs the heart an ampler joy to taste,
And share its feelings with each human breast,
Expand its wish to grasp the total kind
Of sentient soul, of cogitative mind;
Till mutual love commands all strife to cease,
And earth join joyous in the songs of peace.

Thus heard Columbus, eager to behold
The famed Apocalypse its years unfold;
The soul stood speaking thro his gazing eyes,
And thus his voice: Oh let the visions rise!
Command, celestial Guide, from each far pole,
John's vision'd morn to open on my soul,
And raise the scenes, by his reflected light,
Living and glorious to my longing sight.
Let heaven unfolding show the eternal throne,
And all the concave flame in one clear sun;
On clouds of fire, with angels at his side,
The Prince of Peace, the King of Salem ride,
With smiles of love to greet the bridal earth,
Call slumbering ages to a second birth,
With all his white-robed millions fill the train,
And here commence the interminable reign!

Such views, the Saint replies, for sense too bright,
Would seal thy vision in eternal night;
Man cannot face nor seraph power display
The mystic beams of such an awful day.
Enough for thee, that thy delighted mind
Should trace the temporal actions of thy kind;
That time's descending veil should ope so far
Beyond the reach of wretchedness and war,

Till all the paths in nature's sapient plan
Fair in thy presence lead the steps of man,
And form at last, on earth's extended ball,
Union of parts and happiness of all.
To thy glad ken these rolling years have shown
The boundless blessings thy vast labors crown,
That, with the joys of unborn ages blest,
Thy soul exulting may retire to rest.
But see once more! beneath a change of skies,
The last glad visions wait thy raptured eyes.

Eager he look'd. Another train of years
Had roll'd unseen, and brighten'd still their spheres;
Earth more resplendent in the floods of day
Assumed new smiles, and flush'd around him lay.
Green swell the mountains, calm the oceans roll,
Fresh beams of beauty kindle round the pole;
Thro all the range where shores and seas extend,
In tenfold pomp the works of peace ascend.
Robed in the bloom of spring's eternal year,
And ripe with fruits the same glad fields appear;
O'er hills and vales perennial gardens run,
Cities unwall'd stand sparkling to the sun;
The streams all freighted from the bounteous plain
Swell with the load and labor to the main,

Whose stormless waves command a steadier gale
And prop the pinions of a bolder sail:
Sway'd with the floating weight each ocean toils,
And joyous nature's full perfection smiles.
  Fill'd with unfolding fate, the vision'd age
Now leads its actors on a broader stage;
When clothed majestic in the robes of state,
Moved by one voice, in general congress meet
The legates of all empires. Twas the place
Where wretched men first firm'd their wandering pace;
Ere yet beguiled, the dark delirious hordes
Began to fight for altars and for lords;
Nile washes still the soil, and feels once more
The works of wisdom press his peopled shore.
  In this mid site, this monumental clime,
Rear'd by all realms to brave the wrecks of time
A spacious dome swells up, commodious great,
The last resort, the unchanging scene of state.
On rocks of adamant the walls ascend,
Tall columns heave and sky-like arches bend;
Bright o'er the golden roofs the glittering spires
Far in the concave meet the solar fires;
Four blazing fronts, with gates unfolding high,
Look with immortal splendor round the sky:

Hither the delegated sires ascend,
And all the cares of every clime attend.
As that blest band, the guardian guides of heaven,
To whom the care of stars and suns is given,
(When one great circuit shall have proved their spheres,
And time well taught them how to wind their years)
Shall meet in general council; call'd to state
The laws and labors that their charge await;
To learn, to teach, to settle how to hold
Their course more glorious, as their lights unfold:
From all the bounds of space (the mandate known)
They wing their passage to the eternal throne;
Each thro his far dim sky illumes the road,
And sails and centres tow'rd the mount of God;
There, in mid universe, their seats to rear,
Exchange their counsels and their works compare:
So, from all tracts of earth, this gathering throng
In ships and chariots shape their course along,
Reach with unwonted speed the place assign'd
To hear and give the counsels of mankind.
South of the sacred mansion, first resort
The assembled sires, and pass the spacious court.

Here in his porch earth's figured Genius stands,
Truth's mighty mirror poizing in his hands;
Graved on the pedestal and chased in gold,
Man's noblest arts their symbol forms unfold,
His tillage and his trade; with all the store
Of wondrous fabrics and of useful lore:
Labors that fashion to his sovereign sway
Earth's total powers, her soil and air and sea;
Force them to yield their fruits at his known call,
And bear his mandates round the rolling ball.
Beneath the footstool all destructive things,
The mask of priesthood and the mace of kings,
Lie trampled in the dust; for here at last
Fraud, folly, error all their emblems cast.
Each envoy here unloads his wearied hand
Of some old idol from his native land;
One flings a pagod on the mingled heap,
One lays a crescent, one a cross to sleep;
Swords, sceptres, mitres, crowns and globes and stars,
Codes of false fame and stimulants to wars
Sink in the settling mass; since guile began,
These are the agents of the woes of man.
Now the full concourse, where the arches bend,
Pour thro by thousands and their seats ascend.

Far as the centred eye can range around,
Or the deep trumpet's solemn voice resound,
Long rows of reverend sires sublime extend,
And cares of worlds on every brow suspend.
High in the front, for soundest wisdom known,
A sire elect in peerless grandeur shone;
He open'd calm the universal cause,
To give each realm its limit and its laws,
Bid the last breath of tired contention cease,
And bind all regions in the leagues of peace;
Till one confederate, condependent sway
Spread with the sun and bound the walks of day,
One centred system, one all-ruling soul
Live thro the parts and regulate the whole.

Here then, said Hesper, with a blissful smile,
Behold the fruits of thy long years of toil.
To yon bright borders of Atlantic day
Thy swelling pinions led the trackless way,
And taught mankind such useful deeds to dare,
To trace new seas and happy nations rear;
Till by fraternal hands their sails unfurl'd
Have waved at last in union o'er the world.

Then let thy steadfast soul no more complain
Of dangers braved and griefs endured in vain,

Of courts insidious, envy's poison'd stings,
The loss of empire and the frown of kings;
While these broad views thy better thoughts compose
To spurn the malice of insulting foes;
And all the joys descending ages gain,
Repay thy labors and remove thy pain.

THE

COLUMBIAD.

NOTES.

Tho it would be more convenient to the reader to find some of these notes, especially the shorter ones, at the bottom of the pages to which they refer, yet most of them are of such a length as would render that mode of placing them disadvantageous to the symmetry of the pages and the general appearance of the work. It seemed necessary that these should be collected at the end of the Poem; and it was thought proper that the others should not be separated from them.

The notes will probably be found too voluminous for the taste of some readers; but others would doubtless be better pleased to see them still augmented, as several of the philosophical subjects and historical references are left unexplained. Were I to offer apologies in this case, I should hardly know on which side to begin. I will therefore only say that in this appendage, as in the body of the work, I have aimed, as well as I was able, at blending in due proportions the useful with the agreeable.

THE

COLUMBIAD.

NOTES.

No. 1.

One gentle guardian once could shield the brave;
But now that guardian slumbers in the grave.

Book I. Line 105.

The death of queen Isabella, which happened before the last return of Columbus from America, was a subject of great sorrow to him. In her he lost his only powerful friend in Spain, on whose influence he was accustomed to rely in counteracting the perpetual intrigues of a host of enemies, whose rank and fortune gave them a high standing at the court of Valladolid. Their situation and connexions must have commanded a weight of authority not easily resisted by an individual foreigner, however illustrious from his merit.

It was a grievous reflection for Columbus that his services, tho great in themselves and unequalled in their consequences to the world, had been performed in an age and for a nation which knew not their value, as well as for an ungrateful monarch who chose to disregard them.

No. 2.

As, awed to silence, savage bands gave place,
And hail'd with joy the sun-descended race.

Book I. Line 243.

The original inhabitants of Hispaniola were worshippers of the sun. The Europeans, when they first landed there, were supposed by them to be gods, and consequently descended from the sun. See the subject of solar worship treated more at large in a subsequent note.

No. 3.

High lantern'd in his heaven the cloudless White
Heaves the glad sailor an eternal light;
Book I. Line 333.

The White Mountain of Newhampshire, tho eighty miles from the sea, is the first land to be discovered in approaching that part of the coast of North America. It serves as a land-mark for a considerable length of coast, of difficult navigation.

No. 4.

Whirl'd from the monstrous Andes' bursting sides,
Maragnon leads his congregating tides;
Book I. Line 365.

This river, from different circumstances, has obtained several different names. It has been called Amazon, from an idea that some part of the neighboring country was inhabited by a race of warlike women, resembling what Herodotus relates of the Amazons of Scythia. It has been called Orellana, from its having been discovered by a Spanish officer of that name, who, on a certain expedition, deserted from the younger Pizarro on one of the sources of this river, and navigated it from thence to the ocean. Maragnon is the original name given it by the natives; which name I choose to follow.

If we estimate its magnitude by the length of its course and the quantity of water it throws into the sea, it is much the greatest river that has hitherto come to our knowledge. Its navigation is said by Condamine and others to be uninterrupted for four thousand miles from the sea. Its breadth, within the banks, is sixty geographical miles; it receives in its course a variety of great rivers, besides those described in the text. Many of these descend from elevated countries and mountains covered with snow, the melting of which annually swells the Maragnon above its banks; when it overflows and fertilizes a vast extent of territory.

No. 5.

He saw Xaraya's diamond banks unfold,
And Paraguay's deep channel paved with gold.

Book I. Line 435.

Some of the richest diamond mines are found on the banks of the lake Xaraya. The river Paraguay is remarkable for the quantities of gold dust found in its channel. The Rio de la Plata, properly so called, has its source in the mountains of Potosi; and it was probably from this circumstance that it received its name, which signifies River of Silver. This river, after having joined the Paraguay, which is larger than itself, retains its own name till it reaches the sea. Near the mouth, it is one hundred and fifty miles wide; but in other respects it is far inferior to the Maragnon.

No. 6.

Soon as the distant swell was seen to roll,
His ancient wishes reabsorb'd his soul;

Book I. Line 449.

The great object of Columbus, in most of his voyages, was to discover a western passage to India. He navigated the Gulph of Mexico with particular attention to this object, and was much disappointed in not finding a pass into the South Sea. The view he is here supposed to have of that ocean would therefore naturally recal his former desire of sailing to India.

No. 7.

This idle frith must open soon to fame,
Here a lost Lusitanian fix his name,

Book I. Line 491.

The straits of Magellan, so called from having been discovered by a Portuguese navigator of that name, who first attempted to sail round the world, and lost his life in the attempt.

No. 8.

Say, Palfrey, brave good man, was this thy doom?
Dwells here the secret of thy midsea tomb?
Book I. Line 627.

Colonel Palfrey of Boston was an officer of distinction in the American army during the war of independence. Soon after the war he proposed to visit Europe, and embarked for England; but never more was heard of. The ship probably perished in the ice. His daughter, here alluded to, is now the wife of William Lee, American consul at Bordeaux.

No. 9.

The beasts all whitening roam the lifeless plain,
And caves unfrequent scoop the couch for man.
Book I. Line 753.

The color of animals is acquired partly from the food they eat, thro successive generations, and partly from the objects with which they are usually surrounded. Dr. Darwin has a curious note on this subject, in which he remarks on the advantages that insects and other small animals derive from their color, as a means of rendering them invisible to their more powerful enemies; who thus find it difficult to distinguish them from other objects where they reside. Some animals which inhabit cold countries turn white in winter, when the earth is covered with snow; such as the snowbird of the Alps. Others in snowy regions are habitually white; such as the white bear of Russia.

No. 10.

A different cast the glowing zone demands,
In Paria's blooms, from Tombut's burning sands.
Book II. Line 97.

Paria is a fertile country near the river Orinoco; the only

part of the continent of America that Columbus had seen. Tombut, in the same latitude, is the most sterile part of Africa. America embraces a greater compass of latitude by many degrees than the other continent; and yet its inhabitants present a much less variety in their physical and moral character. When shall we be able to account for this fact?

No. 11.

Yet when the hordes to happy nations rise,
And earth by culture warms the genial skies,

Book II. Line 119.

Without entering into any discussion on the theory of heat and cold (a point not yet settled in our academies) I would just observe, in vindication of the expression in the text, that some solid matter, such for instance as the surface of the earth, seems absolutely necessary to the production of heat. At least it must be a matter more compact than that of the sun's rays; and perhaps its power of producing heat is in proportion to its solidity.

The warmth communicated to the atmosphere is doubtless produced by the combined causes of the earth and the sun; but the agency of the former is probably more powerful in this operation than that of the latter, and its presence more indispensable. For masses of matter will produce heat by friction, without the aid of the sun; but no experiment has yet proved that the rays of the sun are capable of producing heat without the aid of other and more solid matter. The air is temperate in those cavities of the earth where the sun is the most effectually excluded; whereas the coldest regions yet known to us are the tops of the Andes, where the sun's rays have the most direct operation, being the most vertical and the least obstructed by vapors. Those regions are deprived of heat by being so far removed from the broad surface of the earth; a body that appears requisite to warm the surrounding atmosphere by its cooperation with the action of the sun.

From these principles we may conclude that cultivation, in a woody country, tends to warm the atmosphere and ameliorate a cold climate; as, by removing the forests and marshes, it opens the earth to the sun, and allows them to act in conjunction upon the air.

According to the descriptions given of the middle parts of Europe by Cesar and Tacitus, it appears that those countries were much colder in their days than they are at present; cultivation seems to have softened that climate to a great degree. The same effect begins to be perceived in North America. Possibly it may in time become as apparent as the present difference in the temperature of the two continents.

No. 12.

A ruddier hue and deeper shade shall gain,
And stalk, in statelier figures, on the plain.

Book II. Line 127.

The complexion of the inhabitants of North America, who are descended from the English and Dutch, is evidently darker, and their stature taller, than those of the English and Dutch in Europe.

No. 13.

Like Memphian hieroglyphs, to stretch the span
Of memory frail in momentary man.

Book II. Line 287.

We may reckon three stages of improvement in the graphic art, or the art of communicating our thoughts to absent persons and to posterity by visible signs. First, The invention of *painting ideas*, or representing actions, dates and other circumstances of historical fact, by the images of material things, drawn usually on a flat surface, or sometimes carved or moulded in a more solid form. This was the state at which the art had arrived in Egypt before the introduction of letters, and in Mexico before the arrival of the Spaniards. The Greeks in Egypt called it hieroglyphic.

Second, The invention of *painting sounds*, which we do by the use of letters, or the alphabet, and which we call writing. This was a vast improvement; as it simplified in a wonderful degree the communication of thought. For ideas are infinite in number and variety; while the simple sounds we use to convey them to the ear are few, distinct and easy to be understood. It would indeed be impossible to express all our ideas by distinct and visible images. And even if the writer were able to do this, not many readers could be made to understand him; since it would be necessary that every new idea should have a new image invented and agreed upon between the writer and the reader, before it could be used. Which preliminary could not be settled without the writer should see and converse with the reader. And he might as well, in this case, convey his ideas by oral speech; so that his writing could be of little use beyond a certain routine of established signs.

The number of simple sounds in human language, used in discourse, is not above eighteen or twenty; and these are so varied in the succession in which they are uttered, as to express an inconceivable and endless variety of thought and sentiment. Then, by the help of an alphabet of about twenty-six letters or visible signs, these sounds are translated from the ear to the eye; and we are able, by thus painting the sound, to arrest its fleeting nature, render it permanent, and talk with distant nations and future ages, without any previous convention whatever, even supposing them to be ignorant of the language in which we write. This is the present state of the art, as commonly practised in all the countries where an alphabet is used. It is called the art of writing; and to understand it is called reading.

Third, Another invention, which is still in its infancy, is the art of *painting phrases*, or sentences; commonly called short-hand writing. This is yet but little used, and only by a few dexterous persons, who make it a particular study. Probably the true principles on which it ought to be founded are yet to be discovered. But it may be presumed, that in this part of the graphic art there remains to the ingenuity of future generations a course of improvements totally inconceivable to the present; by which the whole train of impressions now made upon the mind by reading a long and well written treatise may be conveyed by a few strokes of the pen, and be received at a glance of the eye. This desideratum would be an abridgment of labor in our mental acquisitions, of which we cannot determine the consequences. It might make, in the progress of human knowledge, an epoch as remarkable as that which was made by the invention of alphabetical writing, and produce as great a change in the mode of transmitting the history of events.

One consequence of the invention of alphabetical writing seems to have been to throw into oblivion all previous historical facts; and it has thus left an immense void, which the imagination knows not how to fill, in contemplating the progress of our race. How many important discoveries, which still remain to our use, must have taken their origin in that space of time which is thus left a void to us! A vast succession of ages, and ages of improvement, must have preceded (for example) the invention of the wheel. The wheel must have been in common use, we know not how long, before alphabetical writing; because we find its image employed in painting ideas, during the first stage of the graphic art above described. The wheel was likewise in use before the mysteries of Ceres or those of Isis were established; as is evident from its being imagined as an instrument of punishment in hell, in the case of Ixion, as represented in those mysteries. The taming of the ox and the horse, the use of the sickle and the bow and arrow, a considerable knowledge of astronomy, and its application to the purposes of agriculture and navigation, with many other circumstances, which show a prodigious improvement, must evidently have preceded the date of the zodiac; a date fixed by Dupuis, with a great degree of probability, at about seventeen thousand years from our time. This epoch would doubtless carry us back many thousand years beyond that of the alphabet; the invention of which was sufficient of itself to obliterate the details of previous history, as the event has proved.

How far the loss of these historical details is to be regretted, as an impediment to our progress in useful knowledge, I will not decide; but in one view, which I am going to state, it may be justly considered as a misfortune.

The art of painting ideas, being arrested in the state in which the use of the alphabet found it, went into general disuse for common purposes; and the works then extant, as well as the knowledge of writing in that mode, being no longer intelligible to the people, became objects of deep and laborious study, and known only to the learned; that is, to the men of leisure and contemplation. These men consequently ran it into mystery; making it a holy object, above the reach of vulgar inquiry. On this ground they established, in the course of ages, a profitable function or profession, in the practice of which a certain portion of men of the brightest talents could make a reputable living; taking care not to initiate more than a limited number of professors; no more than the people could maintain as priests. This mode of writing then assumed the name of hieroglyphic, or *sacred painting*, to distinguish it from that which had now become the vulgar mode of writing, by the use of the alphabet. This is perhaps the source of that ancient, vast and variegated system of false religion, with all its host of errors and miseries, which has so long and so grievously weighed upon the character of human nature.

In noticing the distinction of the three stages in the graphic art above described, I have not mentioned the wonderful powers we derive from it in the language of the mathematics and the language of music. In each of these, though its effects are already astonishing, there is no doubt but great improvements are still to be made. Our present mode of writing in these, as in literature, belongs to the *second* or *alphabetical* stage of the graphic art. The ten ciphers, and the other signs used in the mathematical sciences, form the alphabet in which the language of those sciences is written. The few musical notes, and the other signs which accompany them, furnish an alphabet for writing the language of music.

The mode of writing in China is still different from any of those I have mentioned. The Chinese neither paint ideas nor sounds: but they make a character for every word; which character must vary according to the different inflections and uses of that word. The characters must therefore be insupportably numerous, and be still increasing as the language is enriched with new words by the augmentation and correction of ideas.

The English language is supposed to contain about twelve thousand distinct words, and the Italian about seventeen thousand, in the present state of our sciences. I know not how many the Chinese may contain; but if we were to write our languages in the Chinese method, it would be the business of a whole life for a man to learn his mother tongue, so as to read and write it for his ordinary purposes.

As the Chinese have not adopted an alphabet, but have adhered to an invariable state of the graphic art, which is probably more ancient by several thousand years than our present method, may we not venture to conjecture that the traces of their very ancient history have been, for that reason, better preserved? and that their pretensions to a very high antiquity, which we have been used to think extravagant and ridiculous, are really not without foundation? If so, we might then allow a little more latitude to ourselves, and conclude that we are in fact as old as they, and might have been as sensible of it, if we had adhered to our ancient method of writing; and not changed it for a new one which, while it has facilitated the progress of our science, has humbled our pride of antiquity, by obliterating the dates of those labors and improvements of our early progenitors, to which we are indebted for more of the rudiments of our sciences and our arts than we usually imagine.

It is much to be regretted, that the Spanish devastation in Mexico and Peru was so universal as to leave us but few monuments of the history of the human mind in those countries, which presented a state of manners so remarkably different from what can be found in any other part of the world. The pictorial writing of the Mexicans, tho sometimes called hieroglyphic, does not appear to merit that name, as it was not exclusively appropriated by the priests to sacred purposes. Indeed it could not be so appropriated till a more convenient method could be discovered and adopted for common purposes. For a thing cannot become sacred, in this sense of the word, until it ceases to be common.

No. 14.

No Bovadilla seize the tempting spoil,
No dark Ovando, no religious Boyle,

Book II. Line 303.

Bovadilla and Ovando are mentioned in the Introduction as the enemies and successors of Columbus in the government of Hispaniola. They began that system of cruelty towards the natives which in a few years almost depopulated that island, and was afterwards pursued by Cortez, Pizarro and others, in all the first settlements in Spanish America.

Boyle was a fanatical priest who accompanied Ovando, and, under pretence of christianizing the natives by the sword, gave the sanction of the church to the most shocking and extensive scenes of slaughter.

No. 15.

He gains the shore. Behold his fortress rise,
His fleet high flaming suffocates the skies.

Book II. Line 329.

The conduct of Cortez, when he first landed on the coast of Mexico, was as remarkable for that hardy spirit of adventure, to which success gives the name of policy, as his subsequent operations were for cruelty and perfidy. As soon as his army was on shore, he dismantled his fleet of such articles as would be useful in building a new one; he then set fire to his ships, and burnt them in presence of his men; that they might fight their battles with more desperate courage, knowing that it would be impossible to save themselves from a victorious enemy by flight. He constructed a fort, in which the iron and the rigging were preserved.

No. 16.

With cheerful rites their pure devotions pay
To the bright orb that gives the changing day.

Book II. Line 421.

It is worthy of remark, that the countries where the worship of the sun has made the greatest figure are Egypt and Peru; the two regions of the earth the most habitually deprived of rain, and probably of clouds, which in other countries so frequently obstruct his rays and seem to dispute his influence. Tho in the rude ages of society it is certainly natural in all countries to pay adoration to the sun, as one of the visible agents of those changes in the atmosphere which most affect the people's happiness, yet it is reasonable to suppose that this adoration would be more unmixed, and consequently more durable, in climates where the agency of the sun appears unrivalled and supreme.

On the supposition that Greece and Western Asia, regions whose early traditions are best known to us, derived their first theological ideas from Egypt, it is curious to observe how the pure heliosebia of Egypt degenerated in those climates in proportion as other visible agents seemed to exert their influence in human affairs. Greece is a mountainous country, subject to a great deal of lightning and other meteors, whose effects are tremendous and make stronger impressions on rude savages than the gentle energies of the sun.

The Greeks therefore, having forgotten the source of their religious system, ceased to consider the sun as their supreme god; his agency being, in their opinion, subject to a more potent divinity, the Power of the air or Jupiter, whom they styled the Thunderer. So that Apollo, the god of light, became, in their mythology, the subject and offspring of the supreme god of the atmosphere. This religion became extremely confused and complicated with new fables, according to the temperature and other accidents of the different climates thro which it passed. The god of thunder obtained the supreme veneration generally in Europe; known in the south by the name of Jupiter or Zeus, and in the north by that of Thor.

Europe in general has an uneven surface and a vapory sky, liable to great concussions in the lower regions of the atmosphere which border the habitation of man. There is no wonder that in such a region the god of the air should appear more powerful than the god of light. This disposition of the elements has given a gloomy cast to the mind, and in the north more than in the south. The Thor of the Celtic nations was more tremendous, more feared and less beloved, than the Jupiter of the Greeks and Romans; he was worshipped accordingly with more bloody sacrifices. But in all Europe, Western Asia and the northwestern coast of Africa, where the earth is uneven and the climate variable, their religion was more gloomy and their gods more ferocious than among the ancient Egyptians.

A like difference is observed in the religions of the two countries in America where civilization was most advanced before the arrival of the Spaniards. Peru enjoyed a climate of great serenity and regularity. Of all the sensible agents that operated on the earth and air, the sun was apparently the most uniform and energetic. The worship of the sun was therefore the most predominant and durable; and it inspired a mildness of manners analogous to his mild and beneficent influence. In Mexico and other uneven countries, where storms and earthquakes were frequent, the sun, altho he was reckoned among their deities, was not considered so powerful as those of a more boisterous and maleficent nature. The Mexican worship was therefore addressed chiefly to ferocious beings, enemies to human happiness, who delighted in the tears and blood of their votaries. The difference in the moral cast of religion in Peru and Mexico, as well as in Egypt and Greece, must have been greatly owing to climate. Indeed in what else should it be found? since the origin of religious ideas must have been in the energies of those visible agents which form the distinctive character of climates.

No. 17.

Long is the tale; but tho their labors rest
By years obscured, in flowery fiction drest,
Book II. Line 455.

The traditions respecting these founders of the Peruvian empire are indeed obscure; but they excite in us the same sort of veneration that we feel for the most amiable and distinguished characters of remote antiquity. The honest zeal of Garcilasso de la Vega in collecting these traditions into one body of history, as a probable series of facts, is to be applauded; since he has there presented us with one of the most striking examples of the *beau ideal* in political character, that can be found in the whole range of literature. He treats his subject with more natural simplicity, tho with less talent, than Plutarch or Xenophon, when they undertake a similar task, that of drawing traditional characters to fill up the middle space between fable and history.

With regard to the true position that the portrait of Manco Capac ought to hold in this middle space, how near it should stand to history and how near to fable, we should find it difficult to say, and perhaps useless to inquire. Plutarch has gravely given us the lives and actions of several heroes who are evidently more fabulous than Capac, and of others who should be placed on the same line with him. The existence of Theseus, Romulus and Numa is more doubtful and their actions less probable than his. The character of Capac, in regard to its reality, stands on a parallel with that of the Lycurgus of Plutarch and the Cyrus of Xenophon; not purely historical nor purely fabulous, but presented to us as a compendium of those talents and labors which might possibly be crowded into the capacity of one mind, and be achieved in one life, but which more probably belong to several generations; the talents and labors that could reduce a great number of ferocious tribes into one peaceable and industrious state.

Garcilasso was himself an Inca by maternal descent, born and educated at Cusco after the Spanish conquest. He writes apparently with the most scrupulous regard to truth, with little judgment and no ornament. He discovers a credulous zeal to throw a lustre on his remote ancestor Manco Capac, not by inventing new incidents, but by collecting with great industry all that had been recorded in the annals of the family. And their manner of recording events, tho not so perfect as that of writing, was not so liable to error as traditions merely oral, like those of the Caledonian and other Celtic bards, with respect to the ancient heroes of their countries.

His account states, that about four centuries previous to the discovery of that country by the Spaniards, the natives of Peru were as rude savages as any in America. They had no fixed habitations, no ideas of permanent property; they wandered naked like the beasts, and like them depended on the events of each day for a subsistence. At this period Manco Capac and his wife Mama Oella appeared on a small island in the lake Titiaca, near which the city of Cusco was afterwards built. These persons, to establish a belief of their divinity in the minds of the people, were clothed in white garments of cotton, and declared themselves descended from the sun, who was their father and the god of that country. They affirmed that he was offended at their cruel and perpetual wars, their barbarous modes of worship, and their neglecting to make the best use of the blessings he was constantly bestowing, in fertilizing the earth and producing vegetation; that he pitied their wretched state, and had sent his own children to instruct them and to establish a number of wise regulations, by which they might be rendered happy.

By some uncommon method of persuasion, these persons drew

together a few of the savage tribes, laid the foundation of the city of Cusco, and established what is called the kingdom of the Sun, or the Peruvian empire. In the reign of Manco Capac, the dominion was extended about eight leagues from the city; and at the end of four centuries it was established fifteen hundred miles on the coast of the Pacific ocean, and from that ocean to the Andes. During this period, thro a succession of twelve monarchs, the original constitution, established by the first Inca, remained unaltered; and this constitution, with the empire itself, was at last overturned by an accident which no human wisdom could foresee or prevent.

For a more particular detail of the character and institutions of this extraordinary personage the reader is referred to a subsequent note, in which he will find a dissertation on that subject.

In the passage preceding this reference, I have alluded to the fabulous traditions relating to these children of the sun. In the remainder of the second and thro the whole of the third book, I have given what may be supposed a probable narrative of their real origin and actions. The space allowed to this episode may appear too considerable in a poem whose principal object is so different. But it may be useful to exhibit in action the manners and sentiments of savage tribes, whose aliment is war; that the contrast may show more forcibly the advantages of civilized life, whose aliment is peace.

No. 18.

Long robes of white my shoulders must embrace,
To speak my lineage of ethereal race;

Book II. Line 553.

As the art of spinning is said to have been invented by Oella, it is no improbable fiction to imagine that they first assumed these white garments of cotton as an emblem of the sun, in order to inspire that reverence for their persons which was necessary to their success. Such a dress may likewise be supposed to have continued in the family as a badge of royalty.

No. 19.

DISSERTATION ON THE INSTITUTIONS OF MANCO CAPAC.

For the end of Book II.

Altho the original inhabitants of America in general deserve to be classed among the most unimproved savages that had been discovered before those of New Holland, yet the Mexican and Peruvian governments exhibited remarkable exceptions, and seemed to be fast approaching to a state of civilization. In the difference of national character between the people of these two empires we may discern the influence of political systems on the human mind, and infer the importance of the task which a legislator undertakes, in attempting to reduce a barbarous people under the control of government and laws.

The Mexican constitution was formed to render its subjects brave and powerful; but, while it succeeded in this object, it kept them far removed from the real blessings of society. According to the Spanish accounts (which for an obvious reason may however be suspected of exaggeration) the manners of the Mexicans were uncommonly ferocious, and their religion gloomy, sanguinary, and unrelenting. But the establishments of Manco Capac, if we may follow Garcilasso in attributing the whole of the Peruvian constitution to that wonderful personage, present the aspect of a most benevolent and pacific system; they tended to humanize the world and render his people happy; while his ideas of deity were so elevated as to bear a comparison with the sublime doctrines of Socrates or Plato.

The characters, whether real or fabulous, who are the most distinguished as lawgivers among barbarous nations, are Moses, Lycurgus, Solon, Numa, Mahomet, and Peter of Russia. Of these, only the two former and the two latter appear really to deserve the character of lawgivers. Solon and Numa possessed not the opportunity of showing their talents in the work of original legislation. Athens and Rome were considerably civilized before these persons arose. The most they could do was to correct and amend constitutions already formed. Solon may be considered as a wise politician, but by no means as the founder of a nation. The Athenians were too far advanced in society to admit any radical change in their form of government; unless recourse could have been had to the representative system, by establishing an equality of rank, and instructing all the people in their duties and their rights; a system which was never understood by any ancient legislator.

The institutions of Numa (if such a person as Numa really existed) were more effective and durable. His religious ceremonies were, for many ages, the most powerful check on the licentious and turbulent Romans, the greater part of whom were ignorant slaves. By inculcating a remarkable reverence for the gods, and making it necessary to consult the auspices when any thing important was to be transacted, his object was to render the popular superstition subservient to the views of policy, and thus to give the senate a steady check upon the plebeians. But the constitutions of Rome and Athens, notwithstanding the abundant applause that has been bestowed upon them, were never fixed on any permanent principles; tho the wisdom of some of their rulers, and the spirit of liberty that inspired the citizens, may justly demand our admiration.

Each of the other legislators above mentioned deserves a particular consideration, as having acted in stations somewhat similar to that of the Peruvian patriarch. Three objects are to be attended to by the legislator of a barbarous people: First, That his system be such as is capable of reducing the greatest number of men under one jurisdiction: Second, That it apply to such principles in human nature for its support as are universal and permanent, in order to insure the duration of the government: Third, That it admit of improvements correspondent to any advancement in knowledge or variation of circumstances that may happen to its subjects, without endangering the principle of government by such innovations. So far as the systems of such legislators agree with these fundamental principles, they are worthy of respect; and so far as they deviate, they may be considered as defective.

To begin with Moses and Lycurgus: It is proper to observe that, in order to judge of the merit of any institutions, we must take into view the peculiar character of the people for whom they were framed. For want of this attention, many of the laws of Moses and some of those of Lycurgus have been ridiculed and censured. The Jews, when led by Moses out of Egypt, were not only uncivilized, but having just risen to independence from a state of servitude they united the manners of servants and savages; and their national character was a compound of servility, ignorance, filthiness and cruelty. Of their cruelty as a people we need no other proof than the account of their avengers of blood, and the readiness with which the whole congregation turned executioners, and stoned to death the devoted offenders. The leprosy, a disease now scarcely known, was undoubtedly produced by a want of cleanliness continued for successive generations. In this view, their frequent ablutions, their peculiar modes of trial and several other institutions, may be vindicated from ridicule and proved to be wise regulations.

The Spartan lawgiver has been censured for the toleration of theft and adultery. Among that race of barbarians these habits were too general to admit of total prevention or universal punishment. By vesting all property in the commonwealth, instead of encouraging theft, he removed the possibility of the crime; and, in a nation where licentiousness was generally indulged, it was a great step towards introducing a purity of manners, to punish adultery in all cases wherein it was committed without the consent of all parties interested in its consequences.

Until the institution of representative republics, which are of recent date, it was found that those constitutions of government were best calculated for immediate energy and duration, which were interwoven with some religious system. The legislator who appears in the character of an inspired person renders his political institutions sacred, and interests the conscience as well as the judgment in their support. The Jewish lawgiver had this advantage over the Spartan: he appeared not in the character of a mere earthly governor, but as an interpreter of the divine will. By enjoining a religious observance of certain rites he formed his people to habitual obedience; by directing their cruelty against the breakers of the laws he at least mitigated the rancor of private hatred; by directing that real property should return to the original families in the year of Jubilee he prevented too great an equality of wealth; and by selecting a single tribe to be the interpreters of religion he prevented its mysteries from being the subject of profane and vulgar investigation. With a view of securing the permanence of his institutions, he prohibited intercourse with foreigners by severe restrictions, and formed his people to habits and a character disagreeable to other nations; so that any foreign intercourse was prevented by the mutual hatred of both parties.

To these institutions the laws of Lycurgus bear a striking resemblance. The features of his constitution were severe and forbidding; it was however calculated to inspire the most enthusiastic love of liberty and martial honor. In no country was the patriotic passion more energetic than in Sparta; no laws ever excluded the idea of separate property in an equal degree, or inspired a greater contempt for the manners of other nations. The prohibition of money, commerce and almost every thing desirable to effeminate nations, excluded foreigners from Sparta; and while it inspired the people with contempt for strangers it made them agreeable to each other. By these means Lycurgus rendered the nation warlike; and to insure the duration of the government he endeavored to interest the consciences of his people by the aid of oracles, and by the oath he is said to have exacted from them to obey his laws till his return, when he went into perpetual exile.

From this view of the Jewish and Spartan institutions, applied to the principles before stated, they appear in the two first articles considerably imperfect, and in the last totally defective.

Neither of them was calculated to bring any considerable territory or number of men under one jurisdiction; from this circumstance alone they could not be rendered permanent, as nations so restricted in their means of extension must be constantly exposed to their more powerful neighbors. But the third object of legislation, that of providing for the future progress of society, which as it regards the happiness of mankind is the most important of the three, was in both instances entirely neglected. These symptoms appear to have been formed with an express design to prevent future improvement in knowledge or enlargement of the human mind, and to fix those nations in a state of ignorance and barbarism. To vindicate their authors from an imputation of weakness or inattention in this particular, it may be urged that they were each of them surrounded by nations more powerful than their own; it was therefore perhaps impossible for them to commence an establishment upon any other plan.

The institutions of Mahomet are next to be considered. The first object of legislation appears to have been better understood by him than by either of the preceding sages; his jurisdiction was capable of being enlarged to any extent of territory, and governing any number of nations that might be subjugated by his enthusiastic armies; and his system of religion was admirably calculated to attain this object. Like Moses, he convinced his people that he acted as the vicegerent of God; but with this advantage, adapting his religion to the natural feelings and propensities of mankind, he multiplied his followers by the allurements of pleasure and the promise of a sensual paradise. These circumstances were likewise sure to render his constitution durable. His religious system was so easy to be understood, so splendid and so inviting, there could be no danger that the people would lose sight of its principles, and no necessity of future prophets to explain its doctrines or reform the nation. To these advantages if we add the exact and rigid military discipline, the splendor and sacredness of the monarch, and that total ignorance among the people which such a system will produce and perpetuate, the establishment must have been evidently calculated for a considerable extent and duration. But the last and most important end of government, that of mental improvement and social happiness, was deplorably lost in the institution. There was probably more learning and cultivated genius in Arabia, in the days of this extraordinary man, than can now be found in all the Mahometan dominions.

On the contrary, the enterprising mind of the Russian monarch appears to have been wholly bent on the arts of civilization and the improvement of society among his subjects. Established in a legal title to a throne which already commanded a prodigious extent of country, he found the first object of government already secured; and by applying himself with great sagacity to the third object, that of improving his people, it was reasonable to suppose that the second, the durability of his system, would become a necessary consequence. He effected his purposes, important as they were, merely by the introduction of the arts and the encouragement of politer manners. The greatness of his character appears not so much in his institutions, which he copied from other nations, as in the extraordinary measures he followed to introduce them, the judgment he showed in selecting and adapting them to the genius of his subjects, and the surprising assiduity by which he raised a savage people to an elevated rank among European nations.

To the nature and operation of the several forms of government above mentioned I will compare that of the Peruvian lawgiver. I have observed in a preceding note that the knowledge we have of Manco Capac is necessarily imperfect and obscure, derived thro traditions and family registers (without the aid of writing) for four hundred years; from the time he is supposed to have lived, till that of his historian and descendant, Inca Garcilasso de la Vega. About an equal interval elapsed from the supposed epoch of the first kings of Rome to that of their first historians; a longer space from Lycurgus to Herodotus; probably not a shorter one from the time of the great Cyrus to that of Xenophon, author of the elegant romance on the actions of that hero.

I recal the reader's attention to these comparisons, not with a view of contending that our accounts of the actions ascribed to Capac are derived from authentic records, and that he is a subject of real history, like Mahomet or Peter; but to show that, our channels of information with regard to him being equally respectable with those that have brought us acquainted with the classical and venerable names of Lycurgus, Romulus, Numa and Cyrus, we may be as correct in our reasonings from the modern as from the ancient source of reference, and fancy ourselves treading a ground as sacred on the tomb of the western patriarch, as on those more frequented and less scrutinized in the east, consecrated to the demigods of Sparta, Rome and Persia.

It is probable that the savages of Peru before the time of Capac, among other objects of adoration, paid homage to the sun. By availing himself of this popular sentiment he appeared, like Moses and Mahomet, in the character of a divine legislator endowed with supernatural powers. After impressing these ideas on the minds of the people, drawing together a number of the tribes and rendering them subservient to his benevolent purposes, he applied himself to forming the outlines of a plan of policy capable of founding and regulating an extensive empire, wisely calculated for long duration, and well adapted to improve the knowledge, peace and happiness of a considerable portion of mankind. In the allotment of the lands as private property he invented a mode somewhat resembling the feudal system of Europe: yet this system was checked in its operation by a law similar to that of Moses which regulated landed possessions in the year of Jubilee. He divided the lands into three parts; the first was consecrated to the uses of religion, as it was from the sacerdotal part of his system that he doubtless expected its most powerful support. The second portion was set apart for the Inca and his family, to enable him to defray the expenses of government and appear in the style of a monarch. The third and largest portion was allotted to the people; which allotment was repeated every year, and varied according to the number and exigences of each family.

As the Incan race appeared in the character of divinities, it seemed necessary that a subordination of rank should be established, to render the distinction between the monarch and his people more perceptible. With this view he created a band of nobles, who were distinguished by personal and hereditary honors. These were united to the monarch by the strongest ties of interest; in peace they acted as judges and superintended the police of the empire; in war they commanded in the armies. The next order of men were the respectable landholders and cultivators, who composed the principal strength of the nation. Below these was a class of men who were the servants of the public and cultivated the public lands. They possessed no property, and their security depended on their regular industry and peaceable demeanor. Above all these orders were the Incà and his family. He possessed absolute and uncontrolable power; his mandates were regarded as the word of heaven, and the double guilt of impiety and rebellion attended on disobedience.

To impress the utmost veneration for the Incan family, it was a fundamental principle that the royal blood should never be contaminated by any foreign alliance. The mysteries of religion were preserved sacred by the high priest of the royal family under the control of the king, and celebrated with rites capable of making the deepest impression on the multitude. The annual distribution of the lands, while it provided for the varying circumstances of each family, was designed to strengthen the bands of society by perpetuating that distinction of rank among the orders which is supposed necessary to a monarchical government; the peasants could not vie with their superiors, and the nobles could not be subjected by misfortune to a subordinate station. A constant habit of industry was inculcated upon all ranks by the force of example. The cultivation of the soil, which in most other countries is considered as one of the lowest employments, was here regarded as a divine art. Having had no knowledge of it before, and being taught it by the children of their god, the people viewed it as a sacred privilege, a national honor, to assist the sun in opening the bosom of the earth to produce vegetation. That the government might be able to exercise the endearing acts of beneficence, the produce of the public lands was reserved in magazines, to supply the wants of the unfortunate and as a resource in case of scarcity or invasion.

These are the outlines of a government the most simple and energetic, and at least as capable as any monarchy within our knowledge of reducing great and populous countries under one jurisdiction; at the same time, accommodating its principle of action to every stage of improvement, by a singular and happy application to the passions of the human mind, it encouraged the advancement of knowledge without being endangered by success.

In the traits of character which distinguish this institution we may discern all the great principles of each of the legislators above mentioned. The pretensions of Capac to divine authority were as artfully contrived and as effectual in their consequences as those of Mahomet; his exploding the worship of evil beings and objects of terror, forbidding human sacrifices and accommodating the rites of worship to a god of justice and benevolence, produced a greater change in the national character of his people than the laws of Moses did in his; like Peter he provided for the future improvement of society, while his actions were never measured on the contracted scale which limited the genius of Lycurgus.

Thus far we find that altho the political system of Capac did not embrace that extensive scope of human nature which is necessary in forming republican institutions, and which can be drawn only from long and well recorded experience of the passions and tendencies of social man, yet it must be pronounced at least equal to those of the most celebrated monarchical lawgivers, whether ancient or modern. But in some things his mind seems to have attained an elevation with which few of theirs will bear a comparison; I mean in his religious institutions, and the exalted ideas he had formed of the agency and attributes of supernatural beings.

From what source he could have drawn these ideas it is difficult to form a satisfactory conjecture. The worship of the sun is so natural to an early state of society, in a mild climate with a clear atmosphere, that it may be as reasonable to suppose it would originate in Peru as in Egypt or Persia; where we find that a similar worship did originate and was wrought into a splendid system; whence it was probably extended, with various modifications, over most of the ancient world.

Or if we reject this theory, and suppose that only one nation, from some circumstance peculiar to itself, could create the materials of such a system, and has consequently had the privilege of giving its religion to the human race; we may in this case imagine that the Phenicians (who colonized Cadiz and other places in the west of Europe, at the time when they possessed the solar worship in all its glory) must have had a vessel driven across the Atlantic; and thus conveyed a stock of inhabitants, with their own religious ideas, to the western continent.

The first theory is doubtless the most plausible. And the mild regions of Peru, for the reasons mentioned in a former note, became, like Egypt, the seat of an institution so congenial to its climate. But in more boisterous climates, where storms and other violent agents prevail, many different fables have wrought themselves into the system, as remarked in the same note; and the solar religion in such countries has generally lost its name and the more beneficent parts of its influence. Being thus corrupted, religion in almost every part of the earth assumed a gloomy and sanguinary character.

Savage nations create their gods from such materials as they have at hand, the most striking to their senses. And these are in general an assemblage of destructive attributes. They usually form no idea of a general superintending providence ; they consider not their god as the author of their beings, the creator of the world and the dispenser of the happiness they enjoy ; they discern him not in the usual course of nature, in the sunshine and in the shower, the productions of the earth and the blessing of society ; they find a deity only in the storm, the earthquake and the whirlwind, or ascribe to him the evils of pestilence and famine ; they consider him as interposing in wrath to change the course of nature and exercise the attributes of rage and revenge. They adore him with rites suited to these attributes, with horror, with penance and with sacrifice ; they imagine him pleased with the severity of their mortifications, with the oblations of blood and the cries of human victims ; and they hope to compound for greater judgments by voluntary sufferings and horrid sacrifices, suited to the relish of his taste.

Perhaps no single criterion can be given which will determine more accurately the state of society in any age or nation than their general ideas concerning the nature and attributes of deity. In the most enlightened periods of antiquity, only a few of their philosophers, a Socrates, Tully or Confucius, ever formed a rational idea on the subject, or described a god of purity, justice and benevolence. But Capac, erecting his institutions in a country where the visible agents of nature inspired more satisfactory feelings, adopted a milder system. As the sun, with its undisturbed influence, seemed to point itself out as the supreme controller and vital principle of nature, he formed the idea, as the Egyptians had done before, of constituting that luminary the chief object of adoration. He taught the nation to consider the sun as the parent of the universe, the god of order and regularity ; ascribing to his influence the rotation of the seasons, the productions of the earth and the blessings of health ; especially attributing to his inspiration the wisdom of their laws, and that happy constitution which was the delight and veneration of the people.

A system so just and benevolent, as might be expected, was

attended with success. In about four centuries the dominion of the Incas had extended fifteen hundred miles in length, and had introduced peace and prosperity thro the whole region. The arts of society had been carried to a considerable degree of improvement, and the authority of the Incan race universally acknowledged, when an event happened which disturbed the tranquillity of the empire. Huana Capac, the twelfth monarch, had reduced the powerful kingdom of Quito and annexed it to his dominions. To conciliate the affections of his new subjects, he married a daughter of the ancient king of Quito, who was not of the race of Incas. Thus, by violating a fundamental law of the empire, he left at his death a disputed succession to the throne. Atabalipa, the son of Huana by the heiress of Quito, being in possession of the principal force of the Peruvian armies, left at that place on the death of his father, gave battle to his brother Huascar, who was the elder son of Huana by a lawful wife, and legal heir to the crown.

After a long and destructive civil war the former was victorious; and thus was that flourishing kingdom left a prey to regal dissensions and to the few soldiers of Pizarro, who happened at that juncture to make a descent upon the coast. In this manner he effected an easy conquest and an utter destruction of a numerous, brave, unfortunate people.

It is however obvious that this deplorable event is not to be charged on Capac, as the consequence of any defect in his institution. It is impossible that an original legislator should effectually guard against the folly of all future sovereigns. Capac had not only removed every temptation that could induce a wise prince to wish for a change in the constitution, but had connected the ruin of his authority with the change; for he who disregards any part of institutions deemed sacred teaches his people to consider the whole as an imposture. Had he made a law ordaining that the Peruvians should be absolved from their allegiance to a prince who should violate the laws, it would have implied possible error and imperfection in those persons whom the people were ordered to regard as divinities; the reverence due to characters who made such high pretensions would have been weakened; aud instead of rendering the constitution perfect, such a law would have been its greatest defect. Besides, it is probable the rupture might have been healed and the succession settled, with as little difficulty as frequently happens with partial revolutions in other kingdoms, had not the descent of the Spaniards prevented it. And this event, for that age and country, must have been beyond the possibility of human foresight. But viewing the concurrence of these fatal accidents, which reduced this flourishing empire to a level with many other ruined and departed kingdoms, it only furnishes an additional proof that no political system has yet had the privilege to be perfect.

On the whole it is evident that the system of Capac (if the Peruvian constitution may be so called) is one of the greatest exertions of genius to be found in the history of mankind. When we consider him as an individual emerging from the midst of a barbarous people, having seen no example of the operation of laws in any country, originating a plan of religion and policy never equalled by the sages of antiquity, civilizing an extensive empire and rendering religion and government subservient to the general happiness of a great people, there is no danger that we grow too warm in his praise, or pronounce too high an eulogium on his character.

No. 20.

Bade yon tall temple grace their favorite isle,
The mines unfold, the cultured valleys smile,

Book III. Line 5.

One of the great temples of the sun was built on an island in the lake Titiaca near Cusco, to consecrate the spot of ground where Capac and Oella first made their appearance and claimed divine honors as children of the sun.

No. 21.

His eldest hope, young Rocha, at his call,
Resigns his charge within the temple wall;
Book III. Line 29.

The high priest of the sun was always one of the royal family; and in every generation after the first, was brother to the king. This office probably began with Rocha; as he was the first who was capable of receiving it, and as it was necessary, in the education of the prince, that he should be initiated in the sacred mysteries.

No. 22.

A pearl-dropt girdle bound his waist below,
And the white lautu graced his lofty brow.
Book III. Line 135.

The lautu was a cotton band, twisted and worn on the head of the Incas as a badge of royalty. It made several turns round the head; and, according to the description of Garcilasso, it must have resembled the Turkish turban.

It is possible that both the lautu and the turban had their remote origin in the ancient astronomical religion, whose principal god was the sun and usually represented under the figure of a man with the horns of the ram; that is, the sun in the sign of aries. The form of the lautu and of the turban (which I suppose to be the same) seems to indicate that they were originally designed as emblems or badges; and when properly twisted and wound round the head, as Turks of distinction usually wear the turban, they resemble the horns of the ram as represented in those figures of Jupiter Ammon where the horns curl close to the head.

There is an engraving in Garcilasso representing the first Inca and his wife, Capac and Oella; and the heads of both are ornamented with rams' horns projecting out from the lautu. Whether the figures of these personages were usually so represented in Peru previous to the Spanish devastation, would be difficult at this day to ascertain. If it could be ascertained that they were usually so represented there, we might esteem it a remarkable circumstance in proof of the unity of the origin of their religion with that of the ancient Egyptians; from which all the early theological systems of Asia and Europe, as far as they have come to our knowledge, were evidently derived.

No. 23.

Receive, O dreadful Power, from feeble age,
This last pure offering to thy sateless rage;

Book III. Line 181.

Garcilasso declares that the different tribes of those mountain savages worshipped the various objects of terror that annoyed the particular parts of the country where they dwelt; such as storms, volcanos, rivers, lakes, and several beasts and birds of prey. All of them believed that their forefathers were descended from the gods which they worshipped.

No. 24.

Held to the sun the image from his breast
Whose glowing concave all the god exprest;

Book III. Line 273.

The historian of the Incas relates that, by the laws of the empire, none but sacred fire could be used in sacrifices; and that there were three modes in which it might be procured. First, the most sacred fire was that which was drawn immediately from the sun himself by means of a concave mirror, which was usually made of gold or silver highly polished. Second, in case of cloudy weather or other accident, the fire might be taken from the temple, where it was preserved by the holy virgins;

whose functions and discipline resembled those of the vestals of Rome. Third, when the sacrifice was to be made in the provinces at an inconvenient distance from the temple, and when the weather was such as to prevent drawing the fire immediately from the sun, it was permitted to procure it by the friction of two pieces of dry wood.

The two latter modes were resorted to only in cases of necessity. Not to be able to obtain fire by means of the mirror was a bad omen, a sign of displeasure in the god; it cast a gloom over the whole ceremony and threw the people into lamentations, fearing their offering would not be well received.

This method of procuring fire directly from the sun, to burn a sacrifice, must have appeared so miraculous to the savages who could not understand it, that it doubtless had a powerful effect in converting them to the solar religion and to the Incan government.

No. 25.

Dim Paraguay extends the aching sight,
Xaraya glimmers like the moon of night,
Book III. Line 321.

Xaraya is a lake in the country of Paraguay, and is the principal source of the river Paraguay. This river is the largest branch of the Plata.

No. 26.

The Condor frowning from a southern plain,
Borne on a standard, leads a numerous train:
Book III. Line 421.

The Condor is supposed to be the largest bird of prey hitherto known. His wings, from one extreme to the other, are said to measure fifteen feet; he is able to carry a sheep in his talons, and he sometimes attacks men. He inhabits the high mountains of Peru, and is supposed by some authors to be peculiar to the American continent. Buffon believes him to be of the same species with the læmmer-geyer (lamb-vulture) of the Alps. The similarity of their habitations favors this conjecture; but the truth is, the Condor of Peru has not been well examined, and his history is imperfectly known.

No. 27.

So shall the Power in vengeance view the place,
In crimson clothe his terror-beaming face,
Book III. Line 493.

It is natural for the worshippers of the sun to consider any change in the atmosphere as indicative of the different passions of their deity. With the Peruvians a sanguine appearance in the sun denoted his anger.

No. 28.

Thro all the shrines, where erst on new-moon days
Swell'd the full quires of consecrated praise,
Book III. Line 687.

New-moon days were days of high festival with the Incas, according to Garcilasso. Eclipses of the sun must therefore have happened on solemn days, and have interrupted the service of the temple.

No. 29.

Las Casas. Valverde. Gasca.
Book IV. Line 17—27.

Bartholomew de las Casas was a Dominican priest of a most amiable and heroic character. He first went to Hispaniola with Columbus in his second voyage, where he manifested an ardent but honest zeal, first in attempting to instruct the natives in the principles of the catholic faith, and afterwards in defending them against the insufferable cruelties exercised by the Spanish tyrants who succeeded Columbus in the discoveries and settlements in

South America. He early declared himself *Protector of the Indians;* a title which seems to have been acknowledged by the Spanish government. He devoted himself ever after to the most indefatigable labors in the service of that unhappy people. He made several voyages to Spain, to solicit, first from Ferdinand, then from cardinal Ximenes, and finally from Charles V, some effectual restrictions against the horrid career of depopulation which every where attended the Spanish arms. He followed these monsters of cruelty into all the conquered countries; where, by the power of his eloquence and that purity of morals which commands respect even from the worst of men, he doubtless saved the lives of many thousands of innocent people. His life was a continued struggle against that deplorable system of tyranny, of which he gives a description in a treatise addressed to Philip prince of Spain, entitled *Brevissima Relacion de la Destruycion de las Yndias.*

It is said by the Spanish writers that the inhabitants of Hispaniola, when first discovered by the Spaniards, amounted to more than one million. This incredible population was reduced, in fifteen years, to sixty thousand souls.

Vincent Valverde was a fanatical priest who accompanied Pizarro in his destructive expedition to Peru. If we were to search the history of mankind, we should not find another such example of the united efforts of ecclesiastical hypocrisy and military ferocity, of unresisted murder and insatiable plunder, as we meet with in the account of this expedition.

Father Valverde, in a formal manner, gave the sanction of the church to the treacherous murder of Atabalipa and his relations; which was immediately followed by the destruction and almost entire depopulation of a flourishing empire.

Pedro de la Gasca was one of the few men whose virtues form a singular contrast with the vices which disgraced the age in which he lived and the country in which he acquired his glory. He was sent over to Peru by Charles V without any military force, to quell the rebellion of the younger Pizarro and to prevent a second depopulation, by a civil war, of that country which had just been drenched in the blood of its original inhabitants. He effected this great purpose by the weight only of his personal authority and the veneration inspired by his virtues. As soon as he had suppressed the rebellion and established the government of the colony he hastened to resign his authority into the hands of his master. And tho his victories had been obtained in the richest country on earth he returned to Spain as poor as Cincinnatus; having resisted every temptation to plunder, and refused to receive any emolument for his services.

No. 30.

First of his friends, see Frederic's princely form
Ward from the sage divine the gathering storm;
Book IV. Line 157.

Frederic of Saxony, surnamed the Wise, was the first sovereign prince who favored the doctrines of Luther. He became at once his pupil and his patron, defended him from the persecutions of the pope, and gave him an establishment as professor in the university of Wittemburgh.

No. 31.

By all sectarian chiefs he lives approved,
By monarchs courted and by men beloved.
Book IV. Line 165.

Francis I, out of respect to the great learning and moderation of Melancthon, and disregarding the pretended danger of discussing the dogmas of the church, invited him to come to France and establish himself at Paris; but the intrigues of the cardinal de Tournon frustrated the king's intention.

If every leader of religious sects had possessed the amiable qualities of Melancthon, and every monarch who wished to oppose the introduction of new opinions had partaken of the wisdom of Francis, the blood of many hundreds of millions of the human species, which has flowed at the shrine of fanaticism, would have been spared. This circumstance alone would have made of human society by this time a state totally different from what we actually experience; and its influence on the progress of improvement in national happiness and general civilization must have been beyond our ordinary calculation.

No. 32.

While kings and ministers obstruct the plan,
Unfaithful guardians of the weal of man.

Book IV. Line 529.

The British colonies in all their early struggles for existence complained, and with reason, of the uniform indifference and discouragement which they experienced from the government of the mother country. But it was probably to that very indifference that they owed the remarkable spirit of liberty and self-dependence which created their prosperity, by inducing them uniformly to adopt republican institutions. These circumstances prepared the way for that mutual confidence and federal union which have finally formed them into a flourishing nation.

Ministers who feel their power over a distant colony to be uncontrolled are so naturally inclined to govern too much, that it may be a fortunate circumstance for the colony to be neglected altogether. This neglect was indeed fatal to the first Virginia settlers sent out by Sir Walter Raleigh; and the companies who afterwards succeeded in their establishments at Jamestown in Virginia and at Plymouth in Massachusetts were very near sharing the fate of their predecessors. But after these settlements had acquired so much consistence as to assure their own continuance, it may be assumed as an historical fact, that the want of encouragement from government was rather beneficial than detrimental to the British colonies in general.

These establishments were in the nature of private adventures, undertaken by a few individuals at their own expense, rather than organised colonies sent abroad for a public purpose. They were companies incorporated for plantation and trade. All they asked of the mother country (after obtaining acts of incorporation enabling them to acquire property and exercise other *civil* functions, such as incorporated companies at home could exercise) was to give them charters of *political* franchise, ascertaining the extent and limits of their rights and duties as subjects of the British crown forming nations in parts of the earth that had been found in an uncultivated state, and far removed from the mother country.

As they could not in this situation be represented in the parliament of England, these charters stipulated their right of having parliaments or legislative assemblies of their own, with executive and judiciary institutions established within their territories.

The acknowledgment of these rights placed them on a different footing from any other modern colonies; and the restricting clause, by which their trade was confined to the mother country, rendered their situation unlike that of the colonies of ancient Greece. Indeed the British system of colonization in America differed essentially from every other, whether ancient or modern; if that may properly be called a system, which was rather the result of early indifference to the cries of needy adventurers, and subsequent attempts to seize upon their earnings when they became objects of rapacity. This singular train of difficulties must be considered as one of the causes of our ancient prosperity and present freedom.

No. 33.

Where Freedom's sons their high-born lineage trace,
And homebred bravery still exalts the race:

Book V. Line 345.

The author of this poem will not be suspected of laying any stress on the mere circumstance of lineage or birth, as relating either to families or nations. The phrase however in the text is not without its meaning. Among the colonies derived from the several nations of Europe in modern times, those from the English have flourished far better than the others, under a parity of circumstances, such as climate, soil and productions. The reason of this undeniable fact deserves to be explained.

Colonies naturally carry with them the civil, political and religious institutions of their mother countries. These institutions in England are much more favorable to liberty and the development of industry than in any other part of Europe which has sent colonies abroad. But this is not all: when men for several generations have been bred up in the habit of feeling and exercising such a portion of liberty as the English nation has enjoyed, their minds are prepared to open and expand themselves as occasion may offer. They are able to embrace new circumstances, to perceive the improvements that may be drawn from them, and not only make a temperate use of that portion of self-control to which they are accustomed, but devise the means of extending it to other objects of their political relations, till they become familiar with all the interests of men in society.

The habitual use of the liberty of the press, of trial by jury in open court, of the accountability of public agents and of some voice in the election of legislators, must create, in a man or a nation, a character quite different from what it could be under the habitual disuse of these advantages. And when these habits are transplanted with a young colony to a distant region of the earth, enjoying a good soil and climate, with an unlimited and unoccupied country, the difference will necessarily be more remarkable.

A most striking illustration of this principle is exhibited in the colonies of North America. This coast, from the St. Laurence to the Missisippi, was colonized by the French and English. (I make no account of the Dutch establishment on the Hudson nor of the Swedish on the Delaware; they being of little importance, and early absorbed in the English settlements.) If we look back only one hundred years from the present time, we find the French and English dominions here about equally important in point of extent and population. The French Canada, Acadia, Cape Breton, Newfoundland, Florida and Louisiana were then as far advanced in improvement as the English settlements which they flanked on each side. And the French had greatly the advantage in point of soil, interior navigation and capability of extension. They commanded and possessed the two great rivers which almost met together on the English frontier. And the space between the waters of those rivers on the west was planted with French military posts, so as to complete the investment.

New Orleans was begun before Philadelphia, and was much better situated to become a great commercial capital. Quebec and Montreal were older, and had the advantage of most of our other cities. Add to this that the French nation at home was about twice as populous as the English nation at home; and as that part of the increase of colonial population which comes from emigration must naturally be derived from their respective mother countries, it might have been expected that the comparative rapidity of increase would have been in favor of the French at least two to one.

But the French colonists had not been habituated to the use of liberty before their emigration; and they were not prepared nor permitted to enjoy it in any degree afterwards. Their laws were made for them in their mother country, by men who could not know their wants and who felt no interest in their prosperity; and then they were administered by a set of agents as ignorant as their masters; men who, from the nature of their employment and accountability, must in general be oppressive and rapacious.

The result has solved a great problem in political combination. One of these clusters of colonies has grown to a powerful empire, giving examples to the universe in most of the great objects which constitute the dignity of nations. The other, after having been a constant expense to the mother country, and serving for barter and exchange in the capricious vicissitudes of European despotism, presents altogether at this day a mass of population and wealth scarcely equal to one of our provinces.

This note is written at the moment when Louisiana, one of the most extensive but least peopled of the French colonies, is ceded to the United States. The world will see how far the above theory will now be confirmed by the rapid increase of population and improvement in that interesting portion of our continent.

No. 34.

Beneath him lay the sceptre kings had borne,
And the tame thunder from the tempest torn.
Book V. Line 429.

Eripuit cœlo fulmen, sceptrumque tyrannis.

This epigraph, written by Turgot on the bust of Franklin, seems to have been imitated from a line in Manilius; where noticing the progress of science in ascribing things to their natural and proper causes instead of supernatural ones, he says,

Eriput Jovi fulmen, viresque tonandi,
Et sonitum ventis concessit, nubibus ignem.

No. 35.

And Knox from his full park to battle brings
His brazen tubes, the last resort of kings.
Book V. Line 665.

Ultima ratio regum; a device of Louis XIV engraved on his ordnance, and afterwards adopted by other powers. When we consider men as reasonable beings and endowed with the qualities requisite for living together in society, this device looks like a satire upon the species; but in reality it only proves the imperfect state to which their own principles of society have yet advanced them in the long and perhaps interminable progress of which they are susceptible. This *ultima ratio* being already taken out of the hands of individuals and confided only to the chiefs of nations is as clear a proof of a great progress already made, as its remaining in the hands of those chiefs is a proof that we still remain far short of that degree of wisdom and experience which will enable all the nations to live at peace one with another.

There certainly was a time when the same device might have been written on the hatchet or club or fist of every man; and the best weapon of destruction that he could wield against his neighbour might have been called *ultima ratio virorum*, meaning that human reason could go no farther. But the wisdom we have drawn from experience has taught us to restrain the use of mortal weapons, making it unlawful and showing it to be unreasonable to use them in private disputes. The principles of social intercourse and the advantages of peace are so far understood as to enable men to form great societies, and to submit their personal misunderstandings to common judges; thus removing the *ultima ratio* from their own private hands to the hands of their government.

Hitherto there has usually been a government to every nation; but the nations are increasing in size and diminishing in number; so that the hands which now hold the *ultima ratio* by delegation are few, compared with what they have been. I mean this observation to apply only to those extensions of nationality which have been formed on the true principles of society and acquiesced in from a sense of their utility. I mean not to apply it to those unnatural and unwieldy stretches of power, whose overthrow is often and erroneously cited as an argument against the progress of civilization; such as the conquests of Alexander, the Roman generals, Omar, Gengis Khan and others of that brilliant description. These are but meteors of compulsive force, which pass away and discourage, rather than promote, the spirit of national extension of which I speak.

This spirit operates constantly and kindly; nor is its progress so slow but that it is easily perceived. Even within the short memorials of modern history we find a heptarchy in England. Ossian informs us that in his time there was a great number of warlike states in Ireland and as many more in Scotland. Without going back to the writings of Julius Cesar to discover the comparative condition of France, we may almost remember when she counted within her limits six or seven different governments, generally at war among themselves and inviting foreign enemies to come and help them destroy each other. Every province in Spain is still called a kingdom; and it is not long since they were really so in fact, with the *ultima ratio* in the hands of every king.

The publicist who in any of those modern heroic ages could have imagined that all the hundred nations who inhabited the western borders of Europe, from the Orknies to Gibraltar, might one day become so far united in manners and interests as to form but three great nations, would certainly have passed for a madman. Had he been a minister of Pharamond or of Fingal he could no more have kept his place than Turgot could keep his after pointing out the means of promoting industry and preventing wars. He would have been told that the inhabitants of each side of the Humber were natural enemies one to the other; that if their chiefs were even disposed to live in peace they could not do it; their subjects would demand war and could not live without it. The same would have been said of the Seine, the Loire and every other dividing line between their petty communities. It would have been insisted on that such rivers were the natural boundaries of states and never could be otherwise.

But now since the people of those districts find themselves no longer on the frontiers of little warlike states, but in the centre of great industrious nations, they have lost their relish for war, and consider it as a terrible calamity; they cherish the minister who gives them peace, and abhor the one who drives them into unnecessary wars. Their local disputes, which used to be settled by the sword, are now referred to the tribunals of the country. They have substituted a moral to a physical force. They have changed the habits of plunder for those of industry ; and they find themselves richer and happier for the change.

Who will say that the progress of society will stop short in the present stage of its career? that great communities will not discover a mode of arbitrating their disputes, as little ones have done? that nations will not lay aside their present ideas of independence and rivalship, and find themselves more happy and more secure in one great universal society, which shall contain within itself its own principles of defence, its own permanent security? It is evident that national security, in order to be permanent, must be founded on the moral force of society at large, and not on the physical force of each nation independently exerted. The *ultima ratio* must not be a cannon, but a reference to some rational mode of decision worthy of rational beings.

No. 36.

Else what high tones of rapture must have told
The first great action of a chief so bold!

Book V. Line 767.

General Arnold, the leader of this detachment, had acquired by this and many other brilliant achievements a degree of military fame almost unequalled among the American generals. His shameful defection afterwards, by the foulest of treason, should be lamented as a national dishonor; it has not only obliterated his own glory, but it seems in some sort to have cast a shade on that of others whose brave actions had been associated with his in the acquisition of their common and unadulterated fame.

The action here alluded to, the march thro the wilderness from Casco to Quebec, was compared in the gazettes of that day to the passage of the Alps by Hannibal. And really, considered as a scene of true military valor, patient suffering and heroic exertion (detached from the idea of subsequent success in the ulterior expedition) the comparison did not disgrace the Carthaginian. Yet since the defection of Arnold, which happened five years afterwards, this audacious and once celebrated exploit is scarcely mentioned in our annals. And Meigs, Dearborn, Morgan and other distinguished officers in the expedition, whom that alone might have immortalized, have been indebted to their subsequent exertions of patriotic valor for the share of celebrity their names now enjoy.

See the character of Arnold treated more at large in the sixth book.

No. 37.

See the black Prison Ship's expanding womb
Impested thousands, quick and dead, entomb.

Book VI. Line 35.

The systematic and inflexible course of cruelties exercised by the British armies on American prisoners during the three first years of the war were doubtless unexampled among civilized nations. Considering it as a war against rebels, neither their officers nor soldiers conceived themselves bound by the ordinary laws of war.

The detail of facts on this subject, especially in what concerned the prison ships, has not been sufficiently noticed in our annals; at least not so much noticed as the interest of public morals would seem to require. Mr. Boudinot, who was the American commissary of prisoners at the time, has since informed the author of this poem that in one prison ship alone, called the Jersey, which was anchored near Newyork, *eleven thousand* American prisoners died in eighteen months; almost the whole of them from the barbarous treatment of being stifled in a crowded hold with infected air, and poisoned with unwholesome food.

There were several other prison ships, as well as the sugar-house prison in the city, whose histories ought to be better known than they are. I say this not from any sort of enmity to the British nation, for I have none. I respect the Britisth nation; as will be evident from the views I have given of her genius and institutions in the course of this work. I would at all times render that nation every service consistent with my duty to my own; and surely it is worthy of her magnanimity to consider as a real service every true information given her relative to the crimes of her agents in distant countries. These crimes are as contrary to the spirit of the nation at home as they are to the temper of her laws.

No. 38.

Myrtles and laurels equal honors join'd,
Which arms had purchased and the Muses twined;
Book VI. Line 273.

General Burgoyne had gained some celebrity by his pen, as well as by his sword, previous to the American war. He was author of the comedy called *The Heiress*, and of some other theatrical pieces which had been well received on the London theatres.

No. 39.

Deep George's loaded lake reluctant guides
Their bounding barges o'er his sacred tides.
Book VI. Line 285.

The water of Lake George was held in particular veneration by the French catholics of Canada. Of this they formerly made their holy water; which was carried and distributed to the churches thro the province, and probably produced part of the revenues of the clergy. This water is said to have been chosen for the purpose on account of its extreme clearness. The lake was called *Lac du Saint Sacrement.*

No. 40.

His savage hordes the murderous Johnson leads,
Files thro the woods and treads the tangled weeds,
Book VI. Line 389.

This was general sir John Johnson, an American royalist in the British service. He was the son of sir William Johnson, who had been a rich proprietor and inhabitant in the Mohawk country, in the colony of New York, and had been employed by the king as superintendant of Indian affairs. Sir William had married a Mohawk savage wife; and it was supposed that the great influence which he had long exercised over that and the neighboring tribes must have descended to his son. It was on this account that he was employed on the expedition of Burgoyne; in which he had the rank of brigadier general, and the special direction of the savages.

No. 41.

Are these thy trophies, Carleton! these the swords
Thy hand unsheath'd and gave the savage hordes,
Book VI. Line 685.

General sir Guy Carleton, afterwards lord Dorchester, was the British governor of Canada and superintendant of Indian affairs at the time of Burgoyne's campaign. Having great influence with the warlike tribes who inhabited the west of Canada and the borders of the Lakes, he was ordered by the minister to adopt the barbarous and unjustifiable measure of arming and bringing them into the king's service in aid of this expedition.

This was doubtless done with the consent of Burgoyne, tho he seems to have been apprehensive of the difficulty of managing a race of men whose manners were so ferocious, and whose motives to action must have been so different from those of the principal parties in the war. Burgoyne, in his narrative of this campaign, informs us that he took precautions to discourage that inhuman mode of warfare which had been customary among those savages. He ordered them to kill none but such persons as they should find in arms fighting against the king's troops; to spare old men, women, children and prisoners; and not to scalp any but such as they should kill in open war. He intimated to them that he should not pay for any scalps but those thus taken from enemies killed in arms.

It is unfortunate for the reputation of the general and of his government, that they did not reflect on the futility of such an order and the improbability of its being executed. A certain price was offered for scalps; the savages must know that in a bag of scalps, packed and dried and brought into camp and counted out before the commissary to receive payment, it would be impossible to distinguish the political opinions or the occupation, age or sex of the heads to which they had belonged; it could not be ascertained whether they had been taken from Americans or British, whigs or tories, soldiers killed in arms or killed after they had resigned their arms, militia men or peasants, old or young, male or female.

The event proved the deplorable policy of employing such auxiliaries, especially in such multitudes as were brought together on this occasion. No sooner did hostilities begin between the two armies than these people, who could have no knowledge of the cause nor affection for either party, and whose only object was plunder and pay, began their indiscriminate and ungovernable ravages on both sides. They robbed and murdered peasants, whether royalists or others; men, women, children, straggling and wounded soldiers of both armies. The tragical catastrophe of a young lady of the name of Macrea, whose story is almost literally detailed in the foregoing paragraphs of the text, is well known. It made a great impression on the public mind at the time, both in England and America.

General Carleton, in the preceding campaigns, when the war was carried into Canada, had been applauded for his humanity in the treatment of prisoners. But the part he took in this measure of associating the savages in the operations of the British army was a stain upon his character; and the measure was highly detrimental to the royal cause, on account of the general indignation it excited thro the country.

No. 42.

That no proud privilege from birth can spring,
No right divine, nor compact form a king;
Book VII. Line 39.

The assumed right of kings, or that supreme authority which one man exercises over a nation, and for which he is not held accountable, has been contended for on various grounds. It has been sometimes called the *right of conquest;* in which is involved the absolute disposal of the lives and labors of the conquered nation, in favor of the victorious chief and his descendants to perpetuity. Sometimes it is called the *divine right;* in which case kings are considered as the vicegerents of God.

This notion is very ancient, and it is almost universal among modern nations. Homer is full of it; and from his unaffected recurrence to the same idea every where in his poems, it is evident that in his day it was not called in question. The manner in which the Jews were set at work to constitute their first king proves that they were convinced that, if they must have a king, he must be given them from God, and receive that solemn consecration which should establish his authority on the same divine right which was common to other nations, from whom they borrowed the principle.

There are some few instances in history wherein this divine right has been set aside; but it has generally been owing rather to the violence of circumstances, which sometimes drive men to act contrary to their prejudices, tho they still retain them, than to any effort of reasoning by which they convinced themselves that this was a prejudice, and that no divine right existed in reality. For it does not violate this supposed right, to change one king for another, or one race of kings for another, tho done in a manner the most unjust and inhuman. In this case the same divine right remains, and only changes, with the diadem, from one head to another. And tho this change should happen six times in one day (as in one instance it has done in Algiers by the murder of six successive kings) they would still say it was God who did it all; and the action would only tend to prove to the credulous people, that God was made after their own image, as changeable as themselves.

It is only in the case of Tarquin and a few others (whose overthrow has been followed by a more popular form of government) that it can be said that the principle of the divine right has been disregarded, laid aside and forgotten for any length of time.

The English are perhaps the first and only people that ever overturned this doctrine of the divinity of kings, without changing their form of government. This was brought on by circumstances, and took effect in the expulsion of James II. Books were then written to prove that the divine right of kings did not exist; at least, not in the sense in which it had been understood. And these writings completely silenced the old doctrine in England. This indeed was gaining an immense advantage in favor of liberty; tho the effort of reason, to arrive at it, seems to be so small.

But while the English were discarding the old principle they set up a new one; which indeed is not so pernicious because it cannot become so extensive, but which is scarcely more reasonable: it is the right of kings by *compact;* that is, a compact, whether written or understood, by which the representatives of a nation are supposed to bind their constituents and their descendants to be the subjects of a certain prince and of his descendants to perpetuity. This singular doctrine is developed with perspicuity, but ill supported by argument, in Burke's *Reflections on the French Revolution.*

The principle of the American government denies the right of any representatives to make such a compact, and the right of any prince to carry it into execution if it were made. Whatever varieties or mixtures there may be in the *forms* of government, there are but two distinct principles on which government is founded. One supposes the source of power to be *out* of the people, and that the governor is not accountable to them for the manner of using it; the other supposes the source of power to be *in* the people, and that the governor is accountable to them for the manner of using it. The latter is our principle. In this sense no *right divine* nor *compact* can form a king; that is, a person exercising underived and unreverting power.

No. 43.

But while dread Elliott shakes the Midland wave,
They strive in vain the Calpian rock to brave.
Book VII. Line 89.

The English general Elliott commanded the post of Gibraltar, against which the combined forces of France and Spain made a vigorous but fruitless attack in the year 1781. This attack furnished the subjects for two celebrated pictures alluded to in the eighth book: *The burning of the Floating Batteries* painted by Copley; and *The Sortie,* painted by Trumbull.

No. 44.

To guide the sailor in his wandering way,
See Godfrey's glass reverse the beams of day.
Book VIII. Line 581.

It is less from national vanity than from a regard to truth and a desire of rendering personal justice, that the author wishes to rectify the history of science in the circumstance here alluded to. The instrument known by the name of Hadley's Quadrant, now universally in use and generally attributed to Dr. Hadley, was invented by Thomas Godfrey of Philadelphia. See Jefferson's Notes on Virginia; likewise Miller's Retrospect of the Eighteenth Century, in which the original documents relative to Godfrey's invention are fully detailed.

No. 45.

West with his own great soul the canvass warms,
Creates, inspires, impassions human forms,
Book VIII. Line 587.

Benjamin West, president of the Royal Academy in London, was born and educated in Pennsylvania. At the age of twenty-three he went to Italy to perfect his taste in the art to which his genius irresistibly impelled him; in which he was destined to cast a splendor upon the age in which he lives, and probably to excel all his cotemporaries, so far at least as we can judge from the present state of their works. After passing two years in that country of models, where canvass and marble seem to contribute their full proportion of the population, he went to London.

Here he soon rendered himself conspicuous for the boldness of his designs, in daring to shake off the trammels of the art so far as to paint modern history in modern dress. He had already staggered the connoisseurs in Italy while he was there, by his picture of *The Savage Chief taking leave of his family on going to war.* This extraordinary effort of the American pencil on an American subject excited great admiration at Venice. The picture was engraved in that city by Bartolozzi, before either he or West went to England. The artists were surprised to find that the expression of the passions of men did not depend on the robes they wore. And his early works in London, *The Death of Wolfe, The Battles of the Boyne, Lahogue,* &c., engraved by Woollett and others, not only established his reputation, but produced a revolution in the Art. So that modern dress has now become as familiar in fictitious as in real life; it being justly considered essential in painting modern history.

The engraving from his Wolfe has been often copied in France, Italy and Germany; and it may be said that in this picture the revolution in painting really originated. It would now be reckoned as preposterous in an artist to dress modern personages in Grecian or Roman habits, as it was before to give them the garb of the age and country to which they belonged.

The merit of Mr. West was early noticed and encouraged by the king; who took him into pay with a convenient salary, and the title of historical painter to his majesty. In this situation he has decorated the king's palaces, chapels and churches with most of those great pictures from the English history and from the Old and New Testament, which compose so considerable a portion of his works.

The following catalogue of his pictures was furnished me by Mr. West himself in the year 1802. It comprises only his principal productions in *historical* painting, and only his *finished* pictures; without mentioning his numerous portraits, or his more numerous sketches and drawings.

The pictures marked thus * have been engraved. The ciphers express the size of the pictures. When the same subject is mentioned more than once, there is more than one picture on that subject.

IN THE QUEEN'S HOUSE.

* Regulus departing from Rome.
* Death of Wolfe.
* Death of Epaminondas.
* Death of chevalier Bayard.
* Cyrus, with a king and family captives.
* Hannibal sworn when a child.

Damsel accusing Peter.

Apotheosis of the two young princes.

Germanicus, with Segestus and his daughter prisoners.

IN THE KING'S APARTMENTS AT WINDSOR.

Edward III crossing the Somme.

Edward III crowning Ribemond at Calais.

The Six Burgesses of Calais before Edward.

Battle of Cressy, Edward embracing his son.

St. George destroying the Dragon.

Battle of Poictiers, king of France prisoner to the Black Prince.

Institution of the Order of the Garter.
Battle of Nevilcross.
Christ's Crucifixion.
The same on glass for the west window of the church at Windsor, 36 feet by 28.
Peter, John and women at the Sepulchre.
The same on glass for the east window of the same church, 36 feet by 28.
The Angels appearing to the Shepherds.
Nativity of Christ.
Kings presenting gifts to Christ.

IN THE MARBLE GALLERY, WINDSOR CASTLE.

Hymen dancing with the Hours before Peace and Plenty.
Boys with the insignia of Riches.
Boys with the insignia of the Fine Arts.

IN THE KING'S CHAPEL AT WINDSOR.

A complete history of Revealed Religion, divided into four dispensations, and comprised in thirty-eight pictures.

PATRIARCHAL DISPENSATION.

Adam and Eve created. 9 feet by 6.
Adam and Eve driven from Paradise. do.
The Deluge. do.
Noah sacrificing. do.
Abraham going to sacrifice Isaac. do.
Birth of Jacob and Esau. do.
Death of Jacob, surrounded by his sons. do.
Bondage of the Israelites in Egypt. do.

MOSAICAL DISPENSATION.

Moses called. do.
Moses and Aaron before Pharaoh, their rods turned to serpents. 15 feet by 10.
Pharaoh's Army lost in the sea.
Moses receiving the Law. 18 feet by 12.
Moses consecrating Aaron and his sons to the Priesthood. 15 feet by 10.
Moses shows the Brazen Serpent. 15 feet by 10.
Moses on Mount Pisgah sees the Promised Land and dies. 9 feet by 6.
Joshua passing the Jordan. do.
The twelve Tribes drawing their lots. do.
David called and anointed. do.

GOSPEL DISPENSATION.

John Baptist called and named. do.
Christ born. do.
Christ offered gifts by the Wise Men. do.
Christ among the Doctors. do.
Christ baptized, and the Holy Spirit descending on him. 15 feet by 10.
Christ healing the Sick. do.
Christ's last Supper. do.
Christ's Crucifixion. 36 feet by 28.
Christ's Resurrection, Peter, John and the women at the Sepulchre. do.

* Christ's Ascension. 18 feet by 12.

Peter's first Sermon, Descent of the Holy Spirit. 15 feet by 10.

The Apostles preaching and working miracles. do.

Paul and Barnabas turning from the Jews to the Gentiles. do.

APOCALYPTIC DISPENSATION.

John seeing the Son of Man, and called to write. 9 feet by 6.

The Throne surrounded by the Four Beasts, and Saints laying down their crowns. 9 feet by 6.

Death on the Pale Horse, and the Opening of the Seals. do.

The White Horse and his legions, and the Man destroying the Old Beast. do.

General Resurrection, the end of Death. do.

Christ's Second Coming. do.

The New Jerusalem. do.

IN THE COLLECTION OF MR. BECKFORD.

Michael and his angels casting out the Red Dragon and his angels.

The Woman clothed with the Sun.

John called to write the Apocalypse.

The Beast rising out of the sea.

The mighty Angel, one foot on sea the other on land.

St. Anthony of Padua.

The Madre Dolorosa.

Simeon with the Child in his arms.

Landscape, with a Hunt in the back ground.

Abraham and Isaac going to sacrifice.

Thomas à Becket.

Angel in the Sun.

Order of the Garter, differing in composition from that at Windsor.

IN THE COLLECTION OF EARL GROSVENOR.

The Shunamite's son raised to life by Elisha.

Jacob blessing the sons of Joseph.

* Death of Wolfe.

* Battle of Lahogue.

* Battle of the Boyne.

* Restoration of Charles II.

* Cromwell dissolving the Parliament.

The Golden Age.

General Wolfe when a boy.

IN THE COLLECTION OF MR. HOPE.

* Telemachus and Calypso.

* Angelica and Madora.

The Damsel and Orlando.

Cicero at the tomb of Archimedes.

St. Paul's Conversion.

St. Paul persecuting the Christians.

His restoration to sight by Ananias.

Mr. Hope's family; nine figures, size of life.

IN THE HISTORICAL GALLERY, PALLMALL.

Citizens of London offering the crown to William the Conquèror.

The Queen soliciting king Henry to pardon her son John.

IN GREENWICH HOSPITAL.

Paul shaking the Viper from his finger.

Paul preaching at Athens.

Elymas the Sorcerer struck blind.

Cornelius and the Angel.

Peter delivered from prison.

Conversion of St. Paul.

Paul before Felix.

Return of the Prodigal Son.

LARGE FIGURES OF

Faith,	Matthias,	Malachi,
Hope,	Thomas,	Micah,
Charity,	Simon,	Zachariah,
Innocence,	James major,	Daniel,
Matthew,	James minor,	Jude, John,
Mark,	Philip,	Andrew,
Luke,	Peter,	Bartholomew.

IN DIFFERENT CHURCHES.

Michael chaining the Dragon.

Angels announcing the birth of Christ.

St. Stephen stoned to death.

Raising of Lazarus.

Paul shaking off the Viper.

The last Supper.

Resurrection of Christ.

Peter denying Christ.

Moses showing the Brazen Serpent.

John seeing the Lamb of God.

A Mother leading her children to the Temple of Virtue.

IN VARIOUS COLLECTIONS.

Lord Clive taking the duany from the Mogul.

The same.

Christ receiving the Sick.
Pensyl. hospital.

* Leonidas exiling Cleombrotus and family.

The two Marys at the Sepulchre.

Alexander and his Physician.

Cesar reading the Life of Alexander.

Death of Adonis.

Continence of Scipio.

* Savage Warrior taking leave of his family.

Venus and Cupid.

Alfred dividing his loaf with the Beggar.

Helen presented to Paris.

Cupid stung by a bee.

Simeon and the Child.

* William Penn treating with the Savages.

Destruction of the Spanish Armada.

Philippa soliciting of Edward the pardon of the citizens of Calais.

Europa on the Bull.

Death of Hyacinthus.

Death of Cesar.

Venus presenting her cestus to Juno.

Rinaldo and Armida.

Pharaoh's Daughter with the child Moses.

The stolen Kiss.

Angelica and Madora.

Woman of Samaria at the well with Christ.

Agrippina leaning on the urn of Germanicus.

Death of Wolfe.

The same; smaller size.

Romeo and Juliet.

King Lear and his Daughters.

Belisarius and the Boy.

Sir Francis Baring and family.

* Mr. West and family.

A Mother and Child.

Jupiter and Semele.

Petus and Arria.

Venus and Cupid smiling at Europa when Jupiter had left her.

Rebecca coming to Jacob.

Rebecca receiving the bracelets at the well.

Agrippina landing at Brundusium with the ashes of Germanicus.

The same.

The same.

Endymion and Diana.

IN THE COLLECTION OF ROBERT FULTON.

Ophelia distracted, before the king and queen.

* King Lear in the storm.

IN MR. WEST'S OWN COLLECTION.

Hector taking leave of his Wife and Child.

Elisha raising the Shunamite's Son.

The raising of Lazarus.

Macbeth and the Witches.

The return of Tobias.

Return of the Prodigal Son.

Ariadne on the sea shore.

Death of Adonis.

King of France brought to the Black Prince.

* Death of Wolfe.

Venus and Adonis.

Battle of Lahogue.

Edward III crossing the Somme.

Philippa at the Battle of Nevilcross.

Angels announcing the birth of Christ.

Kings bringing presents to Christ.

View on the river Thames.

View on the Susquehanna.

Picture of Tangers Mill at Eton.

Chryseis restored to her Father.

Antiochus and Stratonice.

King Lear and his Daughters.

Chryseus on the sea shore.

Nathan and David. *Thou art the man.*

Elijah raising the widow's Son.

Choice of Hercules.

Venus and Europa.

Daniel interpreting the Writing on the Wall.

Marius on the ruins of Carthage.

* Cymon and Iphigenia.

Cicero at the tomb of Archimedes.

* Alexander, king of Scotland, rescued from the Stag.

Battle of Cressy.

* Mr. West and his family.

* Anthony shows Cesar's Robe and Will.

Egysthus viewing the body of Clytemnestra.

Recovery of king George in 1789.

A large landscape in Windsor Forest.
Ophelia before the King and Queen.
Leonidas taking leave of his family.
Phaeton receiving from Apollo the chariot of the Sun.
The Eagle giving the cup of water to Psyche.
Moonlight and the Beckoning Ghost. *Pope.*
Angel sitting on the stone at the Sepulchre.
The same subject differently composed.
* Angelica and Madora.
The Damsel and Orlando.
The Good Samaritan.
Old Beast and False Prophet destroyed.
Christ healing the sick in the temple.
Death on the Pale Horse.
Jason and the Dragon.
Venus and Adonis seeing the Cupids bathe.
Moses and Aaron before Pharaoh.
Passage boat on the Canal.
Paul and Barnabas rejecting the Jews and turning to the Gentiles.
Diomed, his horses struck with lightning.
Milk-woman in St. James's Park.
Expulsion of Adam and Eve from Paradise.
Order of the Garter.
Orion on the Dolphin's back.
The Deluge.
Queen Elizabeth's Procession to St. Paul's.
Christ showing a child, emblem of heaven.
Harvest Home.
Washing Sheep.
St. Paul shaking off the Viper.
Sun setting at Twickenham on Thames.
Driving sheep and cows to water.
Cattle drinking, and Mr. West drawing, in Windsor Park.
Pharaoh and his host in the Red Sea.
Telemachus and Calypso.
Moses consecrating Aaron and his sons.
A Mother inviting her little boy to come to her thro a brook.
Brewer's porter and hod carrier.
Venus attended by the Graces.
Naming of Samuel.
Birth of Jacob and Esau.
Ascension of Christ.
Samuel presented to Eli.
Moses shown the Promised Land.
Christ among the Doctors.
Reaping scene.
Adonis and his dog.
Mothers with their children in water.
Joshua crossing the Jordan with the Ark.
Christ's Nativity.
* Pyrrhus when a child before king Glaucus.
The Man laying his bread on the bridle of the dead Ass. *Sterne.*
The Captive. *Ditto.*
Cupid letting loose two Doves.
Cupid asleep.
Children eating cherries.
St. Anthony of Padua and the Child.
Jacob and Laban with his two daughters.
The Women looking into the Sepulchre and seeing two Angels where the Lord lay.

The Angel unchaining Peter in prison.
Death of sir Philip Sidney.
Death of Epaminondas.
Death of chevalier Bayard.
Death of Cephalus.
* Kosciusko on a couch.
Abraham and Isaac. *Here is the wood and fire, but where is the lamb to sacrifice?*
Eponina with her children giving bread to her husband when in concealment.
King Henry pardoning his brother John at the prayer of his mother.
Death of lord Chatham.
Presentation of the Crown to William the Conqueror.
Europa crowning the Bull with flowers.
West's garden, gallery and painting room.
Cave of Despair. *Spencer.*
Arethusa bathing.
Cupid shows Venus his finger stung by a bee.
Ubald brings his three daughters to Alfred for him to choose one for his wife.
* Pylades and Orestes.

Besides the two hundred and ninety-nine large finished pictures here mentioned, Mr. West has done about one hundred portraits, and upwards of two hundred drawings with the pen; which last, for sublimity of conception, are among the finest of his works. So that the whole of his pieces amount to above six hundred. Some of them are larger in size than any in the national gallery of France; and he has not been assisted by any other painter.

Mr. West is now about sixty-eight years of age. He discovers no abatement in the activity of his genius, nor in the laborious exercise of his talents. He has painted several fine pictures since the above catalogue was made. Three of which I have particularly noticed in his painting room: Tobet and Tobias with the fish; Abraham sending away Hagar with her child; Achilles receiving from Thetis the new armor; and we hear that he has lately painted the Death of Nelson. He may yet produce many more original works; tho it is presumed he has already exceeded all other historical painters, except Rubens, in the number and variety of his productions. With regard to the merit of his pictures, I cannot pretend to form a judgment that would be of any use in directing that of others. He is doubtless the most classical painter, except Raphael, whose works are known to us.

The critics find fault with the coloring of Mr. West. But in his works, as in those of Raphael, we do not look for coloring. It is dignity of character, fine expression, delicate design, correct drawing and beautiful disposition of drapery which fix the suffrage of the real judge. All which qualities can only spring from an elevated mind.

No. 46.

Nile pours from heaven a tutelary flood,
And gardens grow the vegetable god.
Book IX. Line 287.

O sanctas gentes, quibus hæc nascuntur in hortis
Numina. . Juv. Sat. 15.

No. 47.

Tis to correct their fatal faults of old,
When, caught by tinsel, they forgot the gold.
Book IX. Line 499.

The state of the arts and sciences among the ancients, viewed with reference to the event of universal civilization, was faulty in two respects. First, In their comparative estimation: Second, In their flourishing only in one nation at a time. These circumstances might be favorable to the exertions of individual genius; and they may be assigned both as causes of the universal destruction of the arts and sciences by the Gothic conquest, and as reasons why we should not greatly lament that destruction.

From the political state of mankind in the days of their ancient splendor it was natural that those arts which depend on the imagination, such as Architecture, Statuary, Painting, Eloquence and Poetry, should claim the highest rank in the estimation of a people. In several, perhaps all of these, the ancients remain unrivalled. But these are not the arts which tend the most to the general improvement of society. A man in those days would have rendered more service to the world by ascertaining the true figure and movements of the earth, than by originating a heaven and filling it with all the gods of Homer; and had the expenses of the Egyptian pyramids been employed in furnishing ships of discovery and sending them out of the Mediterranean, the nations called civilized would not have been afterwards overrun by Barbarians.

But the sciences of Geography, Navigation and Commerce, with their consequent improvements in Natural Philosophy and Humanity, could not, from the nature of things at that time, become objects of great encouragement or enterprise. Talent was therefore confined to the cultivation of arts more striking to the senses. As these arts were adapted to gratify the vanity of princes, to help carry on the sacred frauds of priests, to fire the ambition of heroes, or to gain causes in popular assemblies, they were brought to a degree of perfection which prevented their being relished or understood by barbarous neighbors.

The improvements of the world therefore, whether in literature, sciences or arts, descended with the line of conquest from one nation to another, till the whole were concentred in the Roman empire. Their tendency there was to inspire a contempt for nations less civilized, and to teach the Romans to consider all mankind as the proper objects of their military despotism. These circumstances prepared, thro a course of ages, and finally opened a scene of wretchedness at which the human mind has been taught to shudder. But some such convulsion seemed necessary to reduce the nations to a position capable of commencing regular improvements. And, however novel the sentiment may appear, I will venture to say that, as to the prospect of universal civilization, mankind were in a better situation in the time of Charlemagne than they were in the days of Augustus.

The final destruction of the Roman empire left the nations of Europe in circumstances similar to each other; and their consequent rivalship prevented any disproportionate refinement from appearing in any particular region. The principles of government, firmly rooted in the Feudal System, unsocial and unphilosophical as they were, laid the foundation of that balance of power which discourages the Cesars and Alexanders of modern ages from attempting the conquest of the world.

It seems necessary that the arrangement of events in civilizing the world should be in the following order: *first*, all parts of it must be considerably peopled; *second*, the different nations must be known to each other; *third*, their wants must be increased, in order to inspire a passion for commerce. The first of these objects was not probably accomplished till a late period. The second for three centuries past has been greatly accelerated. The third is a necessary consequence of the two former. The spirit of commerce is happily calculated to open an amicable intercourse between all countries, to soften the horrors of war, to enlarge the field of science, and to assimilate the manners, feelings and languages of all nations. This leading principle, in its remoter consequences, will produce advantages in favor of free government, give patriotism the character of philanthropy, induce all men to regard each other as brethren and friends, and teach them the benefits of peace and harmony among the nations.

I conceive it no objection to this theory that the progress has hitherto been slow; when we consider the magnitude of the object, the obstructions that were to be removed, and the length of time taken to accomplish it. The future progress will probably be more rapid than the past. Since the invention of printing, the application of the properties of the magnet, and the knowledge of the structure of the solar system, it is difficult to conceive of a cause that can produce a new state of barbarism; unless it be some great convulsion in the physical world, so extensive as to change the face of the earth or a considerable part of it. This indeed may have been the case already more than once, since the earth was first peopled with men, and antecedent to our histories. But such events have nothing to do with the present argument.

No. 48.

Herschel ascends himself with venturous wain,
And joins and flanks thy planetary train,
Book IX. Line 601.

The planet discovered by Herschel was called by him Georgium Sidus; but in all countries except England it is named Herschel, and probably will be so named there after his death and that of the patron to whom his gratitude led him to make this extraordinary dedication.

I would observe that, besides the impropriety of giving it another name than that of the discoverer, it is inconvenient to use a double name, or a name composed of two words. Let it be either George or Herschel.

The passage referred to in this note was written before the discovery of the three other planets which are now added to our catalogue. Could my voice have weight in deciding on the names to be given to these new children of the sun, I would call them by the names of their respective discoverers, Piazzi, Olbers and Harding, instead of the senseless and absurd appellations of Ceres, Pallas and Juno. The former method would at least assist us in preserving the history of science; the latter will only tend farther to confuse a very ancient mythology which is already extremely confused, and increase the difficulty of following the faint traces of real knowledge that seems couched under the mass of that mythology; traces which may one day lead to many useful truths in philosophy and morals.

No. 49.

To build on ruin'd realms the shrine of fame,
And load his numbers with a tyrant's name.
Book X. Line 261.

A most useful book might be written on this subject. It should be a Review of Poets and Historians, as to the moral and political tendency of their works. It should likewise treat of the importance of the task assigned to these two classes of writers. It might attempt to point out the true object they ought to have in view; perhaps do this with such clearness and energy as to gain the attention of writers as well as readers, and thus serve in some measure as a guide to future historians and poets. At least it would prove a guide to readers; and by teaching them how to judge, and what to praise or blame in the accounts of human actions, whether real or fictitious, the public taste would be reformed by degrees. In this case the recorders of heroic actions, as well as the authors of them, would find it necessary to follow this reform, or they must necessarily fail of obtaining the celebrity to which they all aspire.

I think every person who will give himself the trouble to form an opinion on the manner in which actions, called heroic, have been recorded, must find it faulty; and must lament, as one of the misfortunes of society, that writers of these two classes almost universally, from Homer down to Gibbon, have led astray the moral sense of man. In this view we may say in general of poets and historians, as we do of their heroes, that they have injured the cause of humanity almost in proportion to the fame they have acquired.

I would not be understood by this observation to mean that such writers have done no good. Even the works of Homer, which have caused more mischief to mankind than those of any other, have likewise been a fruitful source of a certain species of benefits. They elevate the mind of every reader; they have called forth great exertions of genius in poets, artists, philosophers and heroes, thro a long succession of ages. But it remains to be considered what a fruitful source they have likewise been of those false notions of honor and erroneous systems of policy which have governed the actions of men from his day to ours.

If, instead of the Iliad, he had given us a work of equal splendor founded on an opposite principle; whose object should have been to celebrate the useful arts of agriculture and navigation; to build the immortal fame of his heroes, and occupy his whole hierarchy of gods, on actions that contribute to the real advancement of society, instead of striking away every foundation on which society ought to be established or can be greatly advanced; mankind, enriched with such a work at that early period, would have given a useful turn to their ambition thro all succeeding ages.

It is not easy to conceive how different the state of nations would have been at this day from what we now find it, had such a bent been given to the pursuits of genius, and such glory cast upon actions truly worthy of imitation. I have treated this subject more at large in the third chapter of *Advice to the Privileged Orders.*

But it will be asked how this kind of censure can attach to the writers of history, whose business is to invent nothing, to confine themselves to the simple narration of facts, and relate the actions of men, not as they should be, but as they are. This is inded a part of the duty of the historian; but it is not his whole duty. His narrative should be clear and simple; but he should likewise develop the political and moral tendency of the transactions he details.

In reviewing actions or doctrines which favor despotism, injustice, false morals or political errors, he should not suffer them to pass without an open and well supported censure. He should show how the authors of such actions might have conducted themselves and succeeded in gaining the celebrity which they sought, by doing good instead of harm to the age and country where they acquired their fame.

The history of human actions, in a political view, has generally been the history of human errors. The writers who have given it to us do not appear to have been sensible of this. How then are young readers to be sensible of it? Their minds are still to be formed; and those who are destined for public life must in a great measure take their bias from the study of history. But history in general, to answer the purpose of sound instruction to the future guides of nations, must be rewritten. For example: among the hundred historians who have treated of what is called the Roman Republic I know not one who has told us this important fact, that Rome never had a republic. The same may be said of Athens, and of several other turbulent associations of men in former ages. And it is for want of this attention or this knowledge in the writers of their histories, that the republican principle of government is so generally associated, even at this day, with the idea of insurrection, anarchy and the desire of conquest. Whereas it is in fact the *want* of the republican principle, not the *practice* of it, which has occasioned all the insurrections, anarchy and desire of conquest, that have disturbed the order of society both in ancient and modern times.

Again: in relating the destruction of Carthage, a measure which the zealous patriots, both before and after, considered so essential to the glory of the Roman state, and which has immortalized so many heroes as the authors and projectors of that destruction, I believe no historian has told us that the disease, decay and downfal of Rome itself were occasioned by that measure, and must be dated from that epoch; and that the actions of Regulus and Scipio, the themes of universal applause, were really more injurious to their country than those of Marius and Sylla, the objects (and justly so) of universal detestation.

If these principles had been understood by Polybius and his successors in the brilliant heritage of history, and had been properly impressed on the minds of their readers, we should not have heard old Cato's vociferation *delenda est Carthago* applied to the American states by an orator of the British parliament, as we did during the war; because every member of that parliament must have understood that the prosperity of these states would be highly advantageous to Britain, from the extensive commercial intercourse that the relative situation of the two countries required. Neither should we see at this day the French and English nations seeking to impoverish and extirpate each other; each of them entertaining the erroneous and absurd opinion that its own prosperity is to be increased by the adversity of its neighbor. We should have learned long ago from the plain dictates of reason, instead of having it beat into us some ages hence by costly experience, that the true dignity of a state is in the happiness of its members; and that their happiness is best promoted by the pursuit of industry at home and the free exchange of their productions abroad.

We should have perceived the real and constant interest that every nation has in the prosperity of its neighbors, instead of their destruction. France would have perceived that the wealth of the English would be beneficial to her, by enabling them to receive and pay for more of her produce. England would have seen the same thing with regard to the French; and such would have been the sentiments of other nations reciprocally and universally.

I know I must be called an extravagant theorist if I insinuate that all these good things would have resulted from having history well written and poetry well conceived. No man will doubt however that such would have been the tendency; nor can we deny that the contrary has resulted, at least in some degree, from the manner in which such writings have been composed. And why should we write at all, if not to benefit mankind? The public mind, as well as the individual mind, receives its propensities; it is equally the creature of habit. Nations are educated, like a single child. They only require a longer time and a greater number of teachers.

No. 50.

For that fine apologue, in mystic strain,
Gave like the rest a golden age to man,

Book X. Line 393.

Absurdities in speculative opinion are commonly considered as innocent things; and we are told every day that they are not worth refuting. So far as opinions are sure to rest merely in speculation, and cannot in any degree become practical, this is doubtless the proper way of treating them. But there are few opinions of this dormant and indifferent kind, especially among those that become general and classical among the nations.

The activity of such, tho imperceptible, is extensive. They get wrought into our intellectual existence, and govern our modes of acting as well as thinking. The interest of society therefore requires that they should be scrutinized, and that such as are erroneous should be exposed, in order to be rejected; when their place may be supplied by truth and reason, which nourish the mind and accelerate the progress of improvement.

Among the absurd notions which early turned the heads of the teachers of mankind, and which are so ridiculous as generally to escape our censure, is that of a Golden Age; or the idea that men were more perfect, more moral and more happy in some early stage of their intercourse, before they cultivated the earth and formed great societies.

The author of Don Quixote has played his artillery upon this doctrine to very good effect; he has summoned against it all the force of our contempt by making it the text of one of the gravest discourses of his hero. But my sensibility is such on moral and political errors, as rarely to be satisfied with the weapon of ridicule; tho I know it to be one of the most mortal of intellectual weapons.

The notion that the social state of men cannot ameliorate, that they have formerly been better than they now are, and that they are continually growing worse, is pregnant with infinite mischief. I know no doctrine in the whole labyrinth of imposture that has a more immoral tendency. It discourages the efforts of all political virtue; it is a constant and practical apology for oppression, tyranny, despotism, in every shape, in every corner of society, as well as from the throne, the pulpit, the tribunal and the camp. It inculcates the belief that ignorance is better than knowledge; that war and violence are more natural than industry and peace; that deserts and tombs are more glorious than joyful cities and cultivated fields.

One of the most operative means of bringing forward our improvements and of making mankind wiser and better than they are, is to convince them that they are capable of becoming so. Without this conviction they may indeed improve slowly, unsteadily and almost imperceptibly, as they have done within the period in which our histories are able to trace them. But this conviction, impressed on the minds of the chiefs and teachers of nations, and inculcated in their schools, would greatly expedite our advancement in public happiness and virtue. Perhaps it would in a great measure insure the world against any future shocks and retrograde steps, such as heretofore it has often experienced.

POSTSCRIPT.

I AM well aware that some readers will be dissatisfied in certain instances with my orthography. Their judgments are respectable; and as it is not a wanton deviation from ancient usage on my part, the subject may justify a moment's retrospect from this place. Since we have arrived at the end of a work that has given me more pleasure in the composition than it probably will in its reception by the public, they must pardon me if I thus linger awhile in taking leave. It is a favorite object of amusement as well as labor, which I cannot hope to replace.

Our language is constantly and rapidly improving. The unexampled progress of the sciences and arts for the last thirty years has enriched it with a great number of new words, which are now become as necessary to the writer as his ancient mother tongue. The same progress which leads to farther extensions of ideas will still extend the vocabulary; and our neology must and will keep pace with the advancement of our knowledge. Hence will follow a closer definition and more accurate use of words, with a stricter attention to their orthography.

Such innovations ought undoubtedly to be admitted with caution; and they will of course be severely scrutinized by men of letters. A language is public property, in the most extensive sense of the word; and readers as well as writers are its guardians. But they ought to have no objection to improving the estate as it passes thro their hands, by making a liberal tho rigid estimate of what may be offered as ameliorations. Some respectable philologists have proposed a total and immediate reform of our orthography and even of our alphabet; but the great body of proprietors in this heritage are of opinion that the attempt would be less advantageous than the slow and certain improvements which are going forward, and which will necessarily continue to attend the active state of our literature.

We have long since laid aside the Latin diphthongs *æ* and *œ* in common English words, and in some proper names tho not in all. Uniformity in this respect is desirable and will prevail. Names of that description which occur in this work I have therefore written with the simple vowel, as *Cesar*, *Phenicia*, *Etna*, *Medea*.

Another class of our words are in a gradual state of reform. They are those Latin nouns ending in *or*, which having past thro France on their way from Rome, changed their *o* into *eu*. The Norman English writers restored the Latin *o*, but retained the French *u*; and tho the latter has been since rejected in most of these words, yet in others it is still retained by many writers. It is quite useless in pronunciation; and propriety as well as analogy requires that the reform should be carried thro. No writer at this day retains the *u* in *actor*, *author*, *emperor* and the far greater part, perhaps nine tenths, of this class of nouns; why then should it be continued in the few that remain, such as *labor*, *honor*? The most accurate authors reject it in all these, and I have followed the example.

I have also respectable authorities in prose as well as poetry for expunging the three last letters in *though* and *through*; they being totally disregarded in pronunciation and awkward in appearance. The long sound of *o* in many words, as *go*, *fro*, puts it out of doubt with respect to *tho*; and its sound of *oo*, which frequently occurs, as in *prove*, *move*, is an equal justification of *thro*. All the British poets, from Pope downwards, and several eminent prose writers, including Shaftsbury and Staunton, have by their practice supported this orthography.

Some verbs in the past tense, where the usual ending in *ed* is harsh and uncouth, have long ago changed it for *t,* as *fixt, capt, meant, past, blest.* Poetry has extended this innovation to many other verbs which are necessarily uttered with the sound of *t,* tho in prose they may still retain for a while their ancient *ed.* I consider this reform as a valuable improvement in the language, because it brings a numerous class of words to be written as they are spoken; and the proportion of the reformed ones is already so considerable that analogy, or regularity of conjugation, requires us to complete the list. I have not carried this reform much farther than other poets have done before me. Examples might perhaps be found for nearly all the instances in which I have indulged it, such as *perisht, astonisht,* tho I have not been solicitous to seek them. The correction might well be extended to several remaining verbs of the same class; but it is difficult in this particular case to fix the proper limit.

With regard to the apostrophe, as employed to mark the elision in the past tense of verbs, I have followed the example of the most accurate poets; who use it where the verb in the present tense does not end in *e,* as *furl'd,* because the *ed* would add a syllable and destroy the measure. But where the present tense ends in *e,* it is retained in the past with the *d,* as *robed,* because it does not add a syllable.

The letter *k* we borrowed from the Greek, and the *c* from the Latin. The power of each of these letters at the end of a word is precisely the same; and the power of one is the same as that of both. Yet our early writers placed them both at the end of certain words, with the *c* before the *k,* as *musick, publick;* why they did not put the *k* first, as being the most ancient character, does not appear. Modern authors have rejected the *k* at the end of this class of words; and no correct writer will think of replacing such an inconvenient appendage.

The idea of putting a stop to innovation in a living language is absurd, unless we put a stop to thinking. When a language becomes fixt it becomes a dead language. Men must leave it for a living one, in which they can express their ideas with all their changes, extensions and corrections. The duty of the critic in this case is only to keep a steady watch over the innovations that are offered, and require a rigid conformity to the general principles of the idiom. Noah Webster, to whose philological labors our language will be much indebted for its purity and regularity, has pointed out the advantages of a steady course of improvement, and how it ought to be conducted. The Preface to his new Dictionary is an able performance. He might advantageously give it more development, with some correction, and publish it as a Prospectus to the great work he now has in hand.

The uniform tendency of our language is towards simplicity as well as regularity. With this view the final *e*, in words where it is quite silent and useless, is dropping off, and will soon disappear. Having long since resigned the place it held in the greater part of these words, as *joye*, *ruine*, and more recently in some others, it must finally quit the remainder where it is still found a superfluous letter, as *active*, *decisive*, *determine*.

We may even hazard a prediction that our whole class of adjectives ending in *ous* will be reformed and brought nearer to their pronunciation by rejecting the *o*. A similar change may be expected in words ending in *ss*. These words have already undergone one reform; they were formerly written with a final *e*, as *wildernesse*. They have lost the *e* because it was useless; and as the final *s* has now become equally useless, it might be dismissed with as little violence to the language. But these two projected innovations have not yet been ventured upon in any degree; and it is not desirable to be the first in so daring an enterprise, when it is not immediately important.

INDEX

TO PASSAGES IN THIS POEM BY PROPER NAMES.

[The Roman Numerals refer to the Book, the Arabic to the Line.]

USEFUL BOOKS

RECENTLY PUBLISHED BY RICHARD PHILLIPS,

No. 6, Bridge-Street, London,

And which may be had of all the Booksellers in the United Kingdom.

LETTERS from PORTUGAL and SPAIN; containing an Account of the Operations of the British Armies under Sir Arthur Wellesley and Sir John Moore, from the day preceding the Battle of Vimiera to the Battle and Embarkation at Corunna, with full and interesting details of the memorable Retreat from Sahagun.

Embellished with 14 Engravings by Heath, from Drawings made on the spot, illustrative of the Campaign. By ADAM NEALE, M.D F.L.S. Physician to His Majesty's Forces. In one elegant Volume, quarto, price two Guineas in boards.

The LIFE of GENERAL WASHINGTON, Commander in Chief of the American forces during the war which established the independence of his country, and First President of the United States; compiled under the inspection of his nephew, the Hon. BUSHROD WASHINGTON, from original papers bequeathed to him by his deceased relative, by JOHN MARSHALL, Chief Justice of the United States, &c. &c. To which is prefixed AN INTRODUCTION, containing a compendious view of the colonies planted by the English on the continent of North America. Five Volumes, elegantly printed in 4to. price 1l. 11s. 6d. each in boards.

Another edition printed in octavo, price 12s. each volume in boards.

TRAVELS in UPPER and LOWER CANADA, with Voyages on the River St. Lawrence, and the Great Lakes; containing a complete Account of the present State and Condition of those immense and valuable Territories. By GEORGE HERIOT, Esq. Deputy Postmaster of British North America. In one elegant volume, Quarto, illustrated with Thirty Engravings from Drawings by the Author, price 2l. 15s. in boards, or 3l. 5s. with the plates coloured.

TRAVELS IN AMERICA, performed in 1806, for the purpose of exploring the Rivers ALLEGHANY, MONONGAHELA, OHIO, and MISSISSIPPI, and ascertaining the produce and social condition of their Banks and Vicinity. By THOMAS ASHE, Esq. in three volumes, small octavo, price 21s. in boards.

TRAVELS through the UNITED STATES of NORTH AMERICA, the country of the IROQUOIS and UPPER CANADA, in the years 1795, 1796, and 1797. By the DUKE of ROCHEFOUCAULT LIANCOURT. With an authentic account of LOWER CANADA. A new edition, in four large volumes, 8vo. 2l. 2s. in boards, with three whole-sheet maps, several large tables, &c. &c.

HELME'S TRAVELS from BUENOS AYRES to LIMA, maps, 6s. bds.

The WEST-INDIA COMMON-PLACE-BOOK, being an Account of the present State of the Commerce, Policy, and Productions, of the West India Islands, deduced from Official Documents, by Sir WILLIAM YOUNG, Bart. M.P. &c. &c. price 1l. 5s. in boards.

THE HISTORY of the LATE WAR, from its commencement in 1792, unto the definitive treaty of peace between Great Britain and France in 1802. To which is annexed, a review of the causes and early progress of the French revolution, together with copious indexes. By ALEXANDER STEPHENS, of the honourable society of the Middle Temple, Esq. In two very large volumes, medium 4to. illustrated with maps, price 3l. 13s. 6d. in boards.

A SYSTEM of MODERN GEOGRAPHY, by JOHN SMITH, LL.D. with views, maps, &c. publishing in parts and numbers, to make two volumes in 4to. at 5s. or 6s. 6d. with a pair of globes.

The SYSTEM of the WORLD, according to Sir Isaac Newton and subsequent Mathematicians. By P. S. LAPLACE, Member of the National Institute. Translated into English by J. POND, F. R. S. 2 vols. 8vo. price 15s.

A JOURNAL of a TOUR through DENMARK and SWEDEN, during the present Winter (1808-9). By JAMES MACDONALD. In two volumes, small 8vo. price 10s. 6d. boards.

The Author of the above-mentioned work was wrecked off the Schaw on the 20th November last, and since that period has travelled through Jutland, Sleswick, Funen, Zealand and Sweden, and left Gottenburgh on the 13th of March.

Richard Taylor and Co., Printers, Shoe Lane, London.

www.ingramcontent.com/pod-product-compliance
Lightning Source LLC
LaVergne TN
LVHW020938110826
845150LV00004B/899

* 9 7 8 1 4 2 5 5 5 1 5 7 5 *